Commemorative Insignia of His Majesty the King's 6th Cycle Birthday, December 5, 1999

ห้ามจำหน่าย

The Must See Sites In
BANGKOK

BANGKOK METROPOLITAN TOURIST BUREAU

Title:	The Must See Site In Bangkok
Date:	September 2000
Printing:	Third Edition
Print run:	7,800
ISBN:	974-86625-9-4

BANGKOK

Produced:	BMA Tourist Promotion Centre
Advisors:	Assoc Prof Manop Pongsatat
	Kraisak Choonhavan
	Narit Le-kakul
	Pol Sub Lt Kriangsak Lohachala
	Nathanon Thavisin
	Wanvilai Promlakano
Editors:	Aswin Aphaiyawong
	Nampol Karomprat
	Dr Sueb-Sak Sirijaraya
	Bernie Cooper
Translators:	Martin R Clutterbuck
	Rattana Thamphakkul
	Thawee Suwanpat
Editorial Staff:	Kita Suchinroj
Photographers:	Manu Manukulkij
	Narin Sermsirimongkol
	Narongchai Wisawawethi
	Nipon Riab-riang
	Prasobsuk Lertwiriyapiti
	Ritthi Ratanapratheep
	Thanawatchara Thanomponsan
	Thawatchai Ramanat
Production:	IMAGE 2727 Co., Ltd.
Design:	M&W
Printed:	A.C.T. Publishing Co., Ltd.
	Bangkok 10250, Thailand
	Tel. (662) 319-2333 318-5862

INTRODUCTION

"The Must See Sites In Bangkok" is a project of the Tourism Promotion Center of the Bangkok Metropolitan Administration, which has been made to introduce the main tourist attractions of Bangkok to both Thai and foreign tourists for them to experience and study. This includes artifacts, art, culture, customs and the real way of life of Bangkok people. I want Thai people, and especially the young, to visit Bangkok more and on a deeper level than at present.

More importantly, I would like foreign visitors to Thailand to stay in Bangkok for many days, and not just a day or two as at present, because Bangkok has more tourist attractions than can be appreciated in a short time. I see both of these benefits, because supporting Thais to visit Bangkok, besides keeping money in the country, is also stimulating the distribution of income from one community to another, while the longer foreigners stay in Bangkok, the greater benefit Bangkokians will receive from their increased spending.

This first edition of the **"The Must See Sites In Bangkok"** has a print run of 7,800 copies, as I see the benefits to both Thai and foreign tourists as I have intended.

Thawatchai Thongsima
BANGKOK METROPOLITAN
ADMINISPRATION COUNCIL

BANGKOK METROPOLIS

    When King Rama I moved his capital across the river from Thonburi, he ordered a new capital to be built on the site of a village known as Bangkok — "the village of the wild plum trees." The plan and architecture of the new city closely followed the traditions of the ancient capital of Ayutthaya, and when the King was enthroned on June 13, 1782, he gave it the auspicious name:

    "Krungthepmahanakhon Amonrattanakosin Mahintharayutthaya Mahadilokphop Noppharatratchathaniburirom Udomratchaniwetma hasathan Amonphiman-Awatansathit Sakkathattiyawitsanukamprasit."

BANGKOK METROPOLITAN TOURIST BUREAU

The city grew steadily in size and importance, and incorporated the provinces of Phra Nakhon and Thonburi, undergoing several changes to its name. Finally, on December 14, 1972, a new administration named it "KRUNGTHEP MAHANAKHON", popularly shortened to "KRUNGTHEP."

Thailand's capital and centre of administration, commerce and communications is one of the most fascinating cities in the world, its 50 districts covering an area of 1,562.2 square kilometres. While local people usually refer to it as Krungthep, it is known around the world by the name of the village that was its original site — BANGKOK

CONTENTS

- 7 Message from the Governor
- 8 Bangkok's History
- 10 Contents

22 Phra Nakhon

- 23 Banglamphu and Phra Athit Road
- 27 Bank of Thailand Museum
- 28 Chalerm Krung Theatre
- 29 Chao Phor Seua Shrine
- 29 Chao Phor Hor Klong Shrine
- 30 Democracy Monument
- 30 Devasathan (Brahman Temple)
- 31 Floating Bank
- 32 Giant Swing
- 33 Lak Muang Shrine (City Pillar Shrine)
- 34 Mahakan Fort
- 34 Memorial of the Expeditionary Force
- 35 Museum of Old Cannon
- 36 National Gallery
- 37 National Museum Bangkok
- 38 National Museum Silpa Bhirasri Memorial
- 39 National Theatre
- 40 Phratamnak Suan Kularb School for Adults
- 41 Rommaninat Park
- 42 Royal Grand Palace and Wat Phra Kaeo
- 46 Royal Memorial to King Puttayodfa (RAMA I)
- 46 Royal Memorial to King Nangklao (RAMA III)
- 47 Royal Thai Army Museum in Honour of HM the King
- 48 Sanam Luang
- 50 Saranrom Park
- 51 Silpakorn University
- 52 Thammasat University
- 53 Thawornwatthu Building
- 54 Wat Bowonniwetwihan Ratchaworawihan

55 Wat Chanasongkhram Ratchaworamahawihan
56 Wat Intharawihan
57 Wat Mahathat Yuwaratrangsarit Ratchaworamahawihan
58 Wat Phrachetuphon Wimonmangkhalaram Ratchaworamahawihan (Wat Pho)
60 Wat Ratchabophit Sathitmahasimaram Ratchaworawihan
62 Wat Ratchaburana Ratchaworawihan
63 Wat Ratchanatdaram Worawihan
64 Wat Ratchapradit Sathitmahasimaram Ratchaworawihan
66 Wat Suthat Thepwararam Ratchaworamahawihan
67 Wat Thepthidaram Worawihan

68 Bang Bon

69 Flower Gardens
71 Wat Bang Bon

72 Bang Kae

73 Birdwatching by a Natural Lake
74 Brass Workshops
74 Orchid Farms
75 Phasicharoen Canal Trip

76 Bang Kapi

77 Huamark Sports Complex
78 Prasart Museum
79 Siberian Duck Pond

80 Bang Khen

81 Wat Phrasrimahathat Woramahawihan

82 Bang Kholaem

83 Krungthep Bridge
84 Wat Ratchasingkorn
85 Wat Worachanyawat

86 Bang Khunthian

87 Art & Cultural Centre of Mon Bangkradee
88 Mangroves at the Bangkok Seaside

90 Bang Na

91 Bangkok International Trade Exhibition Centre (Bitec)

92 Art of Carving
94 Bang Plad
95 Khon Masks and Ornaments
96 Wat Bowonmongkhon Ratchaworawihan
97 Wat Kharuehabodi
98 Bang Rak
99 Bangkok Folk Museum
100 Neilson Hays Library
101 Oriental Hotel
102 Sri Mahamariamman Temple (Wat Khaek)
103 Wat Mahaphruettharam Worawihan
104 Bang Sue
105 Centre of Khon Mask Making at Saphan Mai Community
106 Centre of Wood Carving at Pracha-naruemit Lane
108 Premjai House
109 Rama VI Bridge
110 Bangkok Noi
111 Ban Bu Community: Makers of Stone-Finished Khan
112 Bangkoknoi Canal
114 National Museum of the Royal Barges
116 Siriraj Museum
118 Wat Chinorasaram Worawihan
119 Wat Dusidaram Worawihan
120 Wat Rakhangkhositaram Woramahawihan
121 Wat Suwannaram Ratchaworawihan
122 Bangkok Yai
123 Wangderm Palace
124 Wat Arunratchawararam Ratchaworamahawihan
126 Wat Hongrattanaram Ratchaworawihan
127 Wat Khrueawan Worawihan
128 Wat Molilokkayaram Ratchaworawihan
129 Wat Ratchasittharam Ratchaworawihan
130 Bung Kum
131 Seri Thai Park

132 Chatuchak
133 Bronze Craft Centre
134 Chatuchak Park and Chatuchak Weekend Market
136 Kasetsart University Museums
137 Museum of Thai Banking at Siam Commercial Bank
138 Queen Sirikit Park
140 National Gene Bank of Thailand
141 Thai State Attorney Museum

142 Chom Thong
143 Canal Boat Trip
144 Wat Nangnong Worawihan
145 Wat Ratchaorasaram Ratchaworamahawihan
146 Wat Sai and Floating Market

148 Din Daeng
149 Bangkok Metropolitan Youth Centre (Thai-Japan)

150 Don Muang
151 Bangkok International Airport
151 Royal Thai Air Force Museum

152 Dusit
153 Chang-ton Museum (Royal Elephant National Museum)
154 Chitraladarahotarn Palace
155 Church of the Immaculate Conception
155 Dusit Zoo
156 Government House
157 Model Suphannahong Royal Barge Making Centre
158 Model Warship Craft Centre
159 Museum of the Royal Thai Decorations,
    Exhibition Hall of Thai Cabinet & Royal Gazette
160 National Assembly (Anantasamakom Throne Hall)
162 National Library
164 Parliament House
165 Parus-sakkawan Palace
165 People's Party Marker Plaque
166 Statue of King Rama V (Equestrian Statue)

167 The Royal Turf Club
168 Vimanmek Mansion Museum
180 Wat Benchamabophit Dusitwanaram Ratchaworawihan
181 Wat Rachathiwat Ratchaworawihan

182 Huai Khwang
183 Bangkok Playhouse
184 Tadu Contemporary Art
185 Thailand Cultural Centre

186 Kannayao
187 Wat Rassattadhum

188 Khlong Samwa
189 Pet Fish Farm

190 Khlong San
191 Phattayakul House
191 Monument of King Taksin the Great
192 Somdet Phra Sri Nagarindra the Princess Mother Memorial Park
194 Wat Anongkharam Worawihan
195 Wat Pichayayatikaram Worawihan

196 Khlong Toei
197 Benchasiri Park
198 Plainern Palace
199 Queen Sirikit Convention Centre
200 Science Museum and Planetarium

202 Lak Si
203 Khon Mask Centre
204 Thai Kite Centre

206 Lat Krabang
207 Natural Fish Habitat
208 Phra Nakhon Park
209 Putkao Bird Park

210 Lat Phrao
211 Shrines of Guanyin at Chokchai 4

212 Min Buri

213 Bamboo Birdcage ar
214 Kite Making Centre
215 Miniature Ship Muse
216 Nong Chok
217 Darulmuttageen Mosque
218 Horn Birdcage Making
219 Likae Riab
219 Native Thai Chicken Farm
220 Nong Khaem
221 Pudthaisawan Sword Fighting Institute
222 Pathumwan
223 Chulalongkorn University
224 Erawan Shrine
225 Jim Thompson's House
226 Bangkok Railway Station (Hualampong)
228 Lumphini Park
230 Museum of Imaging Technology
231 Narayana Phand
231 National Stadium
232 Queen Saovabha Memorial Institute (Snake Farm)
233 Wat Boromniwat Ratchaworawihan
234 Phasicharoen
235 Wat Khoohasawan Worawihan
236 Wat Nangchee Shotikaram
237 Wat Upsornsawan Worawihan
238 Phaya Thai
239 Philatelic Museum
240 The Government Savings Bank Museum
242 Phra Khanong
243 Bangchak Birdwatching Club
244 Wat Thammongkhon Thaobunnonthawihan
246 Pomprap Sattruphai
247 Ban Baat Community: Centre of Alms Bowl Making
248 Wat Saket Ratchaworamahawihan (Golden Mount)

250 Wat Sommanatwihan Ratchaworawihan
251 Wat Thepsirintharawat Ratchaworawihan
252 Woradit Palace and Damrong-rajanuphab Library
254 Pravet
255 Gemopolis
256 Suan Luang Rama IX Park
258 Rat Burana
259 Wat Jang-ron
260 Wat Prasertsutthawat
262 Ratchatewi
263 Bangkok Dolls
263 Ban Krua-nua Community: Centre of Silk Weaving
264 Museum of Mineral Resources
265 Phayathai Palace
266 Suan Pakkad Palace
268 Thai Labour Museum
269 Victory Monument
270 Sai Mai
271 Handicrafts Made from Fragrant Clay
272 Swai Fish Habitat at Hok-wa Canal
273 Wat Amarawararam
274 Samphanthawong
275 Thailand's First Commercial Bank
276 Wat Chakkrawatrachawat Woramahawihan
277 Wat Kalawar (The Holy Rosary Church)
278 Wat Trimitwitthayaram Worawihan
280 Yaowarat (Chinatown)
284 Saphan Sung
285 Wat Latbuakhao
286 Sathon
287 Bangkok Fish Market
288 Old Houses on Sathon Road
289 Wat Yannawa
290 Suan Luang

291 Wat Maha But
292 Taling Chan
293 Princess Maha Chakri Sirindhorn Anthropology Center
295 Talingchan Floating Market
297 Wat Ratchadathithan Ratchaworawihan
298 Thawi-Watthana
299 Lord Buddha Images Museum
300 Siamese Cat Farm
301 Utthayan Avenue
302 Thon Buri
303 Bamboo Flute Makers of Ban Laos
304 Bangluang Mosque
305 Santa Cruz Church
306 Silpa Thai House
308 Wat Kanlayanamit Woramahawihan
309 Wat Prayurawongsawat Worawihan
310 Thung Kru
311 Bangmod Tangerines
311 Thonburirom Park
312 Vadhana
313 Ban Chang Thai
313 Pridi Banomyong Institute
314 Siam Society under Royal Patronage
316 Wang Thonglang
317 Chao Phraya Bodindecha (Sing Singhaseni) Museum
318 Yannawa
319 Wat Chongnonsee
320 Wat Bhoman-khunaram

SOME ARCHITECTURAL TERMS

In the descriptions of the temples of Bangkok, the names of the more important elements recur again and again. Here are some of the most common architectural terms:

Chedi: These important Buddhist monuments can be seen in many different forms, depending on history and local preference. They contain sacred relics and other objects of worship, or mark auspicious events.

Chorfah: Curving up from the roof ridge at the gable end, these graceful features represent the naga, the mythical serpent.

Hang Hong: Part of the gable end decoration in Thai architecture. The hang hong is the pointed end piece on the lowest part of the roof.

Hor Trai: A repository for ancient manuscripts. Usually there will be water around it to protect the manuscripts from the ravages of insects.

Kampaeng Kaew: A low wall used to demarcate a special area surrounding either the ubosot or the prayer hall.

Kuti: The monk's residences. Traditionally, they are simple wooden cells.

Mondop: A square form building with a palatial spired roof. This building resembles the "busabok" Royal throne and is used to house highly venerated objects.

Na Ban: The gable end decoration of a palatial of religious building. Ornat gilded designs are usual.

Sala Karnparian: The large hall used by Buddhist monks to preach or study.

Tamnak: A. The residence of high ranking royalty.
B. The residence of high ranking Buddhist monks.

Ubosot: The temple's main chapel where the principal Buddha image is enshrined.

Wihan: The prayer hall. Buddha images are enshrined here as well. During the Sukhothai and Ayutthaya periods, before the ubosot was recognised as an important building, the wihan was mandatory in every temple.

Chedi

Chorfah

Na Ban

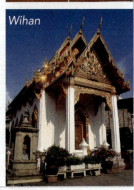
Wihan

The Must See Sites In BANGKOK 21

PHRANAKHON
☎ 282-3367

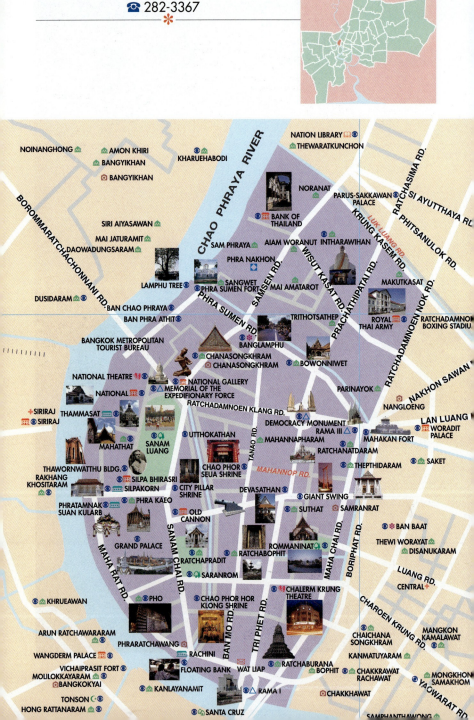

BANGLAMPHU

This old community grew from a village of gardeners in the Ayutthaya period to an important business district of Bangkok.

Near the Royal Grand Palace and the defensive canal linking Banglamphu Canal to Ong-Ang Canal, it was often chosen as land to give to nobles and Royal attendants. Besides being a centre of several communities, markets and temples, it has been an entertainment area since the reign of King Rama IV.

⊙ **Ban Banglamphu:** The community of Thai music is over 100 years old and is a place to study music, singing and making Thai musical instruments. It is also a meeting place for musical activities and rehearsals by such famous groups of musicians as *Khiovichit*, *Duriyaphan* and *Ban Duriyapraneet*.

Khaosan Road: This is a new community of foreign tourists in Bangkok and a meeting place for young travellers from around the world. On either side of the street are cheap guest houses, souvenir, jewellery and clothes stalls, restaurants, bars, book swap shops and travel agents.

★ C9
✉ Phra Athit Road
Banglamphu Sub-District
Phra Nakhon District
Bangkok 10200
🚌 3 6 9 15 19 30 32 33 39 53 64 65 68 82
🚐 6 11 38 68 Mb 8
⚓ 1. Chao Phraya Express Boat: Phra Athit Pier
2. Passenger Boat: Phra Sumen Fort Pier (Phadung Krung Kasem Canal)
🎎 Songkarn Festival: Khaosan Road (Apr 13)
🏛 Phra Sumen Fort: 1949
Ban Phra Athit: 1989
🅿 Behind Phra Sumen Fort
Beside Phra Athit Road
✴ Banglamphu
College of Dramatic Arts
Khaosan Road
National Gallery
National Theatre
Wat Chanasongkhram
Wat Sangwet

PHRA ATHIT ROAD

An important community which grew with the Royal city, it is a centre of government, art and culture. The road lines the Chao Phraya river bank with the palaces of nobles and courtiers and ordinary houses on both sides of the road. The prosperity of the Phra Athit Road community has been intertwined with the history of Bangkok up to the present.

The building of large palaces started in the reign of King Rama III, with architectural influences from China and Europe. Some palaces have been converted into offices and modern buildings, and the community's way of life has been completely transformed from before.

🔵 **Lamphu tree** (*Duabanga grandiflora*): This used to be an area of densely-growing Lamphu trees, so it was called "Banglamphu." At present, there are only two trees left behind Phra Sumen Fort.

Phra Sumen Fort: It was built in the reign of King Rama I on the city's outer wall, which ran along the canal to the Chao Phraya River.

At first, 14 forts were built, but in time they became dilapidated. Eventually, all were demolished, with the exception of Phra Sumen Fort and Mahakan Fort, both of which stand today.

Ban Chao Phraya: It was originally the palace of *HRH Prince Sathit-Thamrongsawat*, a son of the Second King, *Phra Pinklao*. The government of King Rama V subsequently purchased the land and built offices for the Police Department. When *HH Prince Khamrob* entered government service as the Director General of the City Police Department, he requested the house and land as a donation from King Rama VI. It therefore became known as "HH Prince Khamrob's Palace."

Ban Phra Athit: It was formerly the site of the Goethe Institute, and a meeting place for those interested in literature, film, and art. Originally it was the house of *Chao Phraya Worapongpipat (MR Yen Issarasena)*, an important civil servant during the reigns of King Rama V, VI and VII. It is now the office of a private company.

Kurusapha Printing House: Built in 1925, as a printing house for the Ministry of Education, it became a school for students of printing from Wat Sangwetwisayaram in 1933. It was the first school of its kind. After World War II, the teaching stopped but printing continued, and it became known as the "Kurusapha Phra Sumen Printing House."

UNICEF Building: It was originally the palace of *HRH Prince Naresworarit*, a son of King Rama IV. During World War II, *Dr. Pridi Banomyong* lived here when he held the title of Regent for King Rama VIII. It was also the command post for the *Seri Thai*, the Free Thai Movement. It is generally known as Tha Chang Mansion because of its proximity to Tha Chang Sub-District.

Maliwan Mansion is at present the office of the UN Food and Agriculture Organization. The mansion was built in the reign of King Rama VI by the Italian architect, *Ercole Manfredi*.

The Library of the Buddhist Association of Thailand: Contains books and periodicals on the subject of Buddhism in Thai and foreign languages. There are also books on law, Dhamma and history for reference.

- 41 Meeting Bldg. 3rd fl. Buddhist Association of Thailand
- (662) 281-7844
- Mon-Sat 8 am-3 pm
- Sun Public Hols.
- Free Admission
- Buddhist Association of Thailand compound

BANK OF THAILAND MUSEUM

    This is located in Bangkhunphrom Palace, originally the residence of *HRH Prince Baripatra*. After the political changes of 1932, the palace fell to the government, and is now the offices of the Bank of Thailand.

    It was designed in the Renaissance style by the German Architect *Karl Siegfried Döehring*. The windows and window-frame mouldings have been widely praised.

    ◉ Ancient Coins Room: Shows the evolution of Thai money from early beginnings as glass beads and Lanna money to the present day.

    Pot Duang Room: Pot Duang, or bullet coins were circulated in Thailand for over 600 years, and there are examples from the Sukhothai to the Rattanakosin periods on display.

    Thai Coins Room: Shows the evolution of bullet coins to modern type coins.

    Many other rooms should not be missed, such as the Thai Bank Notes Room, Note Printing Works, Gold & Commemorative Coins Room, Bank Note Inspection Room, Royal Thai Government Bonds Room, 50 Years Bank of Thailand Room, Pink Room, Horse Pine Room, and Bangkhunphrom Palace Room, which has been described as "one of the finest examples of past prosperity."

★ G8
✉ 273 Samsen Road
Wat Sam Phraya Sub-District
Phra Nakhon District
Bangkok 10200
☎ (662) 283-5286
FAX (662) 283-5283
🚌 3 6 9 19 30 32 33 43 49 53 64 65
🚐 6 17
⛴ Chao Phraya Express Boat: Wisut Kasat Pier
🕐 Mon-Fri 9-12 noon 2:30-4 pm
⊘ Sat Sun Bank Hol.
🎟 Free admission, but must be group tour with written request one week in advance to the Museum Director
📷 1993
🚫 Taking photo inside Bldg.
🅿 Beside the Museum compound
✚ Banglamphu National Library
Parliament House
Royal Barges Museum
Wat Iamworanut
Wat Intharawihan
Wat Sam Phraya
Vimanmek Mansion Museum

CHALERM KRUNG THEATRE

★ G9
✉ 66 Charoenkrung Road
Wang Burapha Phirom
Sub-District
Phra Nakhon District
Bangkok 10200
☎ (662) 222-1854 222-0434
225-8757
FAX (662) 221-2631
🚌 1 8 10 25 42 43 48 53 73
🅿 1 6 8 25 73 Mb 1
🕒 Daily 10 am-6 pm
ℹ Admission Charge
🅿 The Old Siam Plaza
✚ Central Dept. Store
   Merry King Dept. Store
   Nakhon Kasem Market
   Phahurat Market
   Rommaninat Park
   Sampeng Market
   Saphanhan Market
   Saphanlek Market
   The Old Siam Plaza
   Wat Chakkrawat
   Wat Ratchaburana
   Wat Thipwariwihan

With his enthusiasm for motion pictures, King Rama VII used his private funds to build Chalerm Krung Theatre, the largest and most modern entertainment centre in Asia at that time. He named the theatre in honour of the architect, *MC Samaichalerm Krisdakorn*, and it was a memorial in the celebrations for the 150th anniversary of Bangkok.

When sound films were introduced, the first Thai-language dubbing was originated. When Thailand entered the Second World War in 1941, film activities ceased and the theatre presented stage dramas that were adapted into musicals, which quickly became popular. When the war was over, filmmaking returned and prospered once more.

A major refurbishment in 1992 has ensured that Chalerm Krung Theatre is still an entertainment venue of international standard, presenting shows and films, true to the intentions of its Royal founder.

CHAO PHOR HOR KLONG SHRINE

The Thai tradition of building Hor Klong, or signal towers, has existed since Sukhothai to give messages to the people. When King Rama I was crowned, Thailand was still at war with its neighbours, so the King ordered a signal tower to be built in front of Wat Pho as part of the plans for constructing Bangkok in 1782. It was a copy of a signal tower built in the Ayutthaya period.

Later, King Rama V ordered the tower and the shrine beside it to be dismantled to build Chao Chetu Park. A new shrine and an image of Chao Phor Hor Klong, or the Lord of the Signal Tower were built in the area of the National Security Department, while Hor Klong was built in 1982, the 200th anniversary of the founding of Bangkok.

★ G9
✉ Territorial Defence
   Rim Khlong-Kuderm Road
   Phra Borommaharatchawang
   Sub-District
   Phra Nakhon District
   Bangkok 10200
☎ (662) 222-3347
📠 (662) 222-3347
🚌 2 9 12 43 47 48 60 70 80 86
🚐 1 3 6 7 44 Mb 8
⛴ Chao Phraya Express Boat:
   Tha Chang Pier Tha Tien Pier
🕐 Daily 6 am-8:30 pm
🆓 Free Admission
🎪 Annual Fair (Apr 12)
🅿 In front of the Shrine
✚ City Pillar Grand Palace
   National Museum
   Old Cannon Museum
   Pakkhlong Market
   Sanam Luang Saranrom Park
   Silpa Bhirasri Memorial
   Silpakorn U. Thammasat U.
   Thawornwatthu Bldg.
   Wat Mahathat Wat Pho
   Wat Ratchapradit

CHAO PHOR SEUA SHRINE

This Chinese shrine has a long history and is respected by the Chinese community. It was originally located on Bamrung Muang Road, but when the road was widened in the reign of King Rama V, and lined with new buildings, *Phraya Chodeuk Ratchasetthi (Khien)* rebuilt it on land donated by the King, which is now Tanao Road.

⦿ **The Front Building:** A wooden roof in the Chinese style. On the roof ridge are statues of historic figures. The door frame is painted with the guardians in the Chinese manner. Inside stand Chinese figures of *Chao Phor Seua, Chao Phor Kuan U* and *Chao Mae Tabtim*.

The main arch is decorated with gold-covered wood carved in the form of dragons, fish, gourds, books and swords.

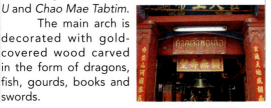

★ G9
✉ 468 Ban Tanao Road
   San Chao Phor Seua
   Sub-District
   Phra Nakhon District
   Bangkok 10200
☎ (662) 224-2110
🚌 10 12 19 35 42 56 96
🚐 42
🕐 Daily 6 am-6 pm
🆓 Free Admission
🎪 Chao Phor Seua Procession
   Ceremony (Oct)
   Coin Casting Ceremony
   Loykrathong Festival
🏛 1988
🅿 Beside the Shrine
✚ Democracy Monument
   Devasathan Giant Swing
   Wat Mahannaparam
   Wat Suthat Wat Theptidaram

★ G9
✉ Ratchadamnoen Klang Avenue
Ban Phanthom Sub-District
Phra Nakhon District
Bangkok 10200
🚌 2 9 12 15 33 35 39 42 44 47 56 59 60 64 68 70 79 82 96 201 203
🚐 Sai 2 3 9 11 12 17 32 Sai 38 39 44 68 Sai 79
⛴ Passenger Boat: Phanfalilat Pier (Sansap Canal)
🅿 Ratchadamnoen Klang Avenue
🚻 Banglamphu Khaosan Road Memorial of King Rama III Wat Bowonniwet Wat Saket
△ 📷

★ G9
✉ 268 Ban Dinsor Road
Sao Chingcha Sub-District
Phra Nakhon District
Bangkok 10200
☎ (662) 222-6951
🚌 10 12 19 35 42 96
🚐 8
🕐 Devasathan: Thu Sun
9 am-4 pm
Ubosot: 8 am-3 pm
🎎 Swing Ceremony (Jan)
🏛 1949
🅿 BMA Bldg.
🚻 Ban Baat Comunity
Wat Ratchanatda Wat Suthat
Wat Thepthidaram
📷

DEMOCRACY MONUMENT

Built in the reign of *F.M. P. Pibulsongkram's* government to commemorate the People's Party requesting a constitution on June 24, 1932, signalling a change of government from absolute monarchy to democracy with the king as head of state.

◉ **Four main wings:** Measuring 25 m. tall. The base has a radius of 25 m., meaning June 25.

75 cannons: Standing in the perimeter mean the year of change of BE 2475 (1932).

Bas relief sculptures: (At the bases of the four wings). They show the operations of the People's Party in changing the government.

Traditional Thai tray: The tray carrying the constitution is 3 m. high, meaning the month of the change, June (3rd lunar month in Thai reckoning).

Six ritual daggers: (At the six gateways). They mean the six principles: independence, internal peace, freedom, equality, economy and education.

DEVASATHAN (BRAHMAN TEMPLE)

Brahmanism was spread in the Indochinese Peninsula before Buddhism came to Thailand and before the foundation of Sukhothai. Both religions are combined in the Thai way of life and its customs and ceremonies.

King Rama I ordered the Devasathan to be built at the same time as the Giant Swing in 1784, according to the ancient custom of building Devalaya in the centre of the city, as in Phimai, Angkor Wat and Angkhor Tom.

◉ **Shrine of Shiva** (Main Chapel): houses bronze images of Shiva in the Blessing posture, and many other images of the Hindu Devas.

Shrine to Ganesha (Middle Chapel): houses five seated images of Ganesha made of granite and sandstone, and two of greenstones and bronze.

Shrine to Vishnu (Outer Chapel): houses images of Vishnu in bronze, and of his consort Laksmi and Savari in plaster. In front of the Devasathan is a small Devalaya, and in the lotus pond there is an image of Brahma.

FLOATING BANK

To encourage saving and to serve people living alongside waterways, the Government Savings Bank started this boat service in 1958, the only waterborne bank in the world. At first, the boats were used to serve people in country districts such as Ban Paew, Damneonsaduak, Bangyai and Khonti.

The bank later established permanent branches and discontinued the boat service when land transport improved. Now Pakkhlong Talat Branch (Mobile) is the only bank boat left.

The boat has a staff of six tellers and a policeman. It starts from Rajini (Pakkhlong Market) Pier at 8:30 in the morning and goes along the Chao Phraya River and Bangkoknoi Canal to Bangyai. When it reaches Nonthaburi it begins its return journey. People waiting for service fly a flag with the bank's logo in white on a blue background in front of their houses. All banking services are available except those needing an online facility. Nowadays two boats, Omsin 33 and Omsin 42, take turns in serving their waterside customers.

★ G9
✉ Government Saving Bank Pakkhlong Talat Branch (Mobile)
☎ (662) 225-5863-4
📠 (662) 225-5863
🏛 Rajini Pier (Pakkhlong Market)
🕐 Mon-Fri 8:30 am-4:30 pm
   Sat Sun Public Hols.
   Bank Mid-year Hol. (Jul 1)
💳 All services are available except online facility

GIANT SWING

The Ceremony of Triyampavai-Tripavai, was one of the 12 Royal ceremonies held in each month since the Sukhothai period. It was carried out in December, the first lunar month. By the Rattanakosin period, it had changed to the second lunar month, January.

It was regarded by the Brahmins as a new year's ceremony. *Shiva* was said to visit the Earth for 10 days every year. Brahmins would meet at Shiva's shrine and wash the bodies and hair of priests to welcome Shiva.

◉ **Swing Ceremony:** Originates from a story in the scriptures. Concerned about the end of the world, *Uma Devi* contrived a bet with Shiva. A serpent was suspended between Putsa trees (*Jujube*) on the river, swinging back and forth between them. Shiva stood in its path on one leg with the other crossed. If the serpent struck Shiva and he fell, that would signify that the world would end. But Shiva did not fall, proving that the whole of creation was secured and strong, so Shiva won.

The Swing Ceremony compares the swing to the Putsa trees, while the space between its posts is the river. Naliwan is the serpent, with Phraya Yuen standing cross-legged on a benjamas wood.

Giant Swing: King Rama I ordered it built in front of the Devasathan at the centre of the city. It was moved to its present position in the reign of King Rama V, to make room for a gas plant.

The ceremony was removed from the list of royal ceremonies in the reign of King Rama VII. At present, it may still be held with Royal sponsorship, but only in the Devasathan.

★ G9
✉ In front of Wat Suthat
Bamrung Muang Road
Sao Chingcha Sub-District
Phra Nakhon District
Bangkok 10200
🚌 10 12 19 35 42 56 96
🚌 42
🕐 Daily 24 hrs.
💲 Free Admission
🏛 1949
🅿 BMA Bldg.
✚ Ban Baat Community
Chao Phor Seua Shrine
Democracy Monument
Devasathan
Rommaninat Park
Wat Mahannaparam
Wat Ratchanatda Wat Suthat
Wat Thepthidaram
📷

LAK MUANG SHRINE (CITY PILLAR SHRINE)

In 1782, King Rama I was crowned as the first monarch of the Chakri dynasty. Having moved his capital from Thonburi to Bangkok, he ordered the ceremony to raise the traditional City Pillar on Sunday, April 21, 1782 at 6:45 am.

⊙ The City Pillar: Made from laburnum wood and decorated with heartwood, it is a decreed 108 inches of it are above ground and 79 inches buried in the soil. The top of the pillar is decorated in shellac and gold leaf and has a pointed tip. Inside is the birth certificate of the city.

When King Rama IV came to the throne, he saw that the Pillar was deteriorating and had it rebuilt. An expert in astrology, he improved the city's fortunes by holding a ceremony to inscribe the city's birth certificate on a gold bar of one baht in weight at the Temple of the Emerald Buddha. The shrine was rebuilt as the top of a prang, as at a pavilion in Ayutthaya, and great festivities were arranged when the city's birth certificate was placed in the City Pillar.

Inside the shrine are the three original gods: *Phra Seua Muang*, *Phra Song Muang* and *Phra Lak Muang*. When Thailand weathered a crisis, King Rama V ordered the building of *Phra Siam Devathiraj* as another god guarding the city.

★ G9
✉ Maha Chai Road
　Phra Borommaharatchawang
　Sub-District
　Phra Nakhon District
　Bangkok 10200
🚌 1 3 6 9 15 19 25 30 32 33
　39 43 44 47 53 59 60 64 65
　70 80 82 91 123 201 203
🚐 1 6 7 8 12 25 Sai 38 39 44
⛴ Chao Phraya Express Boat:
　Tha Chang Pier
🕐 Daily
🆓 Free Admission
🏛 1975
🅿 In front of the Shrine
　Clock Tower Grand Palace
　National Museum
　National Theatre
　Pakkhlong Market
　Phratamnak Suan Kularb School
　Sanam Luang Saranrom Park
　Silpa Bhirasri Memorial
　Silpakorn U. Thammasat U.
　Thawornwatthu Bldg.
　Wat Mahathat Wat Pho
　Wat Phra Kaeo

📷 ℹ

★ H9
✉ Ratchadamnoen Klang Avenue Samranrat Sub-District Phra Nakhon District Bangkok 10200
🚌 2 5 12 15 33 35 39 42 44 47 56 59 60 60 (Exp.) 70 70 (Exp.) 79 201 203
🚐 Sai 2 3 9 11 12 17 32 39 44 68 79 Mb 1 8 10
⛴ Passenger Boat: Phanfalilat Pier (Sansap Canal)
🕐 Daily 24 hrs.
🎟 Free Admission
🏛 1949
🅿 Wat Ratchanatda
✚ Democracy Munoment Memorial of King Rama III Phanfalilat Bridge Wat Ratchanatda Wat Saket
📷

MAHAKAN FORT

This was built in the reign of King Rama I as a fortress on the city wall commanding a view of the canal circling the city as far as to the Chao Phraya River. Originally there were 14 of these forts, but only Mahakan and Phra Sumen Forts remain.

Both are octagonal in shape. While the central tower of both are similar, Mahakan Fort is smaller, being sited on the edge of a canal, with less defensive importance than its neighbour on the river bank.

★ G9
✉ Opposit National Theatre Phra Borommaharat-chawang Sub-District Phra Nakhon District Bangkok 10200
🚌 1 3 7 9 15 25 30 32 33 39 43 44 47 53 59 60 64 65 70 80 82 91 203
🚐 1 6 7 8 12 25 39 44 70 203
🕐 Daily 24 hrs.
🎟 Free Admission
📅 Laying the Wreath: (Nov 11)
🅿 National Theatre
✚ Grand Palace
National Gallery
National Museum
National Theatre
Sanam Luang
Silpa Bhirasri Memorial
Silpakorn U. Thammasat U.
Thawornwatthu Bldg.
Wat Mahathat Wat Pho
Wat Phra Kaeo
△ 📷

MEMORIAL OF
THE EXPEDITIONARY FORCE

During World War I, Thailand joined the Allies and sent a brigade of volunteer soldiers to fight in Europe in 1918. When the war ended with the Allied victory, the brigade of volunteers returned to Thailand in 1919.

The volunteers killed in action were cremated in Europe and their ashes incorporated into this monument which was designed by *HRH Prince Naris* at the behest of King Rama VI.

It is in the form of a round chedi made of polished white stone modelled on those of Srivijaya. On each of the four sides are inscriptions about the war and the names of those who died on the battlefield.

BANGKOK METROPOLITAN TOURIST BUREAU

MUSEUM OF OLD CANNON

The area of the Ministry of Defence was formerly three palaces built by King Rama I for a Royal cousin. The building displaying the cannon was originally a European-style barracks built by King Rama IV for the City Guards.

This open air museum is in front of and to the side of the Defence Ministry. The cannon, 40 in all, are arranged in groups according to their age, starting in the Ayutthaya period and continuing through the Thonburi to Rattanakosin periods. Each has its name and history inscribed on a brass plate.

◉ **Narai Sanghan:** It is the largest and most noteworthy gun. King Rama I had it cast in 1787 to be one of a pair with the Peun Phraya Tani.

Phraya Tani: *Somdet Chao Phraya Maha Surasinghanat* brought this gun from Pattani to present to King Rama I after suppressing a rebellion in the South.

French guns: There are also a number of these guns to be seen such as *Khorm Dam Din, Jeen Sao Sai, Thai Yai Len Na, Java Ratchakris* and *Mu-ngit Taluang Fan.*

★ G9
✉ Ministry of Defence
Sanam Chai Road
Phra Borommaharatchawang
Sub-District
Phra Nakhon District
Bangkok 10200
☎ (662) 226-3814
📠 (662) 255-8262
🚌 1 3 6 9 15 19 25 30 32 33
39 43 44 47 53 59 60 64 65
70 80 82 91 123 201 203
🚖 1 6 7 8 12 25 Sai 38 39 44
⛴ Chao Phraya Express Boat:
Tha Chang Pier
🕐 Daily 24 hrs.
🆓 Free Admission
🅿 In front of Ministry of Defence
✚ City Pillar Grand Palace
National Museum
National Theatre
Pakkhlong Market
Sanam Luang Saranrom Park
Silpa Bhirasri Memorial
Wat Mahathat Wat Pho
Wat Phra Kaeo

★ G9
✉ Chaofa Road
Chanasongkhram Sub-District
Phra Nakhon District
Bangkok 10200
☎ (662) 282-2639 281-2224
📠 (662) 282-2640
🚌 3 6 9 32 33 43 53 64 65
🚐 6 39 80
⛴ Chao Phraya Express Boat:
Pra Athit Pier
🕘 Wed-Sun 9 am-4 pm
🚫 Mon Tue Public Hols.
💰 Thai 10 Bht Foreigner 10 Bht
Free Admission for Monk
Nun Student in Uniform
📷 Exhibition Lecture Seminar
🏛 1978
🖼 1989
📸 Taking photo inside Bldg.
🅿 In the Museum compound
➕ Bangkok Metropolitan
Tourist Bureau Banglamphu
College of Dramatic Arts
Kaosan Road
National Museum
National Theatre
Pra Athit Road
Snam Luang Thammasat U.
Wat Chanasongkhram
Wat Mahathat
Wat Phra Kaeo

NATIONAL GALLERY

With increasing trade with the West resulting in a shortage of traditional bullet coins, King Rama IV ordered the purchase of machinery to mint coins which was installed at the Royal Mint in the Grand Palace. This was replaced in the reign of King Rama V who ordered the construction of an entirely new building for the Royal Mint, which carried on producing coins until its machinery wore out and the Mint moved to Vibhavadi Rangsit Road.

Department of Fine Arts then requested its use from the Royal Mint to create the National Gallery in 1974.

◉ **The Structure:** It contains elements of both Thai and Western architecture and is a *"typical building from the reign of King Rama V."*

Permanent Exhibitions: These include collections of modern art by famous Thai artists both past and present, and includes works by both King Rama VI and His Majesty the present King, traditional murals and all categories of modern art from the first days to the present.

Temporary Exhibitions: Thai and foreign artists arrange revolving exhibitions alternating with annual exhibitions, where the work on display goes through selection, and includes painting, sculpture, prints and installations.

There are also a library and a souvenir shop selling books and postcards. Interested people can listen to lectures, training and seminars about artistic activities arranged by the National Gallery.

NATIONAL MUSEUM BANGKOK

Originally the Personal Museum of King Rama IV with a collection of antiques and Royal Gifts, King Rama V subsequently opened the Sahathai Samakom Pavilion (Concordia Tower) in the Grand Palace grounds as a Public Museum. It was then moved to three palace buildings in the Front Palace (Wang Na). King Rama VII then gave over all buildings in the Front Palace to be the Bangkok Museum.

Exhibition areas are split into three groups:

Gallery of Thai Nation: From the Kingdom of Sukhothai to the Rattanakosin period, in the Sivamokhaphiman Hall.

History of Art and Archaeology in Thailand: Divided into two periods: Prehistory, at the back of the Sivamokhaphiman Hall, and the Historical period, exhibiting sculpture from the 15th century AD to the Rattanakosin period at the Prapat Pipitthapan Building, with sculpture from before this period on display in the Maha Surasinghanat Building.

Fine Arts and Ethnology: Includes displays of musical instruments, nielloware, gold, mother-of-pearl inlay, wood carvings, old textiles, khon masks, puppets, etc. in the group of palace buildings.

Funeral Chariot Hall: Displays funeral carriages such as Phra Mahaphichai Ratcharot, Vejjayantra Ratcharot, the Small Carriage (Ratcharot Noi) and other paraphernalia of Royal Cremations.

In the past, the Front Palace was of secondary importance only to the main palace, and was the residence of Somdet Chao Phraya Maha Surasinghanat, the heir apparent. The many buildings inside include Bhuddhaisawan Chapel, Tamnak Daeng (Red House), Mungkhalaphisek Pavilion, and Sala Longsong Pavilion, considered to be "outstanding examples of traditional Thai architecture."

★ G9
✉ Na Phrathat Road
Phra Borommaharatchawang Sub-District
Phra Nakhon District
Bangkok 10200
☎ (662) 224-1333
FAX (662) 224-1404
🚌 1 3 6 9 15 19 25 30 32 33 39 43 44 47 53 59 60 64 65 70 80 82 91 123 201 203
🚐 1 6 7 8 12 25 Sai 38 39 44
⛴ Chao Phraya Express Boat: Tha Chang Pier
🕐 Wed-Sun 9 am-4 pm
🕐 Mon Tue Public Hols.
🎟 Thai 20 Bht Foreigner 100 Bht
Museum Day (Sep 19)
Krom Phraratchawangboworn Day (Nov 3)
📚 Sat-Sun 9:30 am-3:30 pm
🏛 1961
Free Membership
🗣 English French German Japanese
🕐 Wed Thu 9:30 am-12 noon
🚫 Taking photo inside Bldg.
🅿 In the Museum compound
✚ City Pillar Clock Tower
College of Dramatic Arts
Grand Palace National Theatre
Old Cannon Museum
Silpa Bhirasri Memorial
Silpakorn U. Snam Luang
Thammasat U.
Thawornwatthu Bldg.
Wat Mahathat Wat Pho
Wat Phra Kaeo

NATIONAL MUSEUM SILPA BHIRASRI MEMORIAL

This museum was founded as a memorial to *Prof. Silpa Bhirasri*, who is known as the "father of modern art in Thailand." The building is on the left of the Fine Arts Dept., in the same area as Silpakorn University, where he lived, worked, and taught. He also designed the building.

Prof. Corrado Feroci was born in Florence, Italy and travelled to work as a sculptor at the Fine Arts Dept. in the reign of King Rama VI. He was appointed to teach sculpture at the Royal Academy's Fine Arts section and was later made principal of the Artisan's section of the Fine Arts School. *Luang Vichit-Vadakan* helped him to become a naturalised Thai citizen when Italy surrendered to the Allies in World War II, and gave him the Thai name Silpa Bhirasri.

In 1943 the Fine Arts School was upgraded to university status and given the name Silpakorn University. He was appointed Dean of the Faculty of Sculpture, and his work included building Royal monuments and many important large-scale works.

The interior of the building maintains the atmosphere of the time when *Prof. Silpa* worked there, with contemporary paintings and sculptures as well as implements used by artists and sculptors. The works of artists who were among his first pupils are also displayed here. They include National Artists and famous modern painters such as *Fua Haripitak*, *Khien Yimsiri* and *Sawat Tantisuk* etc.

★ G9
✉ Na Phrathat Road
Phra Borommaharatcha-wang Sub-District
Phra Nakhon District
Bangkok 10200
☎ (662) 223-6162
🚌 1 3 6 9 15 19 25 30 32 33 39 43 44 47 53 59 60 64 65 70 80 82 91 123 201 203
🚌 1 6 7 8 12 25 Sai 38 39 44
⛴ Chao Phraya Express Boat: Tha Chang Pier
🕘 Mon-Fri 9 am-12 noon 1-4 pm
⊘ Sat Sun Public Hols.
🆓 Free Admission
🅿 Fine Arts Dept. Silpakorn U.
✚ College of Dramatic Arts
Grand Palace
National Museum
National Theatre
Old Cannon Museum
Phratamnak Suan Kularb School Silpakorn U.
Snam Luang Saranrom Park
Thammasat U.
Thawornwatthu Bldg.
Wat Mahathat Wat Pho
Wat Phra Kaeo Utthokathan

NATIONAL THEATRE

The original theatre next to Sivamokhaphiman Hall in the National Museum was made of wood. When the government decided to build a National Theatre as a venue for performances of traditional Thai drama, a larger, more sophisticated theatrical complex was called for.

◉ **Theatre Building:** This is divided into three parts. In the right wing is a small theatre, while the left wing contains the workshops of the stage technicians. The central wing is a large auditorium, next to which is the Sankhita Sala for open air musical performances.

Notable among the cultural and dramatic works performed at the National Theatre is the masked Khon, in which episodes from the Ramayana epic drama are enacted to music in highly stylised form. The Lakhon traditional drama can also be seen here, as well as performances of classical music and dance in the traditions both of the court and the villages of the four regions of Thailand.

King Phra Pinklao Monument: This imposing, life-size figure cast in black bronze stands in front of the theatre.

★ G9
✉ 2 Rachini Road
Phra Borommaharatchawang Sub-District
Phra Nakhon District
Bangkok 10200
☎ (662) 221-0174
📠 (662) 221-0171
🚌 3 9 15 30 32 33 53 59 64 65 80 82 91 203
🚐 1 6 7 8 12 25 39 44 80
⛴ Chao Phraya Express Boat: Phra Athit Pier
🎭 Shows: Every Weekend (Nov-May) 4:30 pm
Last Friday of the month
🅿 In front of the Theatre
✚ College of Dramatic Arts
Expeditionary Force Memorial
Grand Palace National Gallery
National Museum
Sanam Luang
Silpa Bhirasri Memorial
Silpakorn U. Thammasat U.
Thawornwatthu Bldg.
Wat Mahathat Wat Phra Kaeo

★ G9
✉ Hor Uthettaksina
(Men's College in the Court)
Former Residences of the
Royal Consorts
(Women's College in the
Court)
Na Phralan Road
Phra Borommaharat-
chawang Sub-District
Phra Nakhon District
Bangkok 10200
☎ Men's College in the Court:
☎ (662) 221-1856 224-3308
FAX (662) 221-8823
Women's College in the Court:
☎ (662) 224-9471
FAX (662) 226-4949
🚌 15 19 25 43 44 47 53
59 82 91 123 203
🚐 1 8 12 Sai 25 39 44 91
⛴ 1. Chao Phraya Express
Boat: Tha Tien Pier
2. Ferry: Tha Chang Pier
Tha Tien Pier
🕘 Mon-Fri 9 am-4 pm
❌ Sat Sun Public Hols.
💲 Free Admission
📋 Enrollment: Mar-Apr
• Must be in group of 10 or
more, with written request
one week in advance to the
Lord Chamberlain.
☎ (662) 224-3273 (Office)
222-6889 (Public Relations)
🅿 Thai Wang Road (Wat Pho)
In front of Saranrom Park
✚ City Pillar Clock Tower
Fine Arts Dept. Grand Palace
National Museum
Old Cannon Museum
Saranrom Park
Silpa Bhirasri Memorial
Silpakorn U. Snam Luang
Tha Tien Market
Thammasat U.
Thawornwatthu Bldg.
Wat Arun Wat Pho
Wat Mahathat

PHRA TAMNAK SUAN KULARB SCHOOL FOR ADULTS

While technology continues its advance, there was a time when Thai arts seemed to have been standing still, almost in danger of disappearing since there were no systems of teaching them and passing on knowledge.

HRH Princess Maha Chakri Sirindhorn thus ordered the foundation of this school to revive Thai craftsmanship and conserve Thai arts as a living force. The emphasis is on teaching those who wish to take up arts as a career, and not simply collect tuition fees. The study of each main subject takes one year, with five months or one term for optional subjects. Candidates for the school must be aged at least 15 years, and must pay the costs of study equipment themselves.

◉ **Men's College in the Court:** Teaches drawing, carving, gold lacquerwork, nielloware, stucco carving, bencharong, industrial sewing and other crafts.

Women's College in the Court: Teaches three subjects: Thai Royal food, including fruit carving; flower arranging, artificial flowers and garlands making and banana leaf weaving; and traditional hand embroidery.

ROMMANINAT PARK

In 1889, King Rama V ordered the purchase of this land to build a place of detention and the training and rehabilitation of the inmates. When construction was complete, it was called, Khuk Mahantathot or "New Prison." The name has been changed many times, the most recent being to Bangkok Special Prison.

To celebrate HM Queen Sirikit's Fifth Cycle birthday in 1992, the Department of Corrections moved the prison out and built Rommaninat Park meaning "*Park of the Queen Our Refuge.*"

◉ **Bronze Sculpture - Conch Shell:** Sited in a commemorative fountain at the highest point of the park. The shell and its platter are cast in alloy and plated with bronze. Inside it are the holy cloth of Mahasolotmongkol and a real shell.

Corrections Museum: Located on Mahachai Road comprises four buildings: Criminal Court, Temporary Building, Shops of the Corrections Department, and Section 9 Building. Inside displays instruments of punishment and evolution of punishment in Thailand.

There is also a multi-purpose space in the park with a children's playground, exercise area, footpaths and jogging tracks .

★ G9
✉ Siriphong Road
   Samranrat Sub-District
   Phra Nakhon Bangkok 10200
☎ (662) 221-5181
📠 (662) 221-5181
🚌 1 5 35 37 42 56 73 96
🚌 7 42
🕐 Office: Mon-Fri 8:30 am-4:30 pm
   Sat Sun Public Hols.
   Park: Daily 5 am- 8 pm
🆓 Free Admission
🏛 Corrections
   ☎(662) 225-1704
   🕐Thu-Sat 8:30 am-4:30 pm
🅿 In front of the Park
✚ Ban Baat Community
   Chao Por Seua Shrine
   Devasathan
   Wat Mahannaparam
   Wat Suthat Wat Theptidaram

ROYAL GRAND PALACE

When King Rama I took the throne as the first monarch of the Chakri Dynasty in 1781, he moved his capital from Thonburi to the other bank. He then ordered the construction of the Royal Grand Palace as the centre of the new city.

Inside the Royal Grand Palace are the Maha Monthien group of buildings, the Throne Halls, and other palaces and buildings. These have been renovated, refurbished, repaired, extended and added to continually as appropriate to every reign since then.

◉ **Chakri Throne Hall:** Hybrid Thai-European architecture built in the reign of King Rama V with the throne hall itself in European style and the roof in a Thai throne hall style.

Chakrapatpiman Throne Hall: The chief throne hall of the Monthien group, and the early Chakri kings mostly stayed in this throne hall.

Dusit Throne Hall: Cruciform style built in the reign of King Rama I. Inside is a Throne decorated in pearl and Phratanratchabanjathorn, a couch of King Rama I.

Royal Decorations & Coins Division: Ranks and coinage has 13 exhibition rooms: Rooms 1-3, royal ranks; Room 6, the apparel of the Emerald Buddha which is changed according to season; Room 7, royal regalia and Room 12, historical money etc.

✉ The Royal Decorations & Cions Division:
On the right side of the main entrance of Wat Phra Kaeo
☎ (662) 224-3328 226-0255
FAX (662) 225-9158
⏰ Daily 9 am-4 pm
💵 Thai 10 Bht
👥 Must be in group of 10 or more, with written request one week in advance to the Director of Currency Management Bureau
📷 Taking photo inside Bldg.
🏢 1st fl.

BANGKOK METROPOLITAN TOURIST BUREAU

WAT PHRA KAEO

The temple is in the outer section of the Royal Enclosure west of the Grand Palace. It was built on the orders of King Rama I along with the Grand Palace and Rattanakosin Island, and is built as a temple in a Royal compound like Wat Sri Sanphet in Ayutthaya. It has no resident monks.

◉ **The Emerald Buddha (Phra Putta Maha Mani Ratana Patimakorn or Phra Kaeo Morakot):** This is a Buddha image in the meditating position in the style of the Lanna school of the north, dating from the 15th century AD. King Rama I brought it from Vientiane, and it is considered to be the most important Buddha image in the country.

Model of Angkor Wat: King Rama IV had this built by *Phra Samphopphai* when Cambodia was under Siamese control. The model was recreated in plaster at the behest of King Rama V to celebrate the first centenary of the Royal city.

Prasat Phra Thepidon: This four-square prang originally called "Puttaprang Prasat" was built in the reign of King Rama IV. Inside are statues of Kings Rama I-King Rama VIII, to which the public pay their respects on Chakri Day, April 6, every year.

Mondop: This structure stands behind Prasat Phra Thepidon, and was built in the reign of King Rama I. Inside is a cabinet holding the Buddhist scriptures beautifully decorated in mother-of-pearl.

Balcony: This can be compared to the temple wall. The murals inside tell the Ramayana story in its entirety. On the columns of the balcony are stone inscriptions of the verses describing the murals.

Phra Sri Ratana Chedi: Built in the style of Wat Sri Sanphet in Ayutthaya, this chedi is to the west of the Monhop. Inside is a small chedi with relics of the Lord Buddha.

Phra Atsada Maha Chedi: This group of eight chedis stands in front of the temple. It was built in the reign of King Rama I and dedicated to the heavens. Six of the group are outside the balcony, two are inside. Each has its own name.

Yaksa Tavarnbal (Gate-keeping Giants): Six pairs of mythical ogres stand at each gate of the Balcony. These are the main Giants of the Ramayana.

Hor Phra Khanthan-rat: Standing in the western corner of the balcony, this is where the Phra Puttakhanthan-rat figure is enshrined. It presides over the Royal rain-making ceremony and the ceremony of the first rice planting. Inside are paintings by the mural artist *Khrua In Khong*.

Hor Phra Ratcha Karamanusorn: Inside this structure are 34 Buddha images in various positions, built by command of King Rama III and dedicated to the kings of Ayutthaya and Thonburi.

Hor Phra Ratcha Pongsanusorn: Built in the reign of King Rama IV, this is the location of the Buddha image of the reigning King of the Rattanakosin Era. Inside are murals of Royal chronicles of Ayutthaya by Khrua In Khong.

Hor Phra Nak: Situated behind the temple, this traditional Thai building roofed with glazed tiles contains the ashes of the Royal family.

★ G9
✉ Na Phralan Road
Phra Borommaharatchawang
Sub-District Phra Nakhon District
Bangkok 10200
☎ (662) 222-8181: 3801 3890
222-2208 623-5500: 3100
🚌 1 3 6 9 15 19 25 30 32 33 39
43 44 47 53 59 60 64 65 70
80 82 91 123 201 203
🚐 1 6 7 8 12 25 Sai 38 39 44
⛴ Chao Phraya Express Boat:
Tha Chang Pier
🕐 Daily 8 am-4 pm
🎟 Foreigner 125 Bht
Sun: Sermon 1 pm
Buddisht Holy Day:
Sermon 9 am 1 am
Guide: 10 am 2 pm
Personal Audio Guide (PAG)
German English French
Japanese Mandarin
Russian Spain Thai
🎧 100 Bht/2 hours
Passport/Credit card
☎(662) 222-2208
Sala Atthawichan
Sala Atthawichan
● Taking photo inside the ubosot
Man: Shorts Pants Slippers
Woman: Undershirt Singlet
Shorts Sandals
🅿 Ratchavoradit Pier
Snam Luang Wat Mahathat
✚ City Pillar Clock Tower
Grand Palace Hor Klong Shrine
National Museum
Old Cannon Museum
Saranrom Park
Silpa Bhirasri Memorial
Silpakorn U. Snam Luang
Thammasat U. Wat Arun
Wat Mahathat Wat Pho
Wat Ratchapradit

★ G9
- Foot of Memorial Bridge Bangkok side Tri Phet Road Phra Borommaharat-chawang Sub-District Phra Nakhon District Bangkok 10200
- 3 4 5 6 7Kor 8 10 19 21 37 40 42 43 53 56 73 82
- 3 5 6 73
- Chao Phraya Express Boat: Memorial Bridge
- Daily 24 hrs.
- Free Admission
- Laying the Wreath: Chakri Day (Apr 6)
- 1988
- Foot of Memorial Bridge
- PakKhlong Market Phahurat Market Suan Kularb Collage Wat Pho Wat Ratchaburana

ROYAL MEMORIAL TO KING PUTTAYODFA (RAMA I)

This was built at the behest of King Rama VIII on the occasion of the city's 150th anniversary together with the Puttayodfa Bridge (Memorail Bridge) across the Chao Phraya River.

HRH Prince Naris designed the memorial, and *Prof. Silpa Bhirasri* sculpted the figure and cast it in bronze. In front of the monument is a concrete wall with a marble plaque bearing the legend, "Pathom Borommaratcha Chakri Wong" (Founder of the Chakri Dynasty) together with a carved depiction of elephants.

★ G9
- Ratchadamnoen Klang Avenue Phra Borommaha-ratchawang Sub-District Phra Nakhon District Bangkok 10200
- 2 2 (Exp.) 5 12 15 33 35 39 42 44 47 56 59 60 60 (Exp.) 70 70 (Exp.) 79 201 203
- Sai 2 Sai 2 (Exp.) 3 9 11 11 (Exp.) 12 17 32 38 (Old 15) 39 44 68 79 Mb 1 8 10
- Passenger Boat: Phanfalilat Pier (Sansap Canal)
- Daily 24 hrs.
- Free Admission
- Wat Ratchanatda
- Democracy Monument Mahakan Fort Phanfalilat Bridge Sangkitasilp Centre Wat Ratchanatda Wat Saket Wat Thepthidaram

ROYAL MEMORIAL TO KING NANG KLAO (RAMA III)

The memorial stands in the open area of Lan Plabpla Maha Chessadabordin in front of Wat Ratchanatda, where the Chalerm Krung Cinema once stood.

The bronze Royal image is approximately one and a half life-size and was designed and cast by the Fine Arts Department. The figure is seated on a throne and holds a sword in the left hand.

The park which surrounds it has three pavilions built for the monarch to welcome foreign guests.

ROYAL THAI ARMY MUSEUM IN HONOUR OF HM THE KING

The museum is in the Royal Thai Army's Headquarters Building and the Armoury of the Chulachomklao Royal Military Academy.

The Office of HM's Principal Private Secretary permitted the use of the name "Royal Thai Army Museum in Honour of HM the King" and the use of the Official Golden Jubilee Seal to decorate the building. The Army opened it to the public in 1996, the year of His Majesty the King's Golden Jubilee.

⦿ Military History Model Room: (1st fl.) Shows the history of military evolution, ancient weapons, and models of important events in the history of the Royal Thai Army.

Weapons Room: (1st fl.) Guns used by the Army from the early Rattanakosin period up to the Vietnam War, and weapons seized from enemy forces are displayed here.

Flag and Equipment Room: (2nd fl.) Displays battle flags, service manuals and various kinds of military equipment and regalia.

Uniforms and Insignia Room: (3rd fl.) The evolution of uniforms from the Sukhothai period to the present day, with insignia, decorations and medals can be seen here.

Other interesting rooms include Barami Pok Klao Room, Evolution of the Army Room, Military Document Search Room and Lecture Hall.

★ H8
✉ 113 Royal Thai Army Headquarters
Ratchadamnoen Nok Avenue
Ban Phanthom Sub-District
Phra Nakhon District
Bangkok 10200
☎ (662) 297-8121-2
📠 (662) 280-2320
12 70 201
🚌 3 9
🕘 Mon-Fri 9 am-4 pm
🚫 Sat Sun Public Hols.
💲 Free Admission, but must be in group of 10 or more, with written request one week in advance to the Director of Directorate of Joint Operations
☎ (662) 297-7859 297-2380
📠 (662) 280-2320
🅿 Behind the Museum
✣ Anantasamakom Throne Hall
Chankasem Palace
Chang-ton Museum
Parliament House
Parus-sakkawan Palace
Ratchadamnoen Boxing Stadium
Royal Thai Decorations Museum
Statue of King Rama V
Wat Benchamabophit

When Bangkok was first built, cremation buildings were erected on this open space and it was used for the cremation ceremonies of monarchs and high-ranking royalty. It was called, "Thung Phramane," or the Phramane Grounds.

In the reign of King Rama III, it was used as a demonstration rice field to display Thailand's prosperity to foreign visitors. The rice grew right up to the palace walls.

SANAM LUANG

King Rama IV chose it as the Royal field for the Peutmongkol or Royal Ploughing Ceremony, and the Rain Making Ceremony. Its name was then changed to Sanam Luang, as its original name was no longer considered to be auspicious.

Originally, Sanam Luang consisted of only a small part of its present southern half. When King Rama V abolished the position of Krom Phra

★ G9
✉ Phra Borommaharat-
chawang Sub-District
Phra Nakhon District
Bangkok 10200
🚌 1 3 6 9 15 19 25 30 32 33
39 43 44 47 53 59 60 64
65 70 80 82 91 201 203
🚐 1 6 7 8 12 25 39 44 70 203
⛴ 1. Chao Phraya Express
Boat: Tha Chang Pier
2. Ferry: Phrachan Nua Pier
Tha Chang Pier
🕐 Daily 24 hrs.
🪁 Kite Festival (Mar)
Songkran Festival (Apr 13)
Royal Ploughing Ceremony
Day (May)
🏛 1977
🅿 In Sanam Luang compound

Ratchawangbowon, he ordered the demolition of the walls, forts and the outside of the Palace to the East, to extend Sanam Luang.

After his first visit to Europe, the king ordered offices to be built for the Ministries of Justice, Transport and Communications. In time, these were demolished and the National Theatre built in their place. King Rama V had tamarind trees planted all around the park for shade, as in the avenues of European capitals.

Sanam Luang has been a multi-purpose area since Bangkok was founded, and the venue for Royal and official ceremonies in every reign. It has been a race track, a golf course, and the famous Weekend Market, which subsequently moved to Chatuchak Park.

At present, Sanam Luang is a park where people can relax in the historic heart of the city, while kite competitions, the ritual bathing of monks in Songkran Festival and the Royal Ploughing Ceremony are still carried out regularly every year.

⊞ Bangkok Metropolitan
Tourist Bureau
City Pillar Clock Tower
College of Dramatic Arts
Expeditionary Force Memorial
Grand Palace
National Gallery
National Museum
National Theatre
Old Cannon Museum
Pratamnak Suan Kularb School
Saranrom Park
Silpa Bhirasri Memorial
Silpakorn U. Thammasat U.
Thawornwatthu Bldg.
Wat Mahathat Wat Pho
Wat Phra Kaeo Utthokathan

★ G9
✉ In Between Rachini Road and Charoenkrung Road
Phraborommaharatchawang Sub-District
Phra Nakhon District
Bangkok 10200
☎ (662) 221-0195 222-1035
FAX (662) 222-1035
🚌 1 3 6 9 12 25 32 43 44 47 48 53 60 82 91 123
🚌 6 7 8 9 12 25 44 91
⛴ Chao Phraya Express Boat: Tha Chang Pier
🕐 Office: Mon-Sat 8:30 am-4:30 pm
Sun Public Hols.
Park: Daily 5 am-8 pm
💲 Free Admission
Plant Doctor: Plant Treatment
🏫 Plant School
☎(662) 246-0283 246-8541
FAX(662) 246-8541
P In front of Saranrom Park
✚ Chao Phor Hor Klong Shrine
City Pillar Clock Tower
College of Dramatic Arts
Grand Palace
National Museum
Old Cannon Museum
Thammasat U.
Thawornwatthu Bldg.
Sanam Luang Silpakorn U.
Wat Mahathat Wat Pho
Wat Phra Kaeo
Wat Ratchapradit

SARANROM PARK

This was originally a Royal Park in Saranrom Palace, which King Rama IV ordered to be built as a residence towards the end of his reign. Sadly, the king passed away before he could take up residence there.

In the reign of King Rama V, it served as a residence for members of the Royal Family and a place to welcome official guests. It became the venue for festivals in the cool season throughout the reign of King Rama VI.

After the change of government, King Rama VII donated it as offices for the People's Party and the location of the People's Party Circle. In 1960, the cabinet presented it to Bangkok Municipality. The Royal Park was then revived as a trefoil garden and public park.

◎ **Monument to HM Queen Sunantha Kumareerat and HRH Prince Kannaporn Phetcharat:** In the reign of King Rama V, the Queen and the young prince died in a boating accident. On the orders of the king, their ashes were kept at the south end of the park in a marble monument dedicated to their memory. Their biographies are carved on the monument, with words of remembrance from King Rama V in both Thai and English.

Chao Mae Takhien Deity: This shrine to the spirit of the takien tree was built in the reign of King Rama VI. It is in the form of a three-level, octagonal Chinese pavilion.

Glass House: This houses a school where botany and such horticultural techniques as hydroponic planting and grafting are taught.

SILPAKORN UNIVERSITY

The original site of this university was Tha Phra Palace, the temple of Royal Grandchildren of King Rama I. It was later used as a residence for the sons of various kings, and HRH *Prince Narissaranuwadtiwongse* was the last prince to stay there.

Silpakorn was the first university of art in Thailand and was founded from the Fine Arts Department school which taught painting and sculpture to civil servants and other students who were accepted without fees. It was *Prof. Silpa Bhirasri* who laid the foundations for the study of European art here, and since then faculties have been opened in more subjects, such as Architecture, Archaeology and Interior Design.

Art Gallery: Temporary exhibitions are held here. It is in three sections: the main audience chamber of the old Tha Phra Palace, and galleries for both the Painting, Sculpture and Prints Faculty, and the Faculty of Interior Design.

Wang Tha Phra Library: Situated at the right of the university gate on Na Phralan Road, this is the biggest art library in the country, and a centre for artistic information.

Monument to Prof. Silpa Bhirasri: This stands in front of the Painting, Sculpture and Prints Faculty.

★ G9
✉ 31 Na Phralan Road
Phraborommaharatchawang Sub-District
Phra Nakhon District
Bangkok 10200
☎ (662) 623-6115-21
FAX (662) 225-8991
🚌 15 19 25 43 44 47 53 59
82 91 123 203
🚐 1 8 12 Sai 25 39 44 91
⚓ 1. Chao Phraya Express Boat:
Tha Chang Pier
2. Ferry: Tha Chang Pier
Phrachan Nua Pier
🕐 University: Daily
Office: Mon-Fri
8:30 am-4:30 pm
Sat Sun Public Hols.
Wang Tha Phra
Mon-Fri 9 am-7:30 pm
Sat 9 am-4 pm
Sun Public Hols.
🏛 1978
🖼 1989
🅿 In the University compound
➕ City Pillar Clock Tower
College of Dramatic Arts
Grand Palace
National Gallery
National Museum
National Theatre
Old Cannon Museum
Pratamnak Suan Kularb School
Sanam Luang Saranrom Park
Silpa Bhirasri Memorial
Silpakorn U. Thammasat U.
Thawornwatthu Bldg.
Wat Arun Wat Mahathat
Wat Pho Wat Phra Kaeo

THAMMASAT UNIVERSITY

★ G9
✉ Na Phrathat Road
Phra Borommaharatchawang Sub-District
Phra Nakhon District
Bangkok 10200
☎ (662) 221-6111-20
📠 (662) 224-8099
🚌 15 30 32 33 47 53 59 64 65 70 80 82 91 203
🚐 1 6 7 8 12 25 39 44 59
⛴ 1. Chao Phraya Express Boat: Tha chang Pier
   2. Ferry: Phrachan Nua Pier
🕐 Mon-Fri 8:30 am-4 pm
   Sat Sun Public Hols.
🎟 Free Admission
🖼 Exhibition Meeting Semenar
📖 Pridi Banomyong
   ☎ (662) 623-5173
   📠 (662) 613-3547
   🕐 Mon-Fri 8:30 am-7 pm
      Sat Sun 8:30 am-4 pm
      Summer Hols: Sat Sun 9:00 am-3 pm
🏛 1976
🅿 In the University compound
✚ City Pillar
   College of Dramatic Arts
   Grand Palace
   National Museum
   Pratamnak Suan Kularb
   School Sanam Luang
   Silpa Bhirasri Memorial
   Silpakorn U. Wat Arun
   Wat Mahathat Wat Pho
   Wat Phra Kaeo Utthokathan

After the change of government in 1932, Thammasat University was founded to service the new political system governing the country.

On June 27, 1934, the day King Rama VIII gave a temporary constitution to the Thai people, the University of Jurisprudence and Politics was founded with *Dr. Pridi Banomyong (Luang Pradit Manutham)* as rector.

In its first period, the university was known as a "knowledge market." It did not receive a state budget, and charged low tuition fees which were used for the university's expenses. The name was later changed to Thammasat University for political reasons.

◉ **Dome Building:** The symbol of the university, this was originally four old military buildings. The architect for the conversion was *Jitsen Aphaiyawong*,

who built a roof joining the four buildings and crowning it with a spire. Now only two buildings remain.

Underneath the roof is a clock, which makes this building the university's clock tower.

The room beneath the clock was formerly the office of Dr. Pridi Banomyong, who founded the university.

BANGKOK METROPOLITAN TOURIST BUREAU

THAWORNWATTHU BUILDING

When *HRH Crown Prince Vajirunhis* passed away, his father King Rama V remarked that it would be inappropriate to build large funeral buildings for a single purpose. He therefore ordered *HRH Prince Naris* to build the Thawornwatthu Building instead of a temporary funeral building. When the Royal funeral was complete, the king donated the building for the purpose of educating monks and novices. It was then named "Sanghisenas Ratcha vitayalai."

Construction of Thawornwatthu Building was completed in the reign of King Rama VI, and it was first given as a Royal library for monks in Bangkok. In the reign of King Rama VII, many more books were added to the library, and the king decided to institute the Vachirayan and Vachiravudh Royal Libraries. He gave Sivamokkhaphiman Hall in the Front Palace to be the Vachirayan Library. Scriptures, state papers and correspondence were kept here. The Thawornwatthu Building itself was used for printed material, photographs and newspapers, and was known as the "Vachiravudh Library."

★ G9
✉ Naradhip Centre for Researches in Social Sciences
Na Phrathat Road
Phraborommaharatchawang Sub-District
Phra Nakhon District
Bangkok 10200
☎ (662) 221-6830
FAX (662) 221-6830
🚌 1 3 6 9 15 19 25 30 32 33 39 43 44 47 53 59 60 64 65 70 80 82 91 123 201 203
🚍 1 6 7 8 12 25 Sai 38 39 44
⛴ Chao Phraya Express Boat: Tha Chang Pier
🕘 Mon Fri 9:00 am-4:30 pm
Sat Sun Public Hols.
💳 Free Admission
🏛 1977
📷 Permission required for taking photo inside Bldg.
🅿 Sanam Luang Wat Mahathat
✚ Fine Arts Dept. City Pillar College of Dramatic Arts Grand Palace Expeditionary Force Memorial National Museum National Theatre Old Cannon Museum Sanam Luang Saranrom Park Silpa Bhirasri Memorial Silpakorn U. Thammasat U. Wat Mahathat Wat Phra Kaeo

★ G9
✉ 248 Phrasumen Road
Bowonniwet Sub-District
Phra Nakhon District
Bangkok 10200
☎ (662) 281-2831-3
FAX (662) 280-0343
🚌 12 15 56 68
🚌 11 11(Exp.) 33 Sai 38 68
🕒 Temple: Daily 8 am-5 pm
Ubosot: Daily 8-8:40 am
8-9 pm
Buddhist Sermon Day:
8 am-12 noon 1-4 pm
💳 Free Admission
📅 Maghapuja Day
Visakhapuja Day
Asalthapuja Day
Atthamipuja Day
📖 Wat Bowonniwet Basement
Sor Wor Bldg.
Thammaniwet: Daily
9 am-5 pm
Funeral Memorial Books
1st fl. Phor Por Row Bldg.
🕒 Sun 1 pm-5 pm
🏛 Kammathan 2nd fl.
Wat Bowonniwet 3rd fl.
Phor Por Row Bldg.
🕒 Sun 1-5 pm
🏛 1949
🏛 First Class
🚌 Mahamakut Buddhist U.
☎ (662) 281-6427
FAX (662) 281-0294
🅿 In the Temple compound
✚ Banglamphu
Democracy Monument
Khaosan Road Mahakan Fort
Phra Athit Road
Phra Sumen Fort Old Wall

WAT BOWONNIWETWIHAN
RATCHAWORAWIHAN

Usually known as Wat Boworn, this temple was built by *HRH Prince Maha Sakdipolsep*, a son of King Rama III, and originally called Wat Mai.

King Rama IV stayed here after he was ordained, and founded the Thammayut Nikai, a more ascetic monastic order. The temple is of special importance because King Rama VI, King Rama VII, and *HM King Bhumibol Adulyadej* were all ordained here.

Ubosot: This is a Trimuk pavilion with wings on both sides and a tiled roof in the Chinese style. The gable end is decorated with glazed ceramics and at centre is the seal of the Royal crown. The doorway arches and windows are in gilded stucco. The murals were painted in European style by *Khrua In Khong*. The important Buddha images are Phra Suwannakhet, Phra Phuttachinnasi, Phra Nirantarai and Phra Phutaninnat.

Sio Kang Gate: The large door framed in the temple wall is carved with gateway guardians in the Chinese style.

Panya Palace: This was built on the orders of King Rama III as the residence of kings and princes who were being ordained.

Petch Palace: The main chamber of this mixed Thai and European-style building was the site of the first printing house in Thailand.

Mahamakut Buddhist University: Founded by King Rama V, this university for monks now has four faculties: Religion and Philosophy, Humanities, Social Studies and Education.

WAT CHANASONGKHRAM
RATCHAWORAMAHAWIHAN

King Rama I appointed a Mon group of monks to look after this Ayutthaya period temple, so it became known in the Mon language as Wat Tong Pu. When *Somdet Chao Phraya Maha Surasinghanat* moved his troops back to Bangkok after victory in the battle of the Nine Armies, there was a ceremony of ritual bathing and changing of robes before he entered the Grand Palace, so the main temple was restored in 1787. After that, King Rama I gave it the name Wat Chanasongkhram.

Ubosot: This dates from the reign of King Rama I. Gable end decoration is a Naga or serpent, a special feature of Front Palace artisans. Behind the chapel walls and window frames are flame motifs. Ogival stones on the temple wall are in the shape of Vishnu mounted on a Garuda. The outside arch has stucco flame motifs, while inside the door frames are coloured paintings. Around the chapel and behind the principal Buddha image are containers of the ashes of the princes of five kings.

Chedi: Two chedis were built in front of the chapel in the early Rattanakosin period. They are in the Jom Hae, or wide base and sharp top shape.

Principal Buddha Image: Phra Putthanorasitrilokachet is an image in the Subduing Mara posture, made of plaster, lined with lead and gilded, in the reign of King Rama I. The base is surrounded by 15 Buddha images which were all made at the same time.

★ G9
✉ Chakkrabongse Road
Banglamphu Sub-District
Phra Nakhon District
Bangkok 10200
☎ (662) 281-8244 281-5056
🚌 3 6 9 15 30 32 33 43 53 64
65 82 123
🚐 6 9 38 (Sai Old 15)
⛴ 1. Chao Phraya Express Boat: Phar Athit Pier
2. Passenger Boat: Phra Sumen Fort Pier
(Phadung Krungkasem Canal)
🕐 Temple: Daily 5 am-8 pm
Ubosot: Daily 6 am-6 pm
💰 Free Admission
🎉 Songkran Festival (Apr 13-15)
🏛 1949
👥 Second Class
🅿 In the Temple compound
✚ Ban Chao Phraya
Banglamphu Ban Phra Athit
Buddhist Association Lib.
College of Dramatic Arts
Lamphu Tree Khaosan Road
Kurusapha Printing House
National Gallery
National Theatre
Phra Sumen Fort
Wat Bowonniwet
Wat Sangwet UNICEF Bldg.

WAT INTRARAWIHAN

★ G8
✉ 114 Wisutkasat Road
Bangkhunphrom Sub-District
Phra Nakhon District
Bangkok 10200
☎ (662) 628-5550-2
📠 (662) 282-8429
🚌 3 9 30 32 33 43 49 53 64 65
🚐 6 17
🕐 Temple: Daily 8:30 am-8 pm
Ubosot: Daily 6 am-6 pm
(Wishing to visit the ubosot should call in advance.)
💳 Free Admission
🎎 Paying respect to Luangpor Toh's Day (Mar 1-10)
Anniversary of Luangphor Toh's Death (Jun 22)
Dhamma Internship for Lay Person:
🕐 Daily Sun 1-4 pm
🏛 In front of the Ubosot
🅿 In the Temple compound
✚ Bank of Thailand Museum
National Library
Wat Iamworanut
Wat Noranat
Wat Sam Phraya

This commoner's temple was built towards the end of the Ayutthaya period. Over the years it was known by various names. King Rama VI eventually ordered the name to be changed finally, as it had the same name as a temple Bang Yireuatai in Thonburi, Wat Inthara. *Somdet Phra Watchirayanwong* (MR *Cheun*) of Wat Bowonniwetwihan gave it the name by which it is known today.

◉ **Phra Si Ariyamettraiya:** Also known as Luangpor Toh, this brick and stucco Buddha image was started in the reign of King Rama IV in 1867 and not completed until 60 years later in the reign of King Rama VII. It is a standing image with the alms bowl in the Sukhothai style, the tallest of its kind in the world. The body is decorated in glass mosaics and 24-carat gold. A staircase at the back of the image enables people to apply gold leaf to the body.

Sema: The alcove features stucco figures caricaturing politicians.

Museum: Historical artifacts from the temple such as old Buddha images and paintings can be seen here.

WAT MAHATHAT YUWARATRANGSARIT
RATCHAWORAMAHAWIHAN

★ G9
✉ 3 Maharat Road
Phraborommaharatchawang Sub-District
Phra Nakhon District
Bangkok 10200
☎ (662) 221-5999 224-1415 222-7984
FAX (662) 623-6282
🚆 1 3 7 9 15 25 30 32 33 39 43 44 47 53 59 60 64 65 70 80 82 91 203
🚌 1 6 7 8 12 25 39 44 70 203
⛴ 1. Chao Phraya Express Boat: Tha Chang Pier
2. Ferry: Phrachan Nua Pier
🕐 Temple: Daily 8 am-5 pm
Ubosot: Mon-Sat 8-9 am 5-6 pm
Sun 7 am-4 pm
Buddhist Sermon Day: 7 am-5 pm
Free Admission
Buddhism Course: 7:30-8:30 pm
Sun 7 am-3 pm (Children)
1949
First Class
Mahachulalongkorn U.
☎ (662) 623-6322-4
Mon-Sat 1-4 pm
Sun Buddhist Sermon Day
P In the Temple compound
City Pillar Clock Tower
College of Dramatic Arts
Expeditionary Force Memorial
Grand Palace National Museum
National Theatre
Old Cannon Museum
Phratamnak Suan Kularb School
Sanam Luang Saranrom Park
Silpa Bhirasri Memorial
Silpakorn U. Thammasat U.
Thawornwatthu Bldg.
Wat Pho Wat Phra Kaeo
Wat Ratchapradit

Built in the Ayutthaya period, this temple was originally named Wat Salak. During restoration in the reigns of King Rama I-King Rama V, it was known by several different names. Eventually it was named Wat Mahathat Yuwaratrangsarit, but it is always known as Wat Mahathat.

Mondop: Inside is a chedi in the style of King Rama I's reign containing Buddha relics. It is the precursor of early Rattanakosin chedis, and completely covered in lacquered gold leaf.

Ubosot: In contrast to most others, this has no front or rear portico. There are entrances on both sides and is large enough for 1,000 monks to gather at one time. The principal Buddha image is covered in gold leaf, and is the work of *Phraya Devarangsan*, a notable craftsman of the Front Palace (Wang Na).

Maha Chulalongkorn Rajavidyalaya: This university was founded by King Rama V as an educational institution for Mahanikai monks.

Wihan Photilangka: The prayer hall was built in the reign of King Rama IV. The principal Buddha image, named Phra Nak, is in the Sukhothai period style and cast in bronze.

Monument to Somdet Chao Phraya Maha Surasinghanat: In front of Photilanga Wihan, the monument is to King Rama I's younger brother, an important army commander when Rattanakosin was founded.

★ G9
✉ 2 Sanamchai Road
Phra Borommaharat-
chawang Sub-District
Phra Nakhon District
Bangkok 10200
☎ (662) 222-5910 226-2942
226-1743 225-9595
📠 (662) 225-9779
🚇 1 3 6 9 12 25 32 43 44 47
48 53 60 82 91 123
🚌 6 7 8 9 12 25 44 91
⛴ 1. Chao Phraya Express Boat:
Rajini (Pakkhlong Talat) Pier
Tha Chang Pier Tha Tien Pier
2. Ferry: Rajini (Pakkhlong
Talat) Pier Tha Chang Pier
Tha Tien Pier
🕒 Temple: Daily 8 am-5 pm
Ubosot: Daily 8 am-5 pm
💵 Foreinger 20 Bht
🏠 Santiwan
🏛 Wat Phrachetuphon:
Wasukree Mansion
🏛 1949
🏛 First Class
🚐 Wat Pho Thai Traditional
Medical and Massage
☎ (662) 221-2874 225-4771
🕒 Enrollment: Daily 8 am-5 pm
Class: Sat Sun 8 am-5 pm
💆 Massage
📷 Permission required for
taking photo inside Bldg.
🅿 In the Temple compound
✚ Clock Tower Grand Palace
Old Cannon Museum
Pakkhlong Market
Saramrom Park Silpakorn U.
Wat Arun Wat Ratchapradit
Wat Phra Kaeo
🏠 🌐

WAT PHRACHETUPHON WIMONMANGKHALARAM RATCHAWORAMAHAWIHAN (WAT PHO)

Of all the monasteries of the first class Royal temples, this is the most important, as it was built by monarchs beside the Royal Grand Palace. Originally, it was an old temple from the Ayutthaya period named Wat Photharam, and people have always called it Wat Pho. We still do today.

In the reign of King Rama III there were no printed books, and people in general did not have access to the education available in temples. Wishing to rectify this, the king ordered texts to be inscribed on stone slabs around the temple which people could read and learn from. As a result, Wat Chetuphon came to be regarded as "the first university in Thailand."

◉ **Reclining Buddha:** This celebrated Buddha image is the work of artisans from the Department of the Ten Crafts. On the soles of the image's feet are the 108 auspicious signs of the Buddha in mother of pearl inlay. In the reign of King Rama III the entire image was gilded with gold leaf.

Chedi: This temple is a veritable kingdom of chedis, as there are 99 of them. There are the four chedis referred to as Phra Maha Chedi of the Four Reigns.

BANGKOK METROPOLITAN
TOURIST BUREAU

Phra Putthadevapatimakorn: The principle Buddha image is enshrined in the ubosot. It contains Buddha relics and the ashes of King Rama I.

Phra Phuttaloknatsasadajan: This image stands in an alcove behind the wihan. It is the tallest example of a bronze standing Buddha image.

Wihan: There are 12 wihan in Wat Pho, more than in any other temple. There are four Phra Wihan Thit, four Phra Wihan Kod, two Phra Wihan Noi, the Wihan of the Reclining Buddha and a Royal Wihan.

Wasukree Mansion or Poet's House: This was the residence of *Somdet Phra Mahasamanachao Krom Phra Paramanuchitchinoros*, one of the finest Rattanakosin era poets.

Wat Pho School of Traditional Medicine and Massage: The preparation of herbal medicines and diagnosis are taught here, as well as the traditional massage seen in the sculptures compiled on King Rama III's orders. The teaching is practical, and every day large numbers of visitors, Thai and foreign, come to study and to be massaged.

Chao Phor Krommaluang Chumporn Shrine: This was moved from Nanglerng Bridge to the Phra Wihan Noi, near the southern gate.

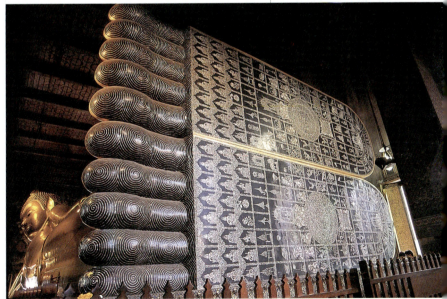

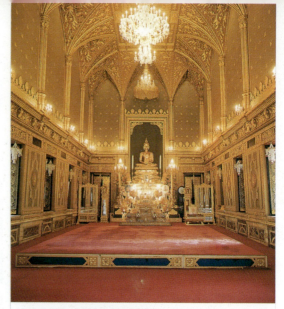

★ G9
✉ 2 Fuang Nakhon Road
Wat Ratchabophit
Sub-District
Phra Nakhon District
Bangkok 10200
☎ (662) 222-3930 221-0904
📠 (662) 222-3922 221-3995
🚌 2 2 (Exp.) 60 60 (Exp.)
🚢 1 2 12
🕐 Temple: Daily 5 am-8 pm
Ubosot: Daily 9-9:30 am
5:30-6 pm
Buddhist Sermon Day:
8 am-1:30 pm
🆓 Free Admission
⊙ Religious rite dedicated to
the late Abbot (Aug 25)
Merit making ceremony on
the anniversary of
King Rama VII (May 30)
Buddhist Lent Commencing
Day: Floral Alming
🏛 1949
🏛 First Class
🅿 Outside the Temple
➕ City Pilllar Clock Tower
Grand Palace
Old Cannon Museum
Saranrom Park Wat Pho
Wat Phra Kaeo
Wat Ratchapradit

📖 Ⓜ 📷

WAT RATCHABOPHIT
SATHITMAHASIMARAM RATCHAWORAWIHAN

King Rama V ordered this to be the first temple built after he came to the throne. It was to commemorate the Queen and his concubines. It later became the temple of King Rama VII.

◉ **Ubosot:** Exterior of the main chapel is Thai, but the interior is European in style. The patterns copy Royal decorations in mother of pearl. The door frames are "an important example of the Rattanakosin style."

Phra Puttha Ankhiros: A Buddha image in the Meditation posture inside the ubosot. It is entirely gilded with gold on a chukchi base, where the ashes of King Rama VII are kept.

Chedi: Built in the Thai style, with a notched base decorated with Bencharong ceramics. The top of the chedi holds relics of the Lord Buddha, and the enclosure around it contains Buddha images in several postures.

Wihan: This prayer hall is in the same style as the ubosot. The window frames are patterned with Royal decorations lacquered with gold leaf.

Royal Cemetery: Monuments containing the ashes of the Queen, concubines, sons and daughters of King Rama V and the Royal Family, are here in the form of Khmer stupas and chedis.

Remarkably, there are no sema, or boundary stones, around the ubosot. Instead, they are set on a circle of columns facing in eight directions.

BANGKOK METROPOLITAN
TOURIST BUREAU

★ G9
119 Chakkraphet Road
Wang Buraphaphirom
Sub-District
Phra Nakhon District
Bangkok 10200
(662) 221-3936 221-9544
(662) 623-7960
6 37 82 88
3 82
Temple: Daily 5 am-8 pm
Ubosot: Daily 9 am-10 am
5:30-6 pm
Free Admission
Religious rite dedicated
to the last Abbot (Apr 17-18)
1949
First Class
In the Temple compound
Chalermkrung Theatre
Chao Mae Tabtim Shrine
Memorial of King Rama I
Phahurat Market
Sapanhan Market
Suan Kularb College
The Old Siam Plaza
Wat Thipwariwihan

WAT RATCHABURANA RATCHAWORAWIHAN

A Chinese trader named *Liap* who lived in the late Ayutthaya period built this temple, so it is called Wat Jeen Liap, Jeen meaning "Chinese." In time, the word Jeen was dropped, leaving only the words Wat Liap.

When King Rama I was crowned, *HSH Prince Thepharipitak* restored it as a Royal temple and named it Wat Ratchaburana, which was the name of capital's temple in the Sukhothai period.

Prang: Built in the reign of King Rama III and has 28 notches on its five-level lotus base. Each level is surrounded by figures of demons, and the top of the prang is a crown with a noppasoon (Siva's weapon).

Ubosot: During World War II, this area was damaged by bombing. The present ubosot was rebuilt to the design of *Prof. Luang Wisan Silpakam (Cheua Patamachinda).*

Part of its historical importance is that *Khrua In Khong,* the monk praised as a master artist at the court, was ordained at this temple. He was "a pioneer of incorporating the European style into traditional Thai art by introducing perspective "

WAT RATCHANATDARAM WORAWIHAN

King Rama III ordered the construction of this temple as a gift to *MC Somanas*, who was later elevated by King Rama IV to the rank of *HRH Princess Somanas Vadhanawadi*.

⦿ Ubosot: The main chapel is built in the style of the Rama III with rectangular pillars and stucco gable ends. The principal Buddha image was cast in copper, and King Rama IV named it Phra Settutamuni.

Loha Prasat: This is the only sanctuary made in Thai style. Building began in the reign of King Rama III, and it was extensively decorated in the reigns of King Rama V and King Rama VI. The 37 spires of the sanctuary represent the 37 Bodhipakkhiyadhamma — the virtues leading to enlightenment. The wooden staircases in the middle room are built around large wooden posts leading upwards. In the centre is an alcove containing relics of the Buddha.

Kuti: The monks' residences are typical of the style of the reign of Rama III.

★ G9
✉ 2 Mahachai Road Bowonniwet Sub-District Phra Nakhon District Bangkok 10200
☎ (662) 224-8807 225-5749
🚌 2 5 12 15 33 35 39 42 44 47 56 59 60 70 79 201 203
🚐 Sai 2 Sai 2 (Exp.) 3 9 11 11 (Exp.) 12 17 32 38 (Old 15) 39 44 68 79 Mb 1 8 10
⛴ Passenger Boat: Panfalilat Pier (Sansap Canal)
🕘 Temple: Daily 9 am-8 pm
   Ubosot: Daily 9 am-5 pm
🎟 Free Admission
🏛 1949
👥 Third Class
🚉 Wat Ratchanatda
🅿 In side the Temple compound
✚ Ban Baat Community
   Democracy Monument
   Mahakan Fort
   Memorial of King Rama III
   Wat Mahanparam
   Wat Saket Wat Teptidaram

★ G9
✉ 2 Saranrom Road
Phra Borommaharat-
chawang Sub-District
Phra Nakhon District
Bangkok 10200
☎ (662) 223-8215 622-0744
🚌 2 60
🚕 1 2 12
🕐 Temple: Daily 5 am-10 pm
Ubosot: Daily 9-9:30 am
5-7 pm
🆓 Free Admission
🎉 Buddhist Lent Commencing Day: Floral Alming
🏛 1949
📷 1989
🏅 First Class
🅿 In the Temple compound
🏯 City Pillar Clock Tower
Grand Palace
Old Cannon Museum
Saranrom Park Wat Pho
Wat Phra Kaeo

WAT RATCHAPRADIT SATHITMAHASIMARAM RATCHAWORAWIHAN

The site of this temple was originally a coffee plantation. King Rama IV believed that traditional Royal ceremonies in the city required three temples, Wat Ratchaburana, Wat Mahathat and Wat Ratchapradit. As Bangkok had neither a Wat Ratchapradit nor a Thammayut Nikai temple near the Grand Palace, the king bought the land to give to the Thammayut sect to build the temple.

◉ **Inscriptions of King Rama IV:** There are two on stone slabs behind the wihan. The first, dated 1864, announces the building of the temple, the second, the laying of the foundation stone in 1865.

Wihan: Decorated with marble, mother-of-pearl and carved wood. Gateways and windows are decorated with stucco crowns, door and window frames with Chinese pearl. There are murals of Royal ceremonies and pictures of a solar eclipse.

Phra Puttasihingkhapatimakorn: A copy of Phra Putthasihing seated on Phra Putta-asana where the ashes of King Rama IV are kept.

Prasat Yod Prang: Two of these are in Khmer style and the front of the arch is decorated in stucco.

Khmer Prang: Contains the ashes of the Supreme Patriarch (*Sa*) and two later abbots.

Belfry: Decorated with Chinese tiles and coloured pottery.

★ G9
146 Bamrung Muang Road
Ratchabophit Sub-District
Phra Nakhon District
Bangkok 10200
☎ (662) 224-9845 222-9632
FAX (662) 222-6935
🚌 10 12 19 35 42 56 96
🚐 42
www.watsuthat.org
info@watsuthat.org
🕐 Temple: Daily 8:30 am-9 pm
Ubosot: Daily 9 am-4 pm
Wihan Luang: Daily
9 am-9 pm
💵 Foreigner 20 Bht
Sermon: Daily 7-9 pm
Songkran Festival (Apr 11-15)
Silcharinee Ceremony
(Aug 10-12 Dec 3-5)
📖 Hor Chantanusorn Public Lib.
☎ (662) 223-6885
🏛 1949
First Class
Buddhist: Sun 1-3 pm
P Inside and beside the Temple
✚ Chao Por Seua Shrine
Chalerm Krung Theatre
Devasathan Giant Swing
Rommaninart Park
Wat Mahannaparam
Wat Thepthidaram

WAT SUTHAT THEPWARARAM
RATCHAWORAMAHAWIHAN

Founded at the centre of Rattanakosin Island, this is one of Thailand's six most important temples. Construction was according to the Treatise on Warfare. King Rama I wished to make it the central temple of Bangkok and building started in 1807.

Construction was completed according to plan in the reign of King Rama VII. Good planning from the beginning earned it praise as *"the most finely proportioned temple."*

Ubosot: It is the longest in Thailand. Murals are by artisans in the reign of King Rama III. The principal Buddha image is named Phra Puttatri Lokachet, and is cast in alloy in the Subduing Mara position. In front are the 80 disciples.

Phra Wihan Luang: Copied from Wat Mongkolbophit in Ayutthaya. The central pair of doors were designed by King Rama II, who started the carving. The murals are considered to be the most beautiful work of the Rattanakosin period.

Phra Wihan Kod: Built in the reign of King Rama III, and surround the Phra Wihan Luang on all four sides. There are 156 Buddha images enshrined inside. The door frames are decorated with lacquered images of Sio Kang.

Phra Sri Sakyamuni: Cast in bronze with the base of pure cloth, in front of Phra Puttabanlang, containing the remains of King Rama VIII.

Satta Mahasathan or "the Seven Places": Represent the places the Lord Buddha resided after enlightenment. King Rama III ordered them to be copied from Phrathat Chedi.

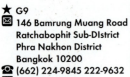

WAT THEPTHIDARAM WORAWIHARN

Originally called Wat Ban Phrayakrai Suanluang, King Rama III ordered its construction to as a gift for *HRH Prince Apsornsudathep.*

⦿ Ubosot: This is characteristic King Rama III period architecture influenced by Chinese art. Gable end is decorated with Chinese ceramics; inside is the principal Buddha image, Luang Phor Khao or Phra Buddha devavilasa.

Wihan: This is in similar style to the ubosot. Inside are images of 43 Bhiksuni — enlightened female disciples — cast in tin alloy.

Prang: Four tall prangs are located at each of the corners of the ubosot, the base of each depicting the four Chinese guardian deities.

Kuti: The monks' residences were build by artisans of King Rama III's reign, with each individual cell or kuti distinctively different.

Decorations in the temple grounds are Chinese stone statues of people and animals such as courtiers seated on the floor.

Sunthorn Phu's quarters : This kuti was occupied by Sunthorn Phu, the major poet of the early Ratanakosin period, who was ordained here as a monk. Sunthorn Phu was honoured for his outstanding cultural works by UNESCO in 1986.

★ G9
✉ 70 Maha Chai Road
   Samranrat Sub-District
   Phra Nakhon Bangkok 10200
☎ (662) 222-5067
📠 (662) 225-9205
🚌 5 35 56
⛴ Passenger Boat: Phanfalilat Pier (Sansap Canel)
🕙 Temple: Daily 5 am-9 pm
   Ubosot: Daily 8-8:30 am
   Buddisht Holy Day 8 am-8 pm
   (Wishing to visit the Ubosot should call in advance.)
🆓 Free Admission
📅 Sunthorn Phu Day (Jun 26)
📖 Sunthorn Phu's Work
🏛 Kuti Sunthorn Phu
🏛 1977
🖼 1994
🐾 Third Class
📷 Permission Required for Taking Photo inside Bldg.
🅿 In the Temple Compound
✚ Ban Baat Community BMA Bldg.
   Chao Phor Seua Shrine
   Democracy Monument
   Devasathan Giant Swing
   Rommaninat Park
   Wat Ratchabophit
   Wat Ratchanatdaram
   Wat Suthat

B A N G B O N

☎ 415-5827

FLOWER GARDENS

Bangbon was once an agricultural zone, but with the arrival of the new road it underwent a change, becoming a residential and light industrial area. Fields which had once grown rice now grow flowers and fruit commercially. The area between Eakkachai-Bangbon Road and Bangbon lane 3 and 5 is now one of the biggest flower-growing areas in Bangkok.

Among the many varieties are white and pink pigeon orchids, and fragrant flowers such as raks (*Calotropis gigantea*) and jumpees (*Michelia alba*). All are much in demand, and purchasers often come to buy the blooms direct from the garden.

★ C13
✉ Bangbon 3 and 5 Lane
Eakkachai Road
Bangbon Sub-District
Bangbon District
Bangkok 10150
🚌 43 120
🚐 Sai 7 Sai 38 Mb 9
✉ Bangbon District Office:
☎ (662) 415-5968 415-5993
📠 (662) 415-5993
🕐 Mon-Fri 8 am-4 pm
🚫 Sat Sun Public Hols.
👤 Mr. Somchai Leudpornsuksawat
Tadsanawarin Garden:
Lotus Farm
☎ (662) 895-0073
🕐 Daily 5-8 pm
👤 Mr. Khunthong Noiraksa
Mango Farm
✉ 30/2 Moo10 Bangbon 3 Lane
Bangbon Sub-District
Bangbon District
Bangkok 10150
☎ (662) 895-0906
✤ Luangpor Khao along
Eakkachai Road

The many orchards specialise in jackfruit, coconut, kathon (*Sandoricum indicum*), and a new strain of mango found in this district which has an average weight of around 700 gramme to 1.5 kilogramme.

The gardeners take their produce to Pak-khlong market as well as the Agricultural Markets Organisation. Since they are small-scale growers, they can sell everything they produce.

WAT BANGBON

Built in 1910 on the bank of Bangbon Canal, the community temple of Bangbon Tai or south Bangbon was formerly called Wat Mai-Ta-Cheuy after its founder, *Ta Cheuy* whose name was carved on the arch of the door to the ubosot, before King Rama VI granted it the official name of Wat Bangbon.

🔵 **Luangphor Gaysorn or Phra Baromsrisukot Udomprotshinkul Budhaboromborpit:** A Sukhothai-style Buddha image in the Subduing Mara posture copied from Luangphor Gaysorn of Wat Taphra in Thonburi. This Buddha image was made at Wat Ratchaorasaram and transported by boat. However, the boat was unable to pass under the raised bridge, so the image had to continue its journey overland.

★ C14
✉ 33 Moo 3 Eakkachai Road
   Bangbon Sub-District
   Bangbon District
   Bangkok 10160
☎ (662) 415-0249 416-6245
📠 43 120
🕐 Temple: 8 am-6 pm
   Wihan: 8 am-6 pm
🆓 Free Admission
🎉 Luangphor Gaysorn Annual Festival (Feb)
🅿 In the Temple compound
✚ Bangbon District Office
   Luangphor Khao along
   Eakkachai Road
   Wat Nongkhaem
Ⓜ 📷

BANGHAE

☎ 830-7231

- SARADEANG
- ORCHID FARMS
- BIRDWATCHING BY A NATURAL LAKE
- BANG WAEK RD.
- PHUTTHA MONTHON SAI 3 RD.
- KHLONG YAIPLUN
- PHASICHAROEN CANAL TRIP
- KHLONG PAI
- LIAP KHLONG THAWI-WATTHANA RD.
- KHOA-TARESAB
- PHROM SUWANSAMAKKE
- MUBAN SETTHAKIT RD.
- KHLONG BANGWAK

BRASS WORKSHOPS
MUBAN SETTHAKIT MARKET

SETTHAKIT VILLAGE

BIRDWATCHING BY A NATURAL LAKE

Every year in December and early January, thousands of Siberian grebes migrate from the bitter cold in Siberia to take refuge at this pond at the intersection of Phuttha Monthon Sai 3 and Bangwaek Road near Suan Saengtham Monastery. This is the ideal time to study the behaviour of these rare migrants.

The vegetation of the surrounding area ranges from tall trees to open fields of different kinds of grasses. It is a natural habitat not only for the Siberian grebes but also for many other species of birds and animals. It is a superb birdwatching site because of its accessibility and the numbers of birds, especially water birds, making their homes there.

★ B9
✉ Phuttha Monthon Sai 3
   Bangpai Sub-District
   Bangkae District
   Bangkok 10160
✉ Bangkae District Office:
   Public Relations
☎ (662) 803-6882
FAX (662) 803-6882
🚌 90
🚐 91
🕐 Mon-Fri 8 am-4 pm
🎟 Free Admission
🅿 In front of the Lake
⊕ Brass Workshops
   Suan Saengtham Monastery

★ B9
✉ Near Wat Saladaeng
Bangwaek Road
Bangkae District
Bangkok 10160
☎ (662) 421-6687
(Mr. Subin Pukkratum)
🚌 91 Kor
🕐 Daily 9 am-5 pm
🅿 At Wat Saladaeng
✚ Brass Workshops
Lord Buddha Images Museum
Phuttha Monthon
Utthayan Avenue

ORCHID FARMS

There are many orchid farms in Bangkae, notably in Bangpai and Laksong Sub-Districts by the Thawi-Watthana and Bangcheucknang Canals. Every morning fresh flowers are cut to sell to traders for sale to buyers at Pakkhlong Market. Big companies also come to buy flowers direct from this garden.

The orchids in this area are of good quality and find a ready market. Local gardeners' associations train growers and share information on improving conditions to help growers to breed better blooms.

★ C9
✉ 250/2 22-27 Lane
Settakit Village
Bangkae Sub-District
Bangkae District
Bangkok 10160
☎ (662) 421-0176
📠 (662) 421-7792
🚌 91
🚌 91
🕐 Mon-Fri 8 am-6 pm
 Sun Public Hols.
🅿 In front of the Workshops
✚ Bangkae District Office
Natural Lake
Phuttha Monthon
Suan Seangtham Monastery

BRASS WORKSHOPS

Mr. Pee Phromsawadht built his brass works with the knowledge that he learned from Ban Changlor Community. At first he copied ancient designs of Buddha images and antique art objects such as the kinnaree, manorah and singha.

Its initial success and diverse development made the brass works a flourishing business for more than 30 years. Mr. Pee's products now decorate many homes and offices in Thailand and overseas.

PASICHAROEN CANAL TRIP

King Rama IV ordered this long canal to be dug, and the work paid for from the opium tax. It was given the name Pasicharoen, and was officially opened in 1872 in the reign of King Rama V.

A trip by long-tail boat to observe the waterside life and nature along both banks of the canals starts from Bolar Pier, Phraya Ratchamontri Canal. It continues to Bangkeekang Canal to visit Emcharoen Art Centre, then to Wat Taaklun and Bangpai Canals.

Visitors can see the orchid farms and canal lifestyle, as well as many vegetable and flower gardens and even rice fields. Growers follow their traditional custom of using the water from the canal for cultivation, transport, bathing and recreation. It conveys the charm of this old Thai way of life.

★ B9
✉ Bangkae District Office
☎ (662) 803-6882
📠 (662) 803-6882
🚌 147
🚐 38
🕐 Mon-Fri 8 am-4 pm
　Sat Sun Public Hols.
　Canal Tour: Sat Sun
✉ Eamcharoen Art Centre
　48/1 Moo 7
　Phet Kasem 68 Lane
　Phet Kasem Road
　Bangkae Nua Sub-District
　Bangkae District
　Bangkok 10160
☎ (662) 454-0769
　7Kor 80 91 101 146
🚌 7 32 80 91 Mb 5 10 12
🕐 Daily 9 am-5 pm
🆓 Free Admission

📷 ℹ️

BANGKAPI

☎ 378-2345

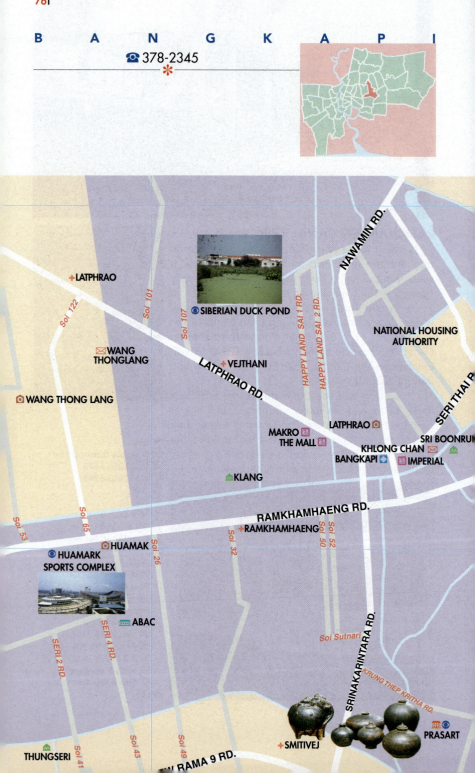

HUAMARK SPORTS COMPLEX

One of the principal sports complexes of the Sports Authority of Thailand, this is the venue for national and international competitions. The complex consists of competition and training buildings, a soccer field, tennis courts and swimming pools, as well as dormitories for athletes.

◉ **Rajamangala National Stadium:** Consists of a soccer field with track and field facilities. Beneath the stadium structure there is an all-purpose area with rooms for athletes and officials. The stadium can accommodate 60,000 spectators.

Velodrome: Consists of standard tracks 7 m. wide by 333.33 m. long. It can accommodate 2,000 spectators.

Indoor Stadium: Used for sports such as boxing and sepak takraw. It can accommodate up to 12,000 spectators.

Shooting Gallery: For both competition and training facilities, and can accommodate 2,000 spectators. The two target ranges contain an automatic dual target launch tower and has space for 500 spectators.

Indoor Sports Training Centre: Provides teaching and training for 12 kinds of sports, ranging from aerobic dance and badminton to volleyball and weight lifting etc.

★ M9
✉ 2088 Ramkhamhaeng Road
  Huamark Sub-District
  Bangkapi District
  Bangkok 10240
☎ (662) 318-0940-6
📠 (662) 318-0937
🚌 22 58 60 61 71 92 93 99 109
  113 115 122 126 137 207
  1 12 14 21 92 126 137
  Mb 3 4 7 10 15 17
⛴ Passenger Boat:
  Ramkhamhaeng Pier
  (Sansap Canal)
🕘 Mon-Fri 8:30 am-4:30 pm
  Sat Sun Public Hols.
🎟 Free Admission
  (Except for sporting event)
  Sport Training Centre:
  Membership only
☎ (662) 314-4678
    318-0904-80: 1068
📠 (662) 314-4678
🕘 Daily 9:30 am-9:30 pm
  Swimming Pool:
☎ (662) 319-9522
🕘 Thu-Sat 10 am-7 pm
  Mon Public Hols.
🅿 Sports Authority of Thailand
🏬 Big C Dept. Store
  Ramkhamhaeng U.

★ N9
✉ 9 Krung Thep Kritha 4A Lane
Krung Thep Kritha Road
Huamark Sub-District
Bangkapi District
Bangkok 10240
☎ (662) 253-9772 (Office)
379-3601 (Museum)
📠 (662) 253-9772
🕐 Office: Mon-Sat 1-6 pm
⊘ Sun
🕐 Museum: Thu-Sun
10 am-3 pm
⊘ Mon
💲 Admission Charge
(Wishing to visit the Museum should call in advance.)
📷 Taking photo inside Bldg.
🅿 In front of the Museum
🚻 ♨

PRASART MUSEUM

Many Thai art objects and antiques are sold overseas, and thus Thai people are denied the chance to seeing them. This inspired *Mr. Prasart Vongsakul* to build his collection of these art objects, and later to open the Prasart Museum. It is a centre for education and research for those interested in Thai antiquity, and a legacy for future generations.

◉ Red Palace: This Thai-style teak house is a replica of the mansion with the same name in the National Museum. Antiques from the Ayutthaya and early Rattanakosin periods are to be found there. They include many domestic items such as furniture and tea sets.

Lanna Pavilion: Situated near the Euro-style Building this Lanna-style wood pavilion is where Lanna-period Buddha images are enshrined.

European-style Building: Thai materials and household utensils used in the past, such as Bencharong and Western art objects are exhibited here.

There are a number of other interesting structures including Chedi, Buddhist Chapel, Hor Kaeow (Teakwood Library), Guanyin Shrine and Lopburi-style Chapel etc.

The garden is the setting for several Sukhothai period terra cotta pieces, and also has a collection of much sought-after Thai and foreign plants.

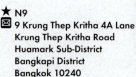

WAT PHRASIMAHATHAT WORAMAHAWIHAN

During the time when *F.M. Plaek Pibulsongkram* was Prime Minister, the government decided to build a temple which was to be called, "Wat Prachathippatai," literally "Democracy Temple" to commemorate the introduction of the democratic system into Thailand. The chosen site was near the Constitutional Defence Monument. While the temple was being built, Thai envoys to India requested the Indian government for some relics of the Lord Buddha, shoots from the sacred Pho tree and soil from the holy places to be brought back to the temple. As a result, the temple's name was changed to Phrasimahathat.

◉ **Pho Tree:** Standing on the Circular Island in front of the chedi. At the foot of the tree is a Buddha image in the Meditation posture.

Chedi Simahathat: A double-layer chedi, the outer layer enclosing a smaller one. Between the two is a corridor with four entrances. The relics of the Lord Buddha and the holy soil were placed in the middle of the chedi. Inside the bigger chedi are 112 apertures for urns containing the bones and ashes of important dignitaries approved by Parliament as having "contributed greatly to the nation."

- ★ K4
- ✉ 1 Moo 6 Phahonyothin Road
  Anusaowari Sub-District
  Bangken District
  Bangkok 10220
- ☎ (662) 521-5974 521-0311
- 📠 (662) 521-3938
- 🚌 26 34 39 59 107 114 126
- 🚐 3 12 13 22 24 39 49 Mb 8
- 🕐 Temple: Daily 5 am-10 pm
  Ubosot: Daily 7:30-8:30 am
  3-6 pm
  Chedi: 5 am-8 pm
- 💲 Free Admission
- 🎉 Songkarn Festival (Apr 13)
  Visakhapuja Day
  Loykrathong Festival
- 🏨 First Class
- 🍽 Buddhist: Sun
- 🅿 In the Temple compound
- ✚ Bangken District Office
  Bangken Police Station
  Central Dept. Store
  Constitutional Defence
  Monument

📖 🚇 📷

BANGKHOLAEM
☎ 291-2341

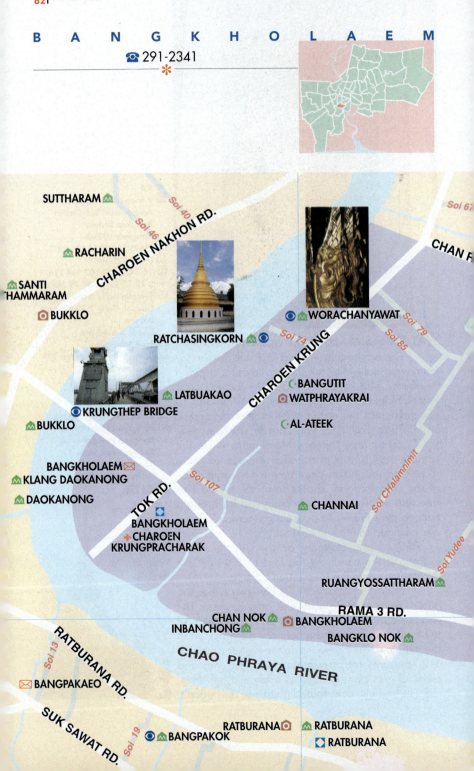

KRUNGTHEP BRIDGE

The 350.80 m. Krungthep Bridge opened on June 25, 1959 was the second bridge to be built across Chao Phraya River, following Puttayodfa or Memorial Bridge. Apart from facilitating communication across the Chao Phraya, the bridge can be opened to allow the passage of ships along the river.

★ G11
- Thanon Tok Intersection
  Bangkholaem Sub-District
  Bangkholaem District
  Bangkok 10210
- 1 15 17 22 75 89 205
- 4 Sai 38 Mb 9 (New Route) 20
- Daily 24 hrs.
- Free Admission
- Small park on Rama III Road
- Central Dept. Store
  Tram at the Yannawa Metro.
  Electricity Authority
  Wat Ratchasingkorn
  Wat Yannawa

★ G11
✉ 2114 Chareonkrung 74 Road
Wat Phraya Krai Sub-District
Bangkholaem District
Bangkok 10120
☎ (662) 289-1414
📠 (662) 289-1414
🚌 1 15 17 22 75
🚐 4 Sai 38 Mb 20
⛴ Chao Phraya Express Boat:
Ratchasingkorn Pier
🕐 Temple: Daily 8 am-5 pm
Ubosot: Daily 8 am-5 pm
💵 Free Admission
🎉 Luangphor Sukhothai
Festival (End of Mar-Apr)
🅿 In the Temple compound
🏨 Maenam Hotel
Wat Ladbuakhao
Wat Phai-ngern-chotinaram
Wat Worachanyawart

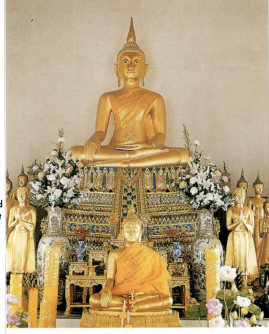

WAT RATCHASINGKORN

The temple is thought to have been built in the reign of King Boromkot (1732-1758) at the end of the Ayutthaya period. Later, *Somdet Krom Phra Ratchawangbowon Maha Surasinghanat*, the Crown Prince in the reign of King Rama I, used his private funds to renovate it without making this public. This we learn from the eight slate Semas attached on each of the eight directions of the outer wall of the main chapel, the religious artifacts were built according to the order of the Crown Prince as a dedication to Buddhism.

Ubosot: It is believed to have been restored by *HSH Princess Pikulthong and Princess Gaysorn*, daughters of the Crown Prince, following the style popular in the reign of King Rama III.

Luangphor Daeng: An Ayutthaya Buddha image with Sukhothai influence made in a mixture of gold and bronze.

Chedi: The two chedis at the back of the ubosot and phra wihan (sermon hall) were built in "haystack" shape, a Rattanakosin chedi style.

The Must See Sites In BANGKOK | 85

WAT WORACHANYAWAT

Formerly called Wat Bangkwang-lang, the temple was built in 1798, during the reign of King Rama II.

Thammas Bussabok: The pulpit where the monks deliver sermons was made by Ayutthaya craftsmen in King Rama III's reign. The finely carved thammas is one of the three most beautiful ancient thammas, and remains in good condition.

Ubosot: The main chapel's roof is covered with tiles, green at the outer rim and yellow at the inner rim. Decorating the roof are chorfa finials and bairaka. At the front and back pediments are pictures of the Hindu god Vishnu. The gilded stucco Buddha image is in the Subduing Mara posture. Its name is unknown. The two mondops in front of the ubosot house several Buddha images in different postures including Nak Prok, Buddha protected by a naga.

- ★ C11
- ✉ 1020/20 Charoenkrung 72 Lane Charoenkrung Road Phraya Krai Sub-District Bangkholaem District Bangkok 10120
- ☎ (662) 289-0415
- 🚌 1 15 17 22 75
- 4 Sai 38 75 Mb 9 20
- ⛴ Chao Phraya Express Boat: Wat Worachanyawat Pier
- 🕐 Temple: Daily 5:30 am-10 pm Ubosot: Daily 8-10 am 4-6 pm
- 💲 Free Admission
- 📅 New Year's Merit Making Festival (Dec 31-Jan 1) Songkran Festival (Apr 13) Loykrathong Festival Buddhist Sermon Days Sun: Sermon Meditation Training: Daily 5-8:30 pm
- Computer & English Centre ☎ (662) 688-1713 BMA Vocational Training Centre ☎ (662) 292-0194
- 🅿 In the Temple compound
- ✚ Bangkok Fish Market Robinson Dept. Store Wat Don Wat Ratchasingkorn Wat Sutthiwararam Wat Yannawa

BANGKHUNTHIAN
☎ 416-5406

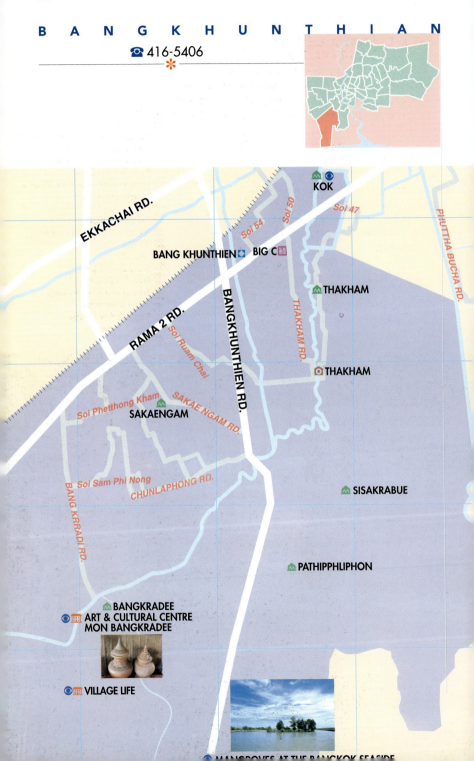

ART & CULTURAL CENTRE OF MON BANGKRADEE

The museum located the house of the headman of a Mon village and was established by a group of people wishing to collect and preserve objects and aspects of Mon art and culture.

The village-style museum contains tools and utensils used by Mon people: Pottery, antique gold ornaments, musical instruments, Mon scriptures and Buddha images.

★ C15
✉ 12 Kor Moo 9
Bangkradee Lane Rama II Road
Samae-dum Sub-District
Bangkhunthian District
Bangkok 10150
✉ Bangkhunthian District Office Development Dept.
☎ (662) 416-1260
FAX (662) 416-1260
☎ (662) 452-2062 (Museum)
🚌 76 105
🚌 140 141
🕐 Daily 8 am-5 pm
💲 Free Admission
✋ Taking photo inside Bldg.
🅿 Wat Bangkradee
⛨ Bangkradee Village
   Wat Bangkradee

BANGKOK METROPOLITAN TOURIST BUREAU

MANGROVES AT THE BANGKOK SEASIDE

Moo 9 and 10 Takham Sub-District of Bangkhunthian District is extended along a 4-km. bay. Nature dominates the surrounding area, an extensive mangrove swamp which is the habitat of seabirds.

The old fishing community, the only one left in Bangkok, still lives in the traditional way. The main income of this community derives from shoreline fishing, shrimp farming, and breeding mussels. Many families process these products to make preserved foods and flavourings like salted fish and fish sauce.

With the increase in the size of the mangrove area, there are plans to develop it as a nursery for aquatic plants and animals, an environmental study centre and an eco-tourism site for Bangkok in the future.

★ D17
✉ Moo 9 and 10 Thakham Sub-District Bangkhunthian District Bangkok 10150
✉ Bangkhunthian District Office Development Dept.
☎ (662) 316-5406
FAX (662) 416-1260
⊙ Mon-Fri 8 am-4 pm
Ⓒ Sat Sun Public Hols.
🅿 Wat Prachabamrung
(Route: Follow the Bangkhunthian-Seaside Road then turn into Wat Prachabamrung and take the boat from Wat Prachabamrung Pier to Chalermchaipattana Canal)
✚ Mangrove Museum
Village Life Museum
Wat Bangkradee Wat Kok

BANGNA

☎ 399-1794

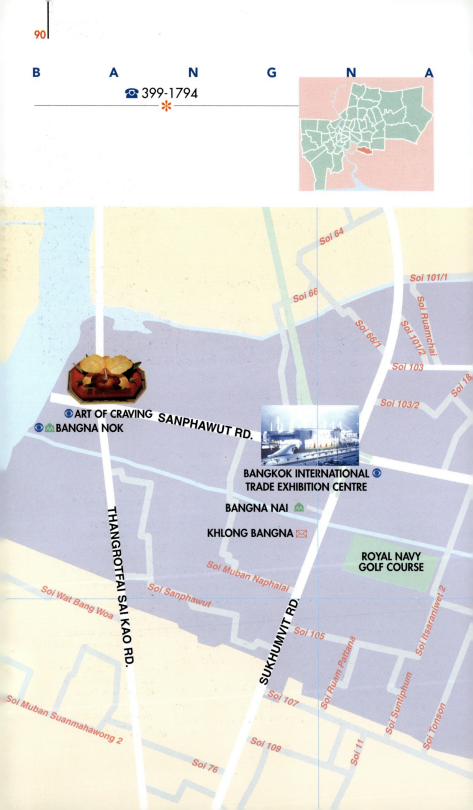

BANGKOK INTERNATIONAL TRADE EXHIBITION CENTRE (BITEC)

The growth of the world economy and industry have led to the exchange of information and technology as well as culture among the countries of the world community. International meetings and exhibitions have become important activities which benefit the country in many ways.

BITEC was specially designed as a multi-purpose centre in response to the demand for exhibition and seminar facilities.

◉ Main Building: This single-level 20,000 sq.m. exhibition hall was built without supporting pillars. It contains seminar, meeting and reception halls of various sizes. The exhibition area can be extended to an open space outside the hall when needed.

Included in the Centre are a bank, a post office, a business centre, a 1,400-seat international food centre, restaurants, a children's play corner, and other services. Delivery area and warehouses are available for exhibitors.

Its location on the Bangna-Trat highway where the expressway ends makes travelling from the Centre to Bangkok business districts very easy and convenient.

★ L12
✉ 8 Bangna (km 1) Road
   Bangna Sub-District
   Bangna District
   Bangkok 10260
☎ (662) 749-3939: 3138
📠 (662) 749-3949
✉ info@bitec.net
🚌 38 46 46 (Exp.) 48 366
🚍 23 38 46 Mb 6
🕙 Office: Mon- Fri 8 am-5 pm
   Sat Sun Public Hols.
   BITEC: Daily
🏢 Organisation Space Rented for Meeting Seminar Training Trade Exhibition
🅿 In the BITEC compound
✚ Bangna District Office
   Central Dept. Store
   Imperial Dept. Store
   Wat Bangna Nok

★ K12
100 The Lane opposite to
Wat Bangna Nok
Sunphawut Road
Bangna Sub-District
Bangna District
Bangkok 10260
☎ (662) 398-7862
🚌 2 23 25 38 129 ←→ Minibus
🚐 Sai 2 7 8 11 13 142 Mb 6
←→ Minibus
🚤 Taxi Boat:
Phra Pradeang Pier ←→
Kongrue Bangna Pier
🕐 Mon-Fri 9 am-5 pm
📚 Teaching Training:
Chatuchak Weekend Market
Project 11 Lock No. 6
Sat Sun 10:30 am-6 pm
Wat Pho Sun 9 am-12 Noon
🅿 In front of the House
✚ Wat Bangna Nai
Wat Bangna Nok

ART OF CARVING

In 1996, *Capt. Ruen Nirun* was presented with an award for his outstanding contribution to the conservation of Thai Culture in the Visual Art (Craftsmanship) category.

Capt. Ruen carves model boats with a specially-designed, single-edged, pointed knife. From studying various kinds of old carving knives and adapting them to suit to his work, *Capt. Ruen* found he could make his own knives by himself, from forging the steel to fixing to the handle.

As a result, he has been able to develop a special knife that is easy to control by the skilled movement of his fingers. It allows him to make his models with speed and accuracy, and produce a uniquely beautiful carving style.

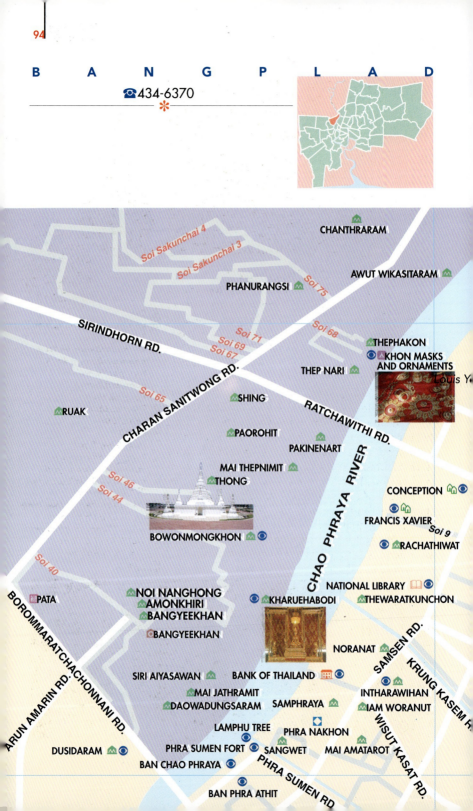

KHON MASKS AND ORNAMENTS

In the classical khon tradition, the masks and costumes on the stage are a colourful expression of the personality of the characters: the charisma of the Hero and Heroine, the power of the Ogre and the shrewdness of the Monkey. The unique costumes are designed to emphasise the characters and the story.

Mr. *Sathaporn Liangsorn* is a former khon actor who learned the art of making costumes from *Master Sakorn Youngkiewsod*. He has used his experience to teach the making of khon masks, ornaments and all the elaborate classical ornaments such as brooches, head dresses, belts, bracelets and anklets, to all who are interested. He hopes that those who learn from him will pass on their knowledge and thus help to preserve this unique Thai cultural heritage.

Today, Mr. Sathaporn still takes part in khon productions, as well as teaching and producing many traditional-style performances.

★ G8
- Wat Thepakorn Occupation Training Centre
  Charansanitwong 68 Lane
  Charansanitwong Road
  Bangplad Sub-District
  Bangplad District
  Bangkok 10700
- (01) 482-0546
- 18 110 203
- Mb 10
- Daily 8 am- 5 pm
- Displays and classes in making khon masks and ornaments: Daily 8 am-8 pm
- Free Admission
  The hall can be hired for khon and likae performances.
- In Wat Thepakorn compound
- Wat Bowonmongkhon
  Wat Kharuehabodi

★ G8
✉ 1265
Charansanitwong 44 Lane
Charansanitwong Road
Bangyeekhan Sub-District
Bangplad District
Bangkok 10700
☎ (662) 424-8074 433-5440
FAX (662) 433-5440
🚌 28 56 66 103 108 203
🚐 10 203 Mb 10
⛴ Ferry: Thewes Pier ◀ ▶
   Wat Bowonmongkon Pier
🕐 Temple: Daily 5 am-10 pm
   Ubosot: Daily 8 am-6 pm
💰 Free Admission
🕯 Candle Festival (Jul)
🏛 Third Class
🏫 Wat Bowonmongkon
   Sirimongkonsueksa
   Kindergarten
🅿 In the Temple compound
✚ Wat Daoduengsarm
   Wat Karuehabodi
   Wat Phakineenat
Ⓜ 📷

WAT BOWONMONGKHON RATCHAWORAWIHAN

This temple, formerly called Wat Lingkob, was restored and given to the Mon people for their religious rites by *Somdet Phra Bowonratchao Krom Phraratchawangbowon Mahasenanurak*, who also gave the temple its present name. In 1919, it was transferred to the Thammayutti sect. It is well-known for the study of Buddhist scripture.

◉ Ubosot: The main chapel has a three-tiered roof decorated with chorfa, garuda head finial and bairaka, a leaf-like ridge on its sloping edge. On the pediments are padyot, embroidered monks' fans, and kruathao, Thai floral motifs. The ceiling, doors and windows are in the Chinese style, and there is a chedi at all four corners to give protection.

Rama IX Celebration Park: In the temple grounds on the bank of Chao Phraya River, this park is used for recreational and religious activities.

Chedi Hongsa: These were built in the Mon style during the reign of King Rama IV. They consist of a main stupa and eight minor stupa on the same square base. The style and the materials all indicate the style of the First Reign.

WAT KARUEHABODI

Phraya Ratchamontriborrirak (Phu), Lord High Chamberlain and minister of the treasury in the reign of King Rama III, donated his old house to be made a temple. King Rama III gave the temple its name and donated its principal Buddha image, Phra Saegkum.

⦿ **Phra Saengkum:** The principal Buddha image was cast in an ancient kind of gold known as noppakun. It is in the late Chiengsaen style called Chiengsaen Singhasam, as is evidenced by its frame-like hair and the edge of the sankati or shawl, which falls to the navel. The image is said to contain relics of the Buddha.

According to the story, this image dates from the Lanna period, but the King of Laos, *Chaichettha* removed it from Chiang Mai and took it to Luang Prabang. When he moved his capital to Vientiane, he took the image with him. Later, when *Chao Phraya Bodindecha* conquered Vientiane, he brought the image back to Siam.

Ubosot: The main chapel has a two-tiered roof of glazed ceramic tiles in the style of the Third Reign. There are none of the traditional roof ornaments, and the pediments are decorated with Chinese porcelain. Traces of murals still remain in the interior, but most of them are damaged.

★ G8
✉ 952 Charansanitwong 44 Lane
Charansanitwong Road
Bangyeekhan Sub-District
Bangplad District
Bangkok 10700
☎ (662) 423-0264 424-0002
FAX (662) 883-3597
28 56 66 103 108 203
🚌 10 203 Mb 10
⛴ Ferry: Thewes Pier ◄ ►
Wat Karuehabodi Pier
🕐 Temple: Daily 5 am-10 pm
Ubosot: Daily 8-9 am 5-6 pm
(Wishing to visit outside these hours should call in advance.)
🎫 Free Admission
🎉 Songkran Festival (Apr 12-13)
Loykrathong Festival
🏛 1949
🚌 Third Class Ordinary
🏛 Wat Karuehabodi
🅿 In the Temple compound
✚ Wat Bangyeekhan
Wat Borwonmongkhon
Wat Noi Nanghong
Wat Paorohit Wat Thong
Ⓜ 📷

BANGRAK

☎ 233-9750

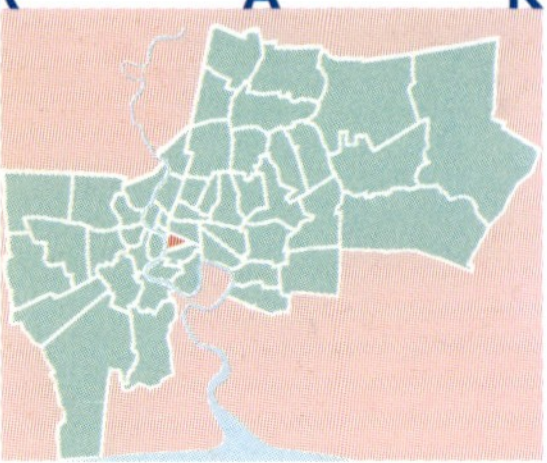

- MAHAPHRUETTHARAM
- SI PHRAYA
- KAEOJAMFA
- ✚ ST. JOSEPH
- BANGRAK
- BANGRAK
- BANGKOK FOLK MUSEUM
- KLANG ✉
- NEILSON HAYS
- ORIENTAL HOTEL
- SRI MAHAM ARIAMMAN TEMPLE
- ✚ LERDSIN
- SUAN PHLU

Roads: MAHA NAKHON RD., Soi Phraya Damrong, Soi Phra Nakharet, RAMA 4 RD., Soi Naras, Soi Jindatawin, SI PHRAYA RD., NARAS RD., CHAROEN KRUNG RD., Soi 45, SURAWONG RD., DECHO RD., MAHESAK RD., SILOM RD., Soi 9, Soi 40, PAN RD., SURASAK RD., SI WIANG RD.

- ★ H10
- ✉ 273 Charoenkrung 43 Lane
  Charoenkrung Road
  Si Phraya Sub-District
  Bangrak District
  Bangkok 10500
- ☎ (662) 233-7027 (Museum)
  231-6930-8: (Office)
  (Mrs. Waraporn Surawadee)
- 🚌 1 35 36 75 93
- 🚐 9 Mb 16
- ⚓ Chao Phraya Express Boat:
  Si Phraya Pier
- 🕒 Contact: Mon-Fri 9 am-5 pm
  Museum: Sat Sun 10 am-5 pm
- 🎟 Free Admission
  (Tour provided, 20 visitors
  limit for each tour.)
- 🅿 In front of the Museum
- ✚ Central Post Office
  Oriental Hotel
  Royal Orchid Sheraton Hotel
  Wat Mahaphruettharam

BANGKOK FOLK MUSEUM

Nowadays, the sight of a wooden Thai-style house in the heart of Bangkok is a rarity. *Ms. Waraporn Surawadee* is the owner of one, her ancestors' home which was built before World War II. She decided to turn it into a private museum, Bangkok Folk Museum, giving Bangkok another historical tourist destination.

In the museum visitors can see a variety of household utensils from former times, items used in ceremonies and collections of antiques.

All the exhibits are classified and categorised according to the standard system used in museums.

NEILSON HAYS LIBRARY

H10
195 Surawong Road
Surawong Sub-District
Bangrak District
Bangkok 10500
(662) 233-1731
FAX (662) 233-1731
1 16 36 75 93
16 36 Mb 3 6 16
Tue-Sat 9:30 am-4 pm
Sun 9:30 am-2 pm
Mon Public Hols.
Non-Member 50 Bht
Art Exhibition
Meeting with the writer
1982
Children 1,300 Bht/year
Adult 1,800 Bht/year
Family 2,000 Bht/year
Permission required for taking photo inside Bldg.
In front of the Libarry
Central Post Office
Phat Phong Road
Silom Road
Wat Mahaphruettharam

The library was founded on January 25, 1869 with the name Bangkok Ladies Library Association. One of the founders was *Mrs. Jennie Neilson Hays*, who devoted much of her life to serving the community. On her death in 1920, her husband built the current library and dedicated the building to her as a permanent symbol of his love.

The Buliding: When the library opened its doors for the fist time, the Bangkok Times reported, "this magnificent building...is a grand palace on a small scale." The Western-style building features domes, stucco pillars, ornate moulding and louvred shutters.

The day-to-day administration of the library is undertaken by the librarian and her staff with twelve volunteers form the Board of the Neilson Hays Library Association, an all-lady team.

Rotunda Gallery: The gallery in the library holds exhibitions by both Thai and foreign artists all year round. It was the brainchild of *Nancy Chandler*, who believes that a library ought to have a gallery in order to support and encourage artists to show their work to the public.

ORIENTAL HOTEL

The opening of the country in the reign of King Rama IV led to important changes to Bangkok with the visits of foreign diplomats, travellers, traders and missionaries, and it brought to the city its first hotel in 1865.

At that time, two Danish seamen, *Captains Jarck* and *Salje*, got together to found the Oriental Hotel on the banks of the Chao Phraya River.

◉ Old Building: S. Cardu, an Italian architect, designed this first building, and its facade is the original symbol of the hotel. The suites in this wing of the hotel are named after writers who have stayed there, such as *Somerset Maugham* and *Joseph Conrad*.

Oriental Hoteliers' School: The school building on the opposite bank of the river was once the house of *Phraya Mahaisawan*, the first mayor of Thonburi. He played a major role in developing the Thonburi side of the city.

★ H10
✉ 48 Chareonkrung 40 Lane
   Chareonkrung Road
   Bangrak Sub-District
   Bangrak District
   Bangkok 10500
☎ (662) 236-0400 236-0420
📠 (662) 236-1937-9
🖱 bscorbkk@loxinfo.co.th
   www.mandarin-oriental.com
🚌 1 15 35 75 77 115
🚐 2 4 15 36 Sai 38 93 75 77
   Mb 17 20
⚓ Chao Phraya Express Boat:
   Oriental Pier
🕘 Office: Mon-Sat 8 am-5 pm
🚫 Sun Public Hols.
📖 Reading Room: Daily
   8 am-8 pm
🚏 Oriental Hoteliers'
🅿 Hotel's parking Bldg.
✚ Bangkok Folk Museum
   French Embassy

SRI MAHAMARIAMMAN TEMPLE

Built in 1879, Brahman (Hindu) temple of the Shakti sect, which reveres this "mother of the gods."

Indians from Tamil Nadu in Southern Indian came to Southern Thailand and established a community on Silom Canal. Traders and labourers, they built Sri Mahamariamman Temple to worship. Later, more land was purchased and a new temple built, which has been developed and renovated to the present day.

Inside is decorated with a principal image of Sri Mahamariamman (Uma Devi), surrounded by Ganesha, Khandakumara, Krisna, Vishnu, Rasmi and Kali. In the courtyard is a small shrine containing a Shiva's Lingam (phallus). Built in Chola and Palva styles to be seen in Tamil Nadu.

Daily rituals are carried out at noon.

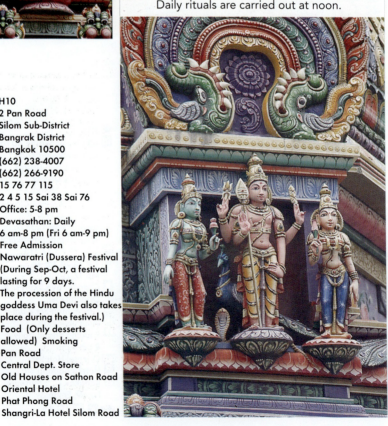

★ H10
- 2 Pan Road
  Silom Sub-District
  Bangrak District
  Bangkok 10500
- ☎ (662) 238-4007
- FAX (662) 266-9190
- 15 76 77 115
- 2 4 5 15 Sai 38 Sai 76
- Office: 5-8 pm
  Devasathan: Daily
  6 am-8 pm (Fri 6 am-9 pm)
- Free Admission
- Nawaratri (Dussera) Festival (During Sep-Oct, a festival lasting for 9 days. The procession of the Hindu goddess Uma Devi also takes place during the festival.)
- Food (Only desserts allowed) Smoking
- P Pan Road
- Central Dept. Store
  Old Houses on Sathon Road
  Oriental Hotel
  Phat Phong Road
  Shangri-La Hotel Silom Road

WAT MAHAPHRUETTHARAM WORAWIHAN

"You will soon be the master of all lives," said the Abbot of this temple to King Rama IV when the king, then in the monkhood, came for the Pha Pa robe offering ceremony. In reply, the king promised the Abbot a new temple if his prediction came true, and, on his accession, he ordered the temple to be entirely renovated.

Murals: The paintings depict Tudonkawatra the 13 ascetic practices of Buddhism, in contrast to most temple murals which tend to depict the story of the Ten Lives, or the life story of the Lord Buddha.

Ubosot: The main chapel has a two-tier roof decorated with traditional chorfa and bairaka. The carving on the gable is of a crown above a throne with two-tier parasols on each side, the Royal insignia of King Rama IV.

Wihan of the Reclining Buddha: The prayer hall dates from the early Rattanakosin period. The Reclining Buddha is in the eastern part, while in the western part is a Buddha image in the Subduing Mara posture.

Prangs: There are four Khmer-style stupas of different sizes.

- ★ H10
- 5/9 Mahapreuttharam Road Mahapruettharam Sub-District Bangrak District Bangkok 10500
- ☎ (662) 236-5678 266-2844
- FAX (662) 233-0059
- 1 16 35 36 75 93
- 93
- 1. Chaophraya Express Boat: Harbour Dept. Pier Si Phraya Pier
  2. Ferry: Si Phraya Pier
- ⏲ Temple: 5 am-10 pm Ubosot: 8 am-6 pm
- Free Admission
- Buddhist Lent Commencing Day: Bathing Robe Draw Rice Alming (Aug 12) Buddhist Lent Final Day: Dhevo Alming
- 1982
- Third Class
- Mahapreuttharam Sattri Mahaphruettharam
- P In the Temple compound
- About Cafe Bangkok Railway Station Wat Trimitr

BANGSUE

☎ 586-9978

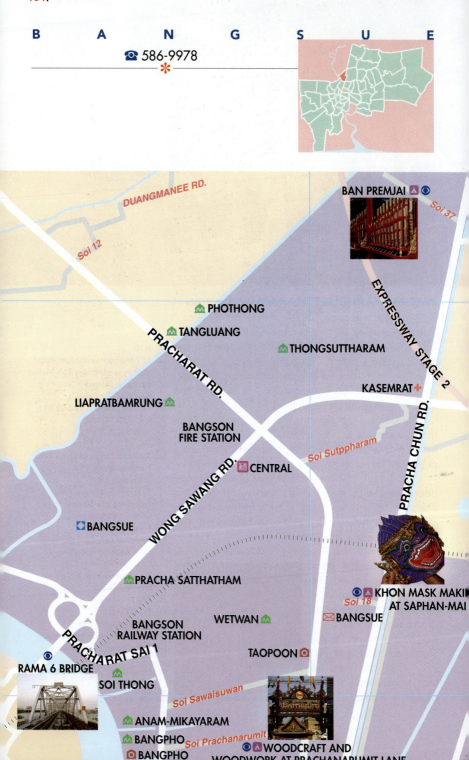

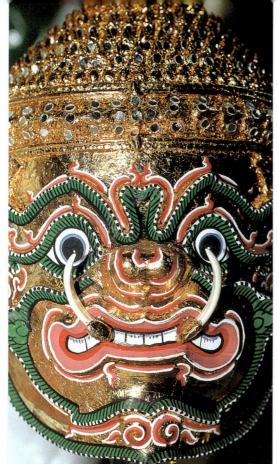

CENTRE OF KHON MASK MAKING AT SAPHAN MAI COMMUNITY

Khon is a branch of traditional theatre in which the performers wear masks called "hua khon" or khon heads. They usually perform scenes from Ramakien, the Thai version of the Ramayana epic.

Khon mask-making has been carried on by National Artist *Louis Youngkiewsod*, for generations. The family were all khon and puppet show players who made and repaired their own costumes. When the popularity of traditional shows gave way to more modern entertainments, the family changed to making khon masks to sell as decoration and gifts.

Mrs. *Sa-ngad Rodpai*, 69, has been making khon masks for about 30 years. Each mask takes approximately three days to finish and the price is between 800-1,000 baht, depending on the design.

★ 16
✉ 602 Saphan Mai Community
  Prachachun 18 Lane
  Prachachun Road
  Bansue Sub-District
  Bansue District
  Bangkok 10800
☏ (662) 585-7693
🚌 16 66 67 70 112
🚌 66 67 70
⏰ Daily 8 am-6 pm
Ⓟ In front of the House
✚ Premjai House
  Wat Thammawat

CENTRE OF WOOD CARVING AT PRACHA-NARUEMIT LANE

    The quiet lanes of Pracha-naruemit and Sawaisuwan were brought to life when a road was built through the area. Chinese families whose forefathers had settled in Wat Yuan, Saphan Kao, Saphan Dum, Dumrongrak Road, Wat Saket, and Banglamphu woodwork centres began to migrate to the new Pracha-naruemit Road.

    The new settlers, most of them furniture makers, brought with them the art of wood carving, and today, there are more than 200 furniture shops

and factories built side by side, one after the other for more than a kilometre along Pracha-naruemit Road.

Not surprisingly, the road became known as "Furniture Street." It is the city's biggest wooden furniture centre, an ideal place to shop for fine wooden crafts and furniture of all kinds, cabinets, doors, window frames, beds and decorative items.

★ H7
- Pracha-naruemit Community
  Pracha-naruemit Lane
  Pracharat Road
  Bangsue Sub-District
  Bangsue District
  Bangkok 10800
- 5 32 33 49 64 90 117
- 6 23
- Daily 8 am-5 pm
- Pracha-naruemit Lane
- Rama VI Bridge
  Rama VII Bridge
  Wat Bangpho-omawad
  Wat Soitong

- ★ 7Chor Moo 14
- ✉ Prachachun 37 Lane
  Prachachun Road
  Bangsue Sub-District
  Bangsue District
  Bangkok 10800
- ☎ (662) 587-8969
- 🚌 66 67 70 112
- 🚕 66 67 70
- ⏲ Daily 8 am-6 pm
- 💰 Free Admission
- 📖 Teaching Thai music
- 🅿 In front of the House
- ✚ Saphan Mai Community

PREMJAI HOUSE (CENTRE FOR MAKING THAI MUSICAL INSTRUMENTS)

Now 61, and head of the family, *Mr. Sumrouy Premjai* is a descendant of *Master Prung Premjai*, a well-known music master in reign of King Rama VI. It was *Master Prung* who invented the three-piece angalung, adapted from the Javanese angalung, an Indonesian musical instrument made of bamboo.

Mr. Sumrouy has been surrounded by Thai musical instruments since birth. Since his father passed away, he has always kept his three-piece angalung in remembrance. From it, he studied the making of other Thai musical instruments and learned how to improve their quality.

Today, his house is well-known for the making and repairing of all kinds of traditional Thai musical instruments, such as *ranard-ek* and *ranard-tum*, the treble and bass xylophones, drums, gong, the small gongs in a tuned circle, *sor*, the stringed gourd played with a bow, *jakae*, (the Thai zither), and *kim*, the Chinese-style zither.

BANGKOK METROPOLITAN
TOURIST BUREAU

RAMA VI BRIDGE

Rama VI bridge was built in 1922 during the reign of King Rama V at Bangson Sub-District. It was designed to be a rail link between the eastern bank of the Chao Phraya River and the western bank, and thus connect the railway systems of Bangkok with the west and south of the country. The bridge has a beam of eight metres, allowing medium-sized ships to pass beneath it.

During World War II, the bridge was severely damaged. Repairs were started in 1950, during the reign of *HM King Bhumibol Adulyadej*.

The present Rama VI Bridge is different from the original one, as it is built in the style of the *Warren Lype* Bridge, and it carries road traffic as well as the railway.

★ H6
✉ Prachachun Road
Bangsue Sub-District
Bangsue District
Bangkok 10800
🚇 18 32 33 49 50 64 90 110 117 203
🚌 6 23 49 25Koe 203 Mb 1
🕐 Daily 24 hrs.
🆓 Free Admission
🅿 Foot of the Bridge
✚ Centre of wood carving at Pracha-naruemit Lane
Wat Prachasatthatham
Wat Soithong
📷

BANGKOK NOI

☎ 434-9077

BAN BU COMMUNITY: MAKERS OF STONE-FINISHED KHAN

★ F8
✉ Ban Bu Community
Charansanitwong 32 Lane
Charansanitwong Road
Siriraj Sub-District
Bangkoknoi District
Bangkok 10700
☎ (662) 424-1689 424-7493
FAX (662) 435-2133
🚌 40 56 57 79 103 108
🚗 9 10 68 80
⏱ Daily 9 am- 6 pm
💰 Free Admission
🅿 Wat Suwannaram
🚻 Bangkoknoi District Office
Wat Suwannaram

Khan are large, earthenware bowls used for storing water. Flowers were sometimes floated in them to give the water a pleasant aroma. They could also be used to hold rice to be donated to monks, as the flowers would impart fragrance to the rice. The most highly regarded khan is the stone-finished type.

Making stone-finished khan has been an industry carried on in the community since the Ayutthaya period. When Ayutthaya fell to the Burmese, the villagers fled to the Banglamphu area before settling in Ban Bu, where they remain to the present day.

The industry relies entirely on human labour. No machinery is used except at the final polishing stage. In the old days, people used *thong mar lor*, believed to be gold sent from China to make khan. Today, they use copper and tin mixed with fragments of gold from old khan thought to be thong mar lor.

The three molten metals are combined in a single mould and fired again. The resulting alloy is hammered into shape and turned on a lathe. In the past, fine crushed stone and water wrapped in a cloth were used to polish the surface of the khan. Today, this is done by crushing the moulds after casting. As they have been in the fire during the casting process, they make a good polishing medium.

Stone-finished khan are still used for their original purpose, but are now mostly in demand as house decorations, and are a favourite gift for foreign visitors.

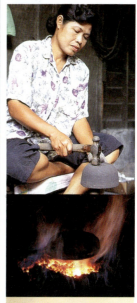

BANGKOKNOI CANAL

In the year 1522, *King Chairachathirat* of Ayutthaya commanded a short canal to be cut at Bangkokyai from the mouth of the Bangkoknoi Canal to the mouth of the Bangkokyai Canal. This later became part of Chao Phraya River, and today it is the section which flows from Thammasat University to Wat Arun. The part of the Chao Phraya River which formerly ran through area of Bangkok then became known as the Bangkoknoi and Bangkokyai canals.

When it was the part of Chao Phraya River, the Bangkoknoi Canal area was an agricultural zone, and the lifestyle of the community was simple. Changes came after the digging of the

The Must See Sites In BANGKOK

★ G9
✉ Bangkoknoi Canal
Siriraj Sub-District
Bangkoknoi District
Bangkok 10700
✉ Mitr Chao Praya Express
Boat Co., Ltd.
☎ (622) 225-6179 623-6169
📠 (662) 221-2297
🚢 Sightseeing Boat:
Tha Chang Pier
🕐 Sat Sun Public Hols.
9 am-3:30 pm
✉ Bangkoknoi Heritage Tour
☎ (662) 424-6189
🚢 Sightseeing Boat:
Wang Na Pier
🕐 Sat 8:30 am-5 pm
✠ Ban Bu Community
Royal Barges Museum
Wat Cheunglane
Wat Nairong Wat Rakhang
Wat Srisudaram
Wat Suwannaram

new canal; the area became more accessible and this led to an increase in the population of the canal-side community.

In 1972, Thonburi Province was combined with Bangkok to become the nation's capital. This brought more roads and public utilities to the Thonburi side and to the canal area. Improved conditions attracted more and more people, and from a small agricultural community it grew into a residential area with industrial and trading zones.

However, there are still places around the banks of the Bangkoknoi Canal where the people maintain their old traditions and lifestyle. Among them are Wat Suwannaram, Wat Srisudaram and the Ban Bu Community.

NATIONAL MUSEUM OF THE ROYAL BARGES

In the past, Thailand was an agricultural society with settled communities growing up beside the waterways. The river was the most important avenue of communication, and boats were the standard form of transport for everyone.

The Royal barges were used only by the King and the Royal family when they travelled. The ceremony of Royal travel by water has been a tradition since the Ayutthaya period. The formation of the Royal barge procession was in accordance with the form laid down in the Strategy Textbook.

The boathouse where the Royal barges were kept was under the control of the Bureau of the Royal Household and the Royal Thai Navy. In 1947, it was transferred to the Department of Fine Arts for the repair and restoration of all the barges, which were registered as a national heritage. The boathouse then became The National Museum of Royal Barges, and since 1974 it has exhibited

the Royal Barges as well as artifacts and accessories used in the ceremony.

⦿ Suphannahong Royal Barge: The prow of the barge was sculpted in a mythological swan figure, and the vessel was completed in the reign of King Rama VI. This is the highest class of Royal barge, and it was awarded the Sea Heritage Medal from the World Ships Organisation of Great Britain in 1981.

Anantanagaraj Royal Barge: The prow of this barge is carved in the form of a seven-head naga. It is used to carry the Buddha image or Phra Krathin, the monks' robes offered during the festival.

Anekchartputchong Royal Barge: This was built in the reign of King Rama V, and is the one Royal barge to be coloured pink.

Among the exhibits in the museum are the Kanya Throne, Budsaba Throne, and many kinds of oars and paddles. Due to lack of space, only eight of the Royal barges can be seen there. The other five are kept at Wasukree Pier and at the Royal Thai Navy Transport Department.

★ G9
✉ Arun Amarin Road
   Siriraj Sub-District
   Bangkoknoi District
   Bangkok 10700
☎ (662) 424-0004
🚌 19 57 79 80 81 91 123 124
   127 147 149
🚌 3 9 11 79 Mb 10
⛴ 1. Passenger Boat: Tha Chang
   Pier (Tha Chang-Bangyai)◄►
   Museum Pier
   2. Ferry: Phrachan Nua Pier ◄►
   Bangkoknoi Railway Station Pier
   ◄►Yaipha Pier◄► walk 300 m.
🕘 Daily 9 am-5 pm
🚫 Dec 31-Jan 1
🎟 Thai 10 Bht
   Foreigner 30 Bht
👥 Guided group tours are
   provided with slide and video
   presentations and free booklet.
📷 Inside Bldg. 100 Bht
   Taking video 200 Bht
🅿 At the foot of Arun-amarin
   Bridge, Phra Pinklao-Pata
   Intersection side.
✚ Siriraj Museum Vichaiprasit Fort
   Wangderm Palace
   Wat Amarintraram Wat Arun
   Wat Khrueawan Wat Rakhang
   Wat Suwannaram

📖 🏛 🏛 ⛴ 🚌

SIRIRAJ MUSEUM

King Rama V founded Siriraj Hospital to provide modern medical treatment for the Thai people. During the time when the hospital was being built, *HRH Prince Sirirajgaguthapan*, the fifth son of *Queen Sri Bajarindra*, fell ill and died of cholera. The King donated the wood used in the Prince's cremation ceremony to the building of the hospital and gave it the name Siriraj in the Prince's memory.

The hospital was Thailand's first medical school, with books and medical specimens collected in several museums established in the hospital help medical students with their studies and research projects.

◉ Congdon Anatomical Museum: (3rd fl. Anatomy Bldg.) This two-room museum was founded in 1927 by *Prof. Dr. Edgar Davidson Congdon*, who was sent by the Rockyfeller Foundation to improve Thai medical studies. It contains 2,000 exhibits, including skeletons, figures of humans and animals, the bodies and organs of Siamese twins, organs preserved in ethyl-alcohol, and most importantly, a display of the peripheral nervous system and blood system which are very difficult to dissect.

Sood Sangvichien Prehistoric Museum & Laboratory: (1st fl. Anatomy Bldg.) The evolution of life forms from 500 million years ago to the beginning of primates 70 million years ago are displayed here, as well as recent material on pre-history and evolution.

Songkran Niyomsane Forensic Medicine Museum: (2nd fl. Adulayadejvikrom Bldg.) This room displays various methods of murder, with skeletons and evidence from past murder cases.

Parasitology Museum: (7th fl. Adulayadejvikrom Bldg.) Here, various kinds of parasites such as whipworms and roundworms are exhibited, with models of their life-cycle.

Ouay Ketusinh Museum of History of Thai Medicine: (1st fl. Physiological Science Bldg.) The history and development of Thai traditional medicine, the treatment of disease and old age, Thai herbal medicines, Thai massage, and other disciplines can be seen here.

Ellis Pathological Museum: (8th fl. Adulayadejvikrom Bldg.) Shows the evolution of medicine, and organs infected with diseases which can be detected with the naked eye or seen only under the microscope.

Veekit Veeranuvati Museum: (1st fl. Paob Bldg.) Medical equipment and books collected over 40 years by *Dr. Veekit Veeranuvati*, the founder of the Gastroenterological Association of Thailand are kept here. Subjects include examination and diagnostic methods and equipment and research work.

★ G9
✉ Siriraj Hospital
Prannok Road
Siriraj Sub-District
Bangkoknoi District
Bangkok 10700
☎ (662) 419-7000: 6547-8
FAX (662) 411-3426
🚌 19 57 81 83 91 146 149
🚐 32 91
⛴ 1. Chao Phraya Express Boat: Wang Lang Pier
2. Ferry: Tha Chang Pier Prachan Nua Pier ◄ ► Siriraj Pier Wang Lang Pier
🕐 Mon-Fri 8:30 am-4:30 pm
Ⓒ Sat Sun Public Hols.
🆓 Free Admission
🅿 In Siriraj Hosp. compound
✚ Grand Palace
Royal Barges Museum
Silpakorn U. Thammasat U.
Wangderm Palace
Wat Amarintraram
Wat Arun Wat Phra Kaeo
Wat Suwannaram

WAT CHINORASARAM WORAWIHAN

The temple was built in 1836 by *Krom Phra Paramanuchitchinoros*, the son of King Rama I, before he entered the monkhood.

It was renovated by command of King Rama IV, who employed artists to carve and paint pictures, especially of naga, the mythological serpent which adorns several parts of the temple.

Ubosot: The main chapel has a tiled roof with traditional decorations. The gables are decorated with gilded stucco ornamented with fragments of glass in the form of branches and flowers. The door and window arches are decorated with gilded stucco and glass mosaics in Western motifs. The interior door and window panels are painted in Chinese motifs. The outside window panels depicts a naga swimming in the clouds. The exterior door panels depict a Chinese deity holding a fan stepping on naga.

Murals: The paintings in the chapel are in several sections. On the wall facing the Buddha image is a map of the temple, the river, canals, the Grand Palace, and another temple in ruins. The outstanding feature of this mural is its black background. On the wall behind the Buddha image, celestial beings fly in a black sky. The pillars are painted red and adorned with Thai motifs.

- ★ F9
- ✉ 3 Itsaraphab 35 Lane
  Itsaraphab Road
  Ban Changlor Sub-District
  Bangkoknoi District
  Bangkok 10700
- ☎ (662) 411-3369 412-0287
- FAX (662) 411-3556
- 40 56 149
- Passenger Boat Tha Tien Pier
  ←→ Wat Krut Pier
- ⏰ Temple: Daily 4:30 am-8 pm
  Ubosot: Daily 8 am-6 pm
- Free Admission
- Third Class
- Wat Chinoros Witthayalai
- P In the Temple compound
- Siriraj Museum
  Wangderm Palace
  Wat Arun Wat Khrueawan
  Wat Rakhang

BANGKOK METROPOLITAN TOURIST BUREAU

WAT DUSIDARAM WORAWIHAN

This temple was founded in the Ayutthaya period on the west bank of Chao Phraya River, near the mouth of Bangkoknoi Canal, and formerly known as Wat Saoprakhon. *HRH Princess Srisunthornthep*, the daughter of King Rama I restored it, and *Krom Phraratchawangbowon Maha Senanurak* refurbished it and gave it its new name.

In the reign of King Rama VI, *Somdet Krom Phraya Vachirayanvarorod* ordered Wat Bhuminrajpaksi, which had only one monk, to merge with Wat Dusidaram. In World War II, Wat Dusidaram and Wat Noithongyu were damaged in an air raid, so these temples were also merged.

Ubosot: The main chapel's three-tiered roof is decorated with chorfa, bairaka and hanghong. The lower part of the gable is made of bricks and mortar and the upper part is decorated with carved wood. The door and window arches are decorated with carved mortar, and inside is a mural painting by an artist of the King Rama I period.

Prarabieng: The balcony surrounding the ubosot has 64 gilded mortar standing Buddha images enshrined in its arches.

Old Ubosot: This chapel comes from Wat Bhuminarajaksi. Its gable decoration shows Narai (the Hindu god, Vishnu) mounted on a garuda with dancing peacocks decorated with coloured mirror glass.

Chedi: The base is in the form of mermaid, with fish and elephants around it, but it is now in very poor condition.

Old Wihan: This prayer hall is built in the form of a boat. The gable shows Narai mounted on a garuda, and there is a standing Buddha image in the Blessing posture.

★ G8
✉ 7 At the foot of Phra Pinklao Bridge Phra Pinklao Road Arun Amarin Sub-District Bangkoknoi District Bangkok 10700
☎ (662) 424-4748 433-9451
🚌 19 30 42 68 79 80 81 91 123 203
🚐 3 7 9 11 17 30 42 68 79 80 91 203
⚓ 1. Chao Phraya Express Boat: Phra Pinklao Bridge Pier
2. Ferry: Phrachan Nua Pier Phra Athit Pier ◄ ► Phra Pinklao Bridge Pier
🕐 Temple: Daily 5 am-9 pm Ubosot: Daily 8 am-6 pm
🆓 Free Admission
🏛 1962
🏷 Third Class
📷 Permission required for taking photo inside Bldg.
🅿 In the Temple compound
✚ Royal Barges Museum
 Siriraj Museum
 Vichaiprasit Fort
 Wangderm Palace
 Wat Arun Wat Khrueawan
 Wat Rakhang
Ⓜ Wat Suwannaram

WAT RAKHANGKOSITARAM
WORAMAHAWIHAN

The temple, formerly named Wat Bangwayai, was built in the Ayutthaya period. It was restored and appointed a Royal temple by *King Taksin* of Thonburi who also sponsored the revision of the tripitaka scriptures at the temple.

During the reign of King Rama I, a melodious rakhang or bell was found in the temple compound. The King order it to be moved to the Temple of the Emerald Buddha, and had five new bells sent back in exchange. The king then changed the temple's name to Wat Rakhangkositaram. In the reign of King Rama IV the name was to be changed again to Wat Rajkanthiyaram ("kanthi" meaning bell). But people did not accept this name, and the temple is still called Wat Rakhang today.

- G9
- 250 Arun Amarin Road
  Siriraj Sub-District
  Bangkoknoi District
  Bangkok 10700
- (662) 411-2255 418-2729
- 19 57 83
- 1. Chao Phraya Express Boat: Railway Station Pier Wang Lang Pier
  2. Ferry: Tha Chang Pier ◄► Wat Rakhang Pier
- Temple: Daily 5 am-9 pm
  Ubosot: Daily 6 am-6 pm
  Wihan Somdet: Daily 8 am-5 pm
- Free Admission
- Songkran Festival (Apr 13-15)
  Commemoration of Somdet Toh (June 22)
- 1949
- Second Class
- Khositsamosorn
  Satri Wat Rakhang
- In the Temple compound
- Royal Barges Museum
  Siriraj Museum
  Wangderm Palace
  Wat Arun Wat Khrueawan
  Wat Suwannaram

Ubosot: This is in the style of King Rama I's reign. Its three-tiered roof is decorated in Thai style, and the murals are by *Phra Wanwadwichit*, a great artist of the King Rama VI era.

Prang: This stupa dates from the reign of King Rama I. It is regarded as *"the finest example of its style."*

Hor Rakhang: The belfry is the symbol of this temple, built in the four-gable style of the late Ayutthaya and early Rattanakosin periods. The bells presented by King Rama I are on the upper floor.

Hor Trai: The scriptures hall consists of three adjoining buildings with a common corridor and is also in the late Ayutthaya/early Rattanakosin style. This former residence of King Rama I has been declared one of *"the most outstanding examples of Thai architecture."*

WAT SUWANNARAM RATCHAWORAWIHAN

During the reign of *King Taksin*, this temple was where Burmese prisoners of war from Bang Kaew Camp were executed. It was founded in the Ayutthaya period and was initially called Wat Thong.

It was dismantled and rebuilt during the restorations made in the reign of King Rama I, and the King renamed it Wat Suwannaram. It was restored again during the reign of King Rama III. It was formerly the site of Royal Cremation Ground for members of the Royal family and high-ranking officers, and was used for this purpose until the reign of King Rama V.

⦿ **Ubosot:** The main chapel has porches at the front and rear. The roof is decorated with chorfa, garuda head finials, bairaka leaf-like decorations and glass mosaic. On the pediments are gilded theppanom, celestial beings, and the figure of Narai mounted on a garuda. Inside the chapel are murals by *Master Thongyu* and *Master Kongpae*, a famous artist of King Rama III's reign. The principal Buddha image from the Sukhothai period is in the Subduing Mara posture and is named "Phra Saadsada."

Wihan: The prayer hall was built during the reign of King Rama V. There are long verandahs on either side and the roof is decorated with chorfa and bairaka, the pediment with theppanom.

Kuti: The monks' residences consist of six buildings with a refectory in the centre. Two smaller buildings with Hor Rakhang and Hor Trai are included in the complex.

★ F8
✉ 33 Soi Charansanitwong 32
  Charansanitwong Road
  Bangkhunnon Sub-District
  Bangkoknoi District
  Bangkok 10700
☎ (662) 434-7790-1
🚌 42 68 79 83 103 108 146
🚍 9 10
⛴ Passenger Boat: Tha Chang Pier Phrachan Nua Pier ‹ ›
  Wat Suwan Pier
🕐 Temple: Daily 5 am-9 pm
  Ubosot: Daily 8-9 am 4-6 pm
🎫 Free Admission
🎉 Songkran Festival (Apr 13-15)
🏛 1949
🏫 Second Class
🚌 Suwannaram Wittayakom
  Wat Suwannaram
🅿 In the Temple compound
➕ Ban Bu Community
  Royal Barges Museum
  Siriraj Museum
  Wangderm Palace
  Wat Khruewan
  Wat Srisudaram
  Wat Amarintararam
🅜 📷

BANGKOK YAI
☎ 457-0069

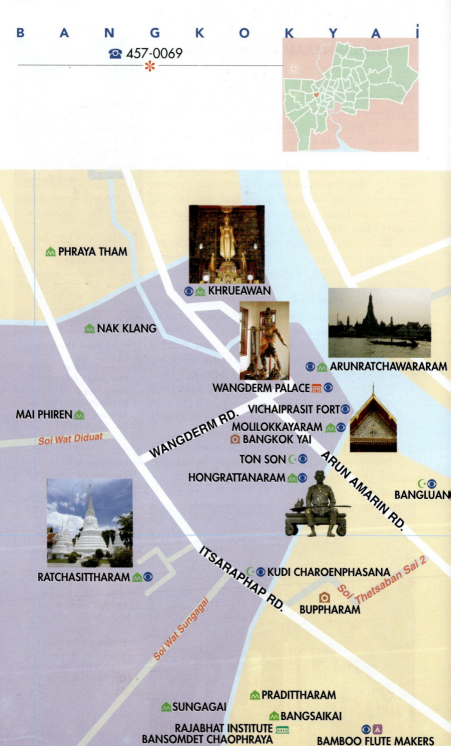

★ G9
✉ Royal Thai Navy
Wangderm Palace
Wangderm Road
Wat Arun Sub-District
Bangkokyai District
Bangkok 10600
☎ (662) 475-4117 466-9355
FAX (662) 466-9355
19 57 83
1. Chao Phraya Express Boat: Tha Tien Pier
2. Ferry: Tha Tien Pier ←→ Wat Arun Pier
🕒 Mon-Fri 8 am-4 pm
Free Admission, but must be in group with written request one week in adcance to the Museum Director
1949
1994
Taking photo inside Bldg.
P Royal Thai Navy
Charoenphasana Bridge
Kudi Charoenphasana
Tonson Mosque
Vichaiprasit Fort Wat Arun
Wat Hongrattanaram
Wat Khrueawan
Wat Molilokkayaram
Wat Rakhang
Wat Ratchasittharam
Wat Sangkrajai

WANGDERM PALACE

The palace was built when King Taksin moved his capital from Ayutthaya to Thonburi.

When King Rama I came to the throne, he moved the capital to Pranakorn and assigned a trusted relative to stay on in Wangderm Palace. King Rama V donated the palace to be used as the School of Naval Education.

⦿ Throne Hall: Built of bricks in the Thai style, this consists of two connected buildings, the north building being the Throne Hall itself and the south building the Pratinang Kwang, or Transverse Building. The Throne Hall is now used for receptions and important ceremonies, while the Transverse Building is used as a reception room for important visitors and for conferences.

The Two Chinese Residences: The larger is a Sino-Thai building. The roof is in the Chinese style and there are frescos on all its gables. The style of the smaller building is Chinese but the doors and windows have been altered to suit the Thai climate.

Adobe of HM King Pinklao: Built in the Western style, this is thought to be "the first building of this kind in the Rattanakosin period."

Shrine of King Taksin the Great: To the north of the two Chinese residences, the shrine is a mixture of Thai and Western styles, and houses the statue of King Taksin.

WAT ARUNRATCHAWARARAM
RATCHAWORAMAHAWIHAN

The prang of Wat Arun on the bank of Chao Phraya River is one of Bangkok's world-famous landmarks. From a French map of Thonburi made in the reign of *King Narai* it can be seen that the temple existed when Ayutthaya was Siam's capital.

The temple was formerly known as Wat Makok, and when *King Taksin* built his palace, he ordered the temple to be annexed to it. The king restored it and renamed it "Wat Jaeng". It was restored again by King Rama II, and renamed "Wat Arunratchatharam". King Rama IV later changed the name to "Wat Arunratchawararam".

Ubosot: This is an outstanding example of Rama II period architecture in late Ayutthaya style. It has a two-tiered roof with glazed ceramics, and pediments decorated with wooden carvings depicting Warunthep. The interior murals were painted during the Third and Fifth Reigns. Phra Phutthathammitsararatchalokthatdilok, the principal Buddha image in the Subduing Mara posture, was cast in the reign of King Rama II and contains relics of King Rama II.

Prang: This brick stupa is decorated with glazed pottery fragments in flower and leaf designs and other Thai patterns. The top is gilded and adorned with the noppasul.

Pra Rabiengkote: This corridor is in place of the kampaeng kaeo found in most other temples. It has a tiled roof with doors opening onto four directions. Inside are 120 Buddha images in the Subduing Mara posture.

★ G9
✉ 34 Arun Amarin Road
Wat Arun Sub-District
Bangkokyai District
Bangkok 10600
☎ (662) 891-1149
📠 (662) 891-1149
19 57 83
⛴ 1. Passenger Boat: Wat Arun Pier
2. Ferry: Tha Tien Pier
Wat Pho Pier ◄► Wat Arun Pier
🕐 Temple: Daily 7:30 am-5:30 pm
Ubosot: Free Admission, but
a written request to the
Temple's Abbot is required
💰 Prang: 10 Bht
🎉 Thod Kratin Festival:
9 days after Buddhist Lent
Final Day (Nov)
📖 Loykrathong Festival
Somdet (Wanathitiyanatera)
🕐 Mon-Tue Thu-Sun
8:30 am-5:30 pm
🚫 Wed Public Hols.
💰 Membership 10 Bht
1949
🏛 First Class Special
🎓 Prathomthawithaphisek
🅿 In the Temple compound
✚ Kudi Charoenphasana
Tonson Mosque
Wangderm palace
Wat Hongrattanaram
Wat Khrueawan
Wat Molilokkayaram
Wat Rakhang Wat Sangkrajai
Vichaiprasit Fort
Ⓜ 📷

Mondop of the Buddha's Footprint: A chapel surmounted by a spire, this stands between the ubosot and the wihan. It was built during the Third Reign and houses a copy of the footprint of the Buddha carved in Kwantong stone and decorated with colourful porcelain.

Ogre Statues: Guarding at the gate are two ogres (yaksha). The white yaksha is Sahassadecha and its green partner Thossakun, the villain of the Ramakien, the Thai version of the Ramayana epic.

The temple has flourished throughout the Rattanakosin period. The beauty of the architecture and the fine craftsmanship declare its status as a temple of the first grade and one of the most outstanding temples of Thailand. In a long tradition, every king of the Chakri Dynasty has presided over important ceremonies here, including the Royal barge processions to offer Pra Krathin or monks' robes, during the Thod Krathin Festival.

WAT HONGRATTANARAM
RATCHAWORAWIHAN

★ G9
✉ 102 Wangderm Road
Wat Arun Sub-District
Bangkokyai District
Bangkok 10600
☎ (662) 466-8126 472-0743
🚌 19 40 56 57 149
⛴ Passenger Boat: Tha Tien Pier Memorial Bridge Pier
◄► Wat Hong Pier
🕐 Temple: Daily 5 am-10 pm
Ubosot: Daily 8:30-9 am
5-5:30 pm
🆓 Free Admission
🎉 Songkran Festival (Apr 13)
🏛 1949
🅿 In the Temple compound
📍 Wangderm Palace
Wat Arun
Wat Hongrattanaram
Wat Kanlayanamit
Wat Khrueawan
Wat Rakhang
Wat Ratchasittharam
Wat Sangkrajai

Ⓜ 📷

Built in the Ayutthaya period by a wealthy Chinese named *Hong*, the temple was known as Wat Jaosua or Jeasua Hong. When Thonburi became the capital, the temple was made a centre of education under the patronage of King Taksin, who was of Chinese descent himself. It was renovated in the reign of King Rama III.

Ubosot: The combination of Chinese and European style stucco reliefs adorning the door and window arches of the ubosot are some of the finest of their kind. The interior murals painted in the Third and Fourth Reigns tell the story of Ratthanapimphawong, or the Emerald Buddha story.

Hor Trai: The room housing the Buddhist scripture has gilded black lacquer panels. The door was carved in a kruathao-style scroll of floral motifs in the reign of King Rama I.

Golden Buddha Image: For many years it was believed that the ancient Golden Buddha image was made of limestone, but when the casing fell off and the inside was revealed it was seen to be made of high quality gold in Sukhothai style. The old U-thong alphabet was found inscribed at the base.

BANGKOK METROPOLITAN
TOURIST BUREAU

- ★ G9
- 36 Arun Amarin Road
  Wat Arun Sub-District
  Bangkokyai District
  Bangkok 10600
- ☎ (662) 466-3653 472-6699
  465-3565
- FAX (662) 465-3565
- 19 57 83
- 1. Chao Phraya Express Boat:
  Tha Tien Pier
  2. Ferry: Wat Arun Pier
- Temple: Daily 5 am-8 pm
  Ubosot: Daily 7-8 am
  4-5 pm
- Free Admission
- Songkran Festival (Apr 13)
- Thrid Class
- In the Temple compound
- Charoenphasana Bridge
  Kudi Charoenphasana
  Tonson Mosque
  Vichaiprasit Fort
  Wangderm Palace Wat Arun
  Wat Hongrattanaram
  Wat Molilokkayaram
  Wat Ratchasittharam
  Wat Rakhang Wat Sangkrajai

WAT KHRUEAWAN WORAWIHAN

Built in the Ayutthaya period, this temple was restored by *Phrya Abhaibhuthorn* and his daughter *Chaochom Khrueawan*, the Royal consort of King Rama III. They presented it to the king, who designated it a Royal temple and named it Wat Khrueawan.

Ubosot: The pediments of the ubosot are decorated with stucco in the krauthao floral style. The gilded and painted window and door panels are also decorated with stucco. The murals painted in the reign of King Rama III period depict former incarnations of the Lord Buddha. The principal Buddha image resembles Pra Luangroatjanarit in the Great Pagoda.

Wihan: It is similar to the ubosot, but its 12-sided pillars were replaced by square pillars.

WAT MOLILOKKAYARAM RATCHAWORAWIHAN

The original name of this temple was Wat Tai Talat. Since it was built in the palace grounds, King Rama I invited monks to take up residence in it.

King Rama II restored the temple and named it Wat Phutthaisawan. He later sent his son to be educated there. The name was changed to Wat Moliloksuttharam by King Rama III.

Ubosot: The main chapel has a three-tiered roof decorated with traditional ornaments such as chorfa finials and bairaka at the sloping edge. The window and pediments are decorated with stucco, and the wooden door and window panels are finely carved with tree and flower patterns.

Somdet Phra Phutthakosajarn Mansion: This was a famous spiritual master's residence. Its doors and windows are painted in the kammalor style.

Wihan: The sermon hall was built in the Ayutthaya period and the stucco reliefs on the pediments, doors, and windows were added during the reign of King Rama III.

Kuti: The monks' residences were built of wood and are in the Thai-Chinese style.

Hor Trai: The scripture building is also of wood, and its window panels are decorated with gilded lacquer.

★ G9
✉ 2 Wangderm Road
Wat Arun Sub-District
Bangkokyai District
Bangkok 10600
☎ (662) 472-5038 472-3183
🚌 19 57
⛴ Passenger Boat: Rajini Pier (Pakkhlong Talat) ◄►
Wat Moli Pier
🕐 Temple: Daily 5 am-8 pm
Ubosot: Daily 8:30-9 am
5-6 pm
(Wishing to visit the ubosot should call in advance.)
🎫 Free Admission
🎉 Songkran Festival (Apr 13)
🏛 1949
👥 Second Class
🅿 In the Temple compound
🚇 Charoenphasana Bridge
Kudi Charoenphasana
Tonson Mosque Wat Arun
Wangderm Palace
Wat Hongrattanaram
Wat Kanlayanamit
Wat Khruewan
Wat Rakhang
Wat Ratchasittharam
Wat Sangkrajai

BANGKOK METROPOLITAN TOURIST BUREAU

WAT RATCHASITTHARAM
RATCHAWORAWIHAN

King Rama I had this temple built beside the old Wat Plub, and later merged the two. The temple was restored during the reign of King Rama III. Tamnak Chan, the mansion given to King Rama II when he entered the monkhood, was also restored, and the name of the temple was changed to Wat Ratchasittharam

⦿ **Ubosot:** The brick and stucco main chapel has a two tiered roof. On the pediments are depictions of Narai (Vishnu) mounted on a garuda, with flower motifs and coloured glass mosaics. The murals depict the penultimate life of the Lord Buddha and the Tribhumikatha, the Buddhist cosmology of the three worlds, Heaven, Earth and Hell.

Tamnak Chan: The ground floor was built of brick and stucco while the upper floor is of chan, or sandal wood. During restoration in King Rama III's reign, the mansion was moved to the side of the Keng Jeen, the Chinese style mansion.

Sala Karnparian: The instruction hall has a two-tiered roof and contains two preaching chairs, 14 gilded lacquer painted cabinets and the chair given by the king.

Chedi: The two chedi are named Phra Sirasana Chedi and Phra Sirajumphot Chedi. Their bases are decorated with ropes of stucco.

 G10
3 Itsaraphap 23 Lane
Itsaraphap Road
Wat Arun Sub-District
Bangkokyai District
Bangkok 10600
(662) 465-4527 465-4646
466-6680
19 40 56 57 149
Passenger Boat:
Wat Arun Pier
Wat Sangkrajai Pier
Temple: Daily 5 am-10 pm
Ubosot: Daily 8-8:30 am
5-5:30 pm
Buddisht Sermon Day:
8:30-10:30 am
Free Admission
Visakhapuja Day: Sermon
Songkran Festival (Apr 13)
1949
Second Class
Wat Ratsittharam
In the Temple compound
Charoenphasana Bridge
Kudi Charoenphasana
Tonson Mosque
Vichaiprasit Fort Wat Arun
Wat Hongrattanaram
Wat Khrueawan
Wat Molilokkayaram
Wat Rakhang
Wat Sangkrajai

BUENG KUM
☎ 374-8017

SERI THAI PARK

Once known as Buengkum or Bueng-ta-thong Pond, this was abandoned reservoir until it was incorporated into the flood prevention project of HM the King. It was then transformed into a park, as well as a reservoir to hold excess water before its release into natural canals.

On the 52nd anniversary of the end of World War II, August 16, 1997, the park was officially given the name Seri Thai Park in honour of the *Seri Thai* or Free Thai Movement whose members fought alongside the Allies during the Japanese occupation.

It is the only public water park in Bangkok and covers an area of 360 rai (about 145 acres). The 9 km. long reservoir is linked with Sansap Canal, and many native plants grow in the park area. The island pavilion has 10 varieties of palm tree.

◉ Three Forest Parks: *Thaveesuk, Romsai* and *Charoenkarn*, with a variety of perennial trees such as Banyan, Royal Poinciana, Cassia and Borneo Mahogany.

In the flower and fruit gardens, most of the plants are of Thai origin. Among the flowering shrubs are pikul and moke, while fruit trees include pomelo, santol, custard apple and jackfruit.

Apart from being a water park in the middle of the city, Seri Thai Park is also an outdoor classroom displaying different varieties of Thai plants and trees for those who have both education and recreation in mind.

★ O8
✉ Sukhaphiban 2 Road
Khlongkum Sub-District
Buengkum District
Bangkok 10240
☎ (662) 378-7884
📠 (662) 379-7884
🚌 27 60 71 109 151
   2 27 Mb 3
🕐 Office: Mon-Sat 8 am-4 pm
   Sun Public Hols.
   Park: Daily 5 am-8 pm
🆓 Free Admission
🅿 Entrance of Buengkum school
   or Sahakorn Village
✚ Buengkum District Office
   Siam Park

CHATUCHAK

☎ 513-9954

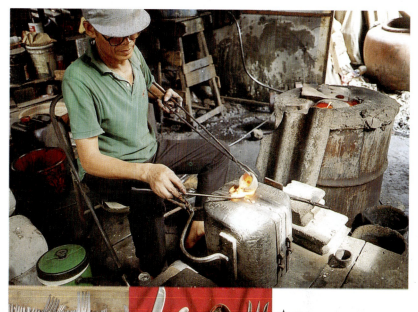

BRONZE CRAFT CENTRE

In times past, the bronze khan or drinking bowl, was the drinking vessel of choice in wealthy Siamese homes. Bronze was preferred to pottery or other materials as it made the water seem cooler and sweeter. Craftsmen also used bronze to fashion cutlery, plates and other tableware as well as candelabra, vases and other decorative objects for the home.

Thai bronze tableware has proved to be popular with foreign visitors. It is admired for its appearance and style, and for the quality of the metal itself, which will not contaminate food. Today, it seems that most of the bronze tableware and decorative items made in Thailand are for export to dining rooms overseas.

★ J5
✉ Pradit-torakarn Community
13 Phahonyothin 47 Lane
Phahonyothin Road
Ladyao Sub-District
Chatuchak District
Bangkok 10900
☎ (662) 579-2861
✉ Bangkok Community Handicraft Promotion Centre (BCHPC) Service Cooperative, Ltd.
13/2 Phahonyothin 47 Lane
Phahonyothin Road
Ladyao Sub-District
Chatuchak District
Bangkok 10900
☎ (662) 940-6929
FAX (662) 579-1445
🚌 26 34 39 59 107 114 126
🚌 3 12 22 39 126 Mb 8 16
🕐 Community: Daily 10 am-5 pm
Co-op: Mon-Fri 10 am-5 pm
Sun Public Hols.
Free Admission
P In front of Co-op
✚ Freshwater Fish Aquarium
Kasetsart U. Museums
National Genebank

CHATUCHAK PARK AND CHATUCHAK WEEKEND MARKET

The State Railway of Thailand donated this land to build a park according to the wish of HM the King on the occasion of his 4th Cycle birthday in 1976.

Inside the park are many varieties of trees and plants in gardens with different themes. There is a herbal garden, for instance, and another devoted to flowers in literature.

◉ Chatuchak Market: A heaven for shoppers, especially if they are ready to bargain. The plant market is held every Wednesday and Thursday, while at the weekend it becomes the biggest market in Thailand, bringing together 8,000 stalls from all parts of the country.

A look at the plan of the market shows that it is divided into 26 areas. The kinds of products to be found include antiques, books and magazines, fashions, food, furniture, handicrafts, jewellery, paintings, pets, plants, and miscellaneous items.

Six Asean Sculptors: This exhibition shows the work of artists from the six countries of the Asean region: Brunei, Indonesia, Malaysia, The Philippines, Singapore and Thailand.

Prestigious Train Hall: Located near Gate 2, this is the place to study history and view displays of past forms of transport, from London taxis to Japanese patrol cars used during World War II.

★ 17
✉ Kamphaengphet 3 Road
Ladyao Sub-District
Chatuchak District
Bangkok 10900
☎ (662) 272-4575
FAX (662) 272-4575
🚌 3 8 26 27 28 29 34 39
44 52 55 59 63 77 90
96 104 112 122 138 145
🚐 2 3 9 10 12 13 18 Mb 2
🕐 Office: Mon-Fri
7:30 am-3:30 pm
Sat Sun Public Hols.
Park: Daily 4:30 am-8 pm
🎫 Free Admission
🏛 Railway Hall of Fame:
Sat-Sun 5 am-6 pm
We Love Train Association:
☎(662) 243-2037
FAX(662) 243-2037
🅿 Behind the Park on
Kamphaengphet 3 Road
✚ Aw Taw Khor Market
Central Plaza
Queen Sirikit Park
Railway Park

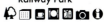

KASETSART UNIVERSITY MUSEUMS

Kasetsart University focuses its teaching on agriculture, science and nature. Because so many samples and specimens are needed for teaching and research, several museums have to accommodate these samples.

◉ **Agriculture Museum:** (2nd fl., Exhibition Bldg. behind the Office of Agricultural Museum and Culture). Containing traditional equipment used in agriculture and the making of agricultural products, such as an ancient sugar cane press.

Veterinary Museum: (Pathology Bldg.). A collection of animal skeletons, abnormally developed animals, animal organs, etc.

Fishery Museum: (ground fl., Department of Fishery). A collection of skeletons of fish species, shells, fishing equipment and stuffed marine animals.

Entomology Museum: (2nd fl., Charas Soonthornsingha Bldg.). A collection of many insect species.

Office of Agricultural Museum and Culture: Providing information relating to the development of agriculture and culture. The office also holds exhibitions on the development of agriculture and its relationship to Thai society, emphasising Thai traditional wisdom and basic technologies.

Other museums in the university include Rattanakosin Bicentennial Museum of Nature Study, Archive Hall, Anthropology Park, Traditional Textile Museum, and Museum of Zoology.

★ J5
✉ The Office of Agricultural Museum and Culture
Kasetsart University
Bangken District
Bangkok 10900
☎ (662) 942-8680 942-8711-2
FAX (662) 742-8713
✉ uvnm@nontri.ku.ac.th
🚌 26 39 59 104 107 114 126
🚐 3 9 12 13 22 24 39 126
🕘 Mon-Fri 8:30 am-4 pm
⊘ Sat Sun Public Hols.
ⓘ Free Admission
🎦 Exhibition Seminar Training
📷 Permission required for taking photo inside Bldg.
🅿 Kasetsart University
✚ Bronze Craft Centre
Freshwater Fish Aquarium
National Genebank
Thai State Attorney Museum

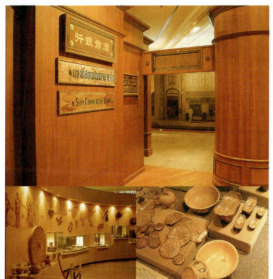

MUSEUM OF THAI BANKING AT SIAM COMMERCIAL BANK

The first bank in Thailand was opened by the British in 1868. After this, Thailand's financial and banking systems evolved along internationally recognised forms. Financial documents from the period are thus extremely valuable for the history of Thai banking

⦿ **Part 1. Evolution of Currency:** This starts with prehistoric items of barter and ancient media of exchange, showing how currency developed alongside the accumulation and storage of goods, and the exchange of different currencies until the introduction of modern banking systems.

Part 2 Evolution of Banks: The need for financial institutions led to the adoption of the banking system. This shows start with foreign bank operations in Thailand, and the evolution of the country's first bank, known as the "Book Club".

Part 3 Start of Banking: The success of the Book Club led to the foundation of other banks, and there are some fascinating historical documents from this era.

Part 4 Siam Commercial Bank to the Present Day: The rise of one of Thailand's leading banks and how it became an international institution.

★ J6
✉ 9 Ratchadaphisek Road
Ladyao Sub-District
Chatuchak District
Bangkok 10900
☎ (662) 544-4504 544-4525
544-4462-3
FAX (662) 937-7454
🚌 26 28 39 108 112 126 206
🚌 38 49 126 206Por 25Kor
🕐 Tue-Sat 10 am-5 pm
Mon Sun Public Hols.
Bank Mid-year Hol.
Free Admission
Must be in group
(Please call in advance)
Siam Commercial Bank:
Multiform information and
Data Financial Banking
Management Economics
🕐 Mon-Fri 8 am-5 pm
Sat Sun Public Hols.
Bank Mid-year Hol.
☎ (662) 544-3615-9
FAX (662) 544-3620
P Parking Bldg.
Central Plaza
Kasetsart U. Museums
SCB Park Plaza

QUEEN SIRIKIT PARK

    Another green area, the forest park was built to commemorate the 60th birthday anniversary of *HM Queen Sirikit*. Besides serving as a "lung" for Bangkokians the park also used to conserve plants both of local and foreign origins.

    The combining of letter "Sor seua" and "S" shape pool: The first Thai and English alphabets of

the name of the queen. The pool is decorated with flowers and three fountains.

Lotus Garden: A big concrete pool contains local and foreign lotuses planted in ancient water jar . Also decorating the area are various kinds of flowers arranged in European-style.

Botanical Garden: The garden was built on a 30-rai plot of land for conservation of plants.

17
820 Phahonyothin Road
Ladyao Sub-District
Chatuchak District
Bangkok 10900
(662) 272-4358-9
(662) 272-4343
Office: Mon-Sat 8 am-4 pm
Sun Public Hols.
Park: Daily 5 am-6:30 pm
3 8 28 29 52 59 69 77 104
108 122 134 138 145
2 3 9 10 12 18 23 38
38 (Exp.) 39 44 134 145
Mb 2 5 8 12 15
Free Admission
Must be in group, with written request one week in advance to the Chief of the Park.
Food Drink Sport Equipment Pet Bike
Permission required for taking photo inside the Park.
In front of the Park
Aw Taw Khor Market
Central Plaza Chatuchak Park
Railway Park

THE NATIONAL GENEBANK OF THAILAND

★ J5
✉ Industrial and Technical
   Consultancy Department
   Thai Institue of Scientific
   and Technological Research
   196 Phaholyothin Road
   Ladyao Sub-District
   Chatuchak District
   Bangkok 10900
☎ (662) 579-1121-30: 5101
FAX (662) 561-4771
🚌 26 34 39 59 107 114
   126 129
🚐 3 12 22 39 126 Mb 8 16
🕐 Mon-Fri 8 am-4 pm
🕐 Sat Sun Public Hols.
🆓 Free Admission
   Seeds Storage Service
🅿 In front of the Bldg.
✚ Kasetsart U. Museums
   Bronze Craft Centre
   Freshwater Fish Aquarium

Thailand is an agricultural country with many famous plants as export commodities, while other plants are overlooked as being not commercial plants.

That is one reason Science and Technology Research Institute of Thailand set up a Genebank in 1984, with support from International Board for Plant Genetic Resources, IBPGR, to protect genetic resources, as a location to exchange plant strains and as an information service, and to develop strains, and support research into agriculture and biotechnology. Sells, stores and exchanges samples for interested people.

◉ **Storage Methods:** Two kinds: Permanent, which will sprout after 50 years, and functional, which will still sprout after 5 years. After recording details, cleaning and testing sprouting and moisture in the lab, they are vacuum packed in tins, and put in cold storage, being tested for sprouting every year.

At present, the Bank contains seeds of over 50 families and over 200 varieties in 4,000 samples, packed in aluminium cans and envelopes.

THAI STATE ATTORNEY MUSEUM

The museum was established in 1993 to commemorate the 100th anniversary of the establishment of the Thai institution of attorneys in order to collect valuable legal items.

The Exhibits are old documents and office equipment which were collected from attorney's offices throughout the country.

Attorney's Office Corner: Displays the general atmosphere of an attorney's office. The corner comprises an eight-legged table, document trays, legal gowns, office equipment, etc.

Ancient Legal Book Library: Collects rare legal books such as Volume One of "Thai Law," two works by Dr. Bradley, works by HRH Prince Rabi, the Father of Thai Law, 1st-25th Royal Gazettes, Official Records of attorneys' offices from 1914- present, and documents from historical and interesting cases, etc.

Antique Buddha Image Room: Displays Buddha images from the Dvaravati to the Early Rattanakosin period and a statue of King Rama I.

Past Attorney Generals Room: Displays pictures of the first Attorney General to the present.

Chalermphrakiat Public Legal Library: Contains books for legal research.

★ J6
✉ 11th fl., Office of the Attorney General Bldg. Ratchadaphisek Road Lardyao Sub-District Chatuchak District Bangkok 10900
☎ (662) 541-2951 541-2934
FAX (662) 541-2951 541-2934
🖱 http://www.inet.co.th/org/oag
🚌 38 136 206
🚌 22 Por 25Kor 38 126 136
🕘 Mon-Fri 9 am-4 pm
✕ Sat Sun Public Hols.
ⓘ Free Admission
📖 Ancient Legal Book Lib.
   Chalermphrakiat Public Legal Lib.
👥 Must be in group
📷 Permission required for taking photo inside Bldg.
🅿 In front of the Bldg.
✚ SCB Park Plaza
   Thai Banking Museum

JOMTHONG
☎ 427-6672

CANAL BOAT TRIP

The life-style of the Thai people has always been associated with waterways. With the coming of roads and tall commercial buildings, the view along Bangkok waterways has been constantly changing over the years.

◉ Canal Boat Trip: The best time to make a canal boat trip would be around six o'clock in the morning in order to capture the authentic atmosphere and the varied activity which begins early in the day: Monks receiving alms, children hurrying to school, and boats delivering vegetables from farms to markets.

Boat trips in the afternoon are best taken after two p.m. to avoid the heat of the mid-day sun. The traditional Thai lifestyle can still be found along several waterways such as the Daokanong, Bangkhunthien and Lart canals. Here visitors can discover the more tranquil face of life in Bangkok.

A tour might begin with a visit to the National Museum of the Royal Barges, then to see the murals at Wat Suwannaram. After that, go to see the Guanyin, feed the Swai fish (*Pangasius foroleri*), and visit Sala Karnparian at Wat Shepakhao. Then go to Khlong Chakpra for lunch at Talingchan Floating Market. From there, go to the floating ubosot of Wat Phigunthong. Finally, pay a visit to the Sukhothai ubosot in the old merchant ship, Sumpaoshape at Wat Chalor.

★ F12
1. Passenger Boat:
Tha Chang Pier
Rajini Pier (Pakkhlong Talat)
Memorial Bridge Pier
Oriental Pier
Daily 6 am-2 pm
Price according to hours used.
2. Mitr Chao Phraya Express
Boat: Daily 8 am
☎ (662) 225-6179
P At the Pier compound
Wat Kaewpaitoon
Wat Nangnong Wat Nung
Wat Ratchaorasaram
Wat Sai

WAT NANGNONG WORAWIHAN

This temple is thought to have been built in the Ayutthaya period during the reign of *King Srisanpetch VIII (Khunluang Sorasak)*.

◉ **Ubosot:** The main chapel dates from the reign of King Rama III. The exterior door panels are inlaid with mother-of-pearl, the interiors painted with gilded lacquer. Murals depict stories and characters from Chinese literature, and pictures of the virtuous Chinese holy men, Hok, Lok and Siew.

Chedi: Built during the reign of King Rama III, the 20-sided chedi stands on an octagonal base. An image Luangpor Toh is enshrined at the front.

Wihan: The pediments are decorated with stucco dragons and the chedi with coloured ceramics. The old wihan contains two Buddha images said to have been found protruding from a mound in the earth.

★ F11
✉ 76 Wutthakat Road
Bangkhor Sub-District
Chomthong District
Bangkok 10150
☎ (662) 468-6876 476-2612
FAX (662) 875-4828
🚌 10 43 111
⛴ Passenger Boat: Rajini (Pakkhlong Talat) Pier
Memorial Bridge Pier ◄ ►
Talat Phlu Pier ◄ ► Bus
🕐 Temple: Daily 5 am-8 pm
Ubosot: Daily 8 am-8:30 am
(Wishing to visit the ubosot should call in advance.)
💰 Free Adminission
🎎 Annual festival (Mar.)
Serm Duangchata (Dec 31)
🏛 1977
🏯 Third Class
🏫 Nangnongphiphat
Nangnong Kindergarten
📷 Permission required for taking photo inside Bldg.
🅿 In the Temple compound
✚ Wat Nung
Wat Ratchaorasaram
Wat Sai

WAT RATCHAORASARAM
RATCHAWORAMAHAWIHAN

Formerly named Wat Jomthong, this small but historically important temple was built on the western bank of Sanamchai Canal in the Ayutthaya period, and later appointed as the Royal temple of King Rama III. The King favoured the Chinese style, and this distinguishes its buildings and interiors.

This is the first temple without such traditional decorations as chorfa, bairaka or hanghong. However, the Thai and Chinese styles harmonise well.

 Ubosot: The main chapel has a Chinese-style roof, but Thai coloured tiles. The tiles on the upper part of the pediment feature offerings; landscapes are on the lower part. Stucco chrysanthemum motifs surround the doors and windows. The principal Buddha image is one of the finest of its period. It is seated under the nine-tiered parasol seen only in temples where the ashes of kings are laid to rest.

The Throne beneath the Pikul Tree: At the left hand corner of the ubosot under an old pikul tree is the large stone on which King Rama III as Crown Prince was always seated when he came to visit the temple or to inspect the restoration work.

Wihan of the Reclining Buddha: The sermon hall contains a reclining Buddha image made of stucco. Descriptions of traditional medicine and massage are inscribed on the outer wall along the verandah. The exterior door and window panels have stucco reliefs of a Chinese guardian deity.

Wihan of the Standing Buddha: The prayer hall contains a bronze standing Buddha image in the Forgiving posture, thought to have been cast in the U-thong period.

John Crawford Britain's Ambassador to the Court of King Rama II once described this temple as "the most beautifully built in Bangkok."

- ★ F11
- 258 Ekkachai 4 Lane Ekkachai Road Bangkor Sub-District Jomthong District Bangkok 10150
- (662) 415-2286 893-7274
- FAX (662) 893-7273
- 10 43 120
- Mb 9
- 1. Passenger Boat: Rajini (Pakkhlong Talat) Pier ◄ ► Wat Ratchaorasaram Pier Departure 8 am Return 5 pm
  2. Passenger Boat: Rajini (Pakkhlong Talat) Pier ◄ ► Wat Paknum ◄ ► Bus
- Temple: Daily 5 am-8 pm Ubosot: Daily 8-9 am 4:30-6 pm
- Free Admission
- Annual Festival (Mar)
- Bhadraramongkol: Collection of religious texts Documents for research In Bali language.
- 1949
- First Class
- Wat Ratchaorasaram Institute
- Permission required for taking photo inside Bldg.
- In the Temple compound
- Wat Nangnong Wat Nung Wat Sai

WAT SAI AND FLOATING MARKET

This Mahanikai sect temple was built in the Ayutthaya period and restored during the reigns of King Rama IV and King Rama V.

◉ **Tamnak Thong:** "the Golden Mansion," was thought to have been dedicated by *Phra Chao Sua*, King of Ayutthaya, as a monks' residence. The wooden house is raised high on pillars in the Thai tradition, and the interior is divided by wooden partitions. One of the rooms contains a Chinese-style

wooden bed with carved flower motifs patterned with glass, and a painting of a Chinese lady. On the door panels are pictures of the guardian deity, and on the outside wall is a gilded lacquer painting of the traditional kanok or flame-like motif.

Old Belfry: This circular tower stands on a lotus-shaped base, and the finial of the bell is in the form of a lotus bud. Its original bell has now been replaced by a drum.

Wihan: Built in Rattanakosin style with a two-tiered roof. Inside are sandstone, stucco, and bronze Buddha images in the Ayutthaya and Rattanakosin styles.

Wat Sai Floating Market: Images of people young and old paddling boats laden with fruit, vegetable and other produce, traders greeting each other with smiling faces, buyers bargaining, sellers inviting — these are only pictures of a way of life in the past which is now gone forever. With the building of Rama II Road and the extension of Eakkachai Road to Samut Sakhorn, the transport of agricultural produce shifted from waterways to roads.

The wooden shop houses have been replaced by concrete commercial buildings and a few gift shops. The canal bank has been concreted over and a new pier added. The once busy and well-known floating market is now only of passing interest to tourists taking a canal trip.

★ F11
✉ 11 Moo 2
Thavorn-wattana Lane
Ekkachai Road
Bangkhunthian Sub-District
Jomthong District
Bangkok 10150
☎ (662) 415-7173 415-1926
FAX (662) 415-7173
🚍 10 43 120
Mb 9
⛵ Long-tail Boat: Rajini Pier (Pakkhlong Talat) Tha Chang Pier Memorial Bridge Pier Si Phraya Pier, Oriental Pier etc. ◄►Wat Sai
🕐 Temple: Daily 5 am-8 pm Ubosot: Daily 8-8:30 am (Wishing to visit the ubosot should call in advance.)
💳 Free Admission
🎉 Songkran Festival (Apr 13) Merit making ceremony dedicated to the late Abbot (Oct 20)
🏛 1962
📷 Permission required for taking photo inside Bldg.
Ⓟ In the Temple compound
✚ Wat Sai Floating Market Wat Nangnong Wat Nung Wat Ratchaorasaram

DIN DAENG
☎ 246-8547

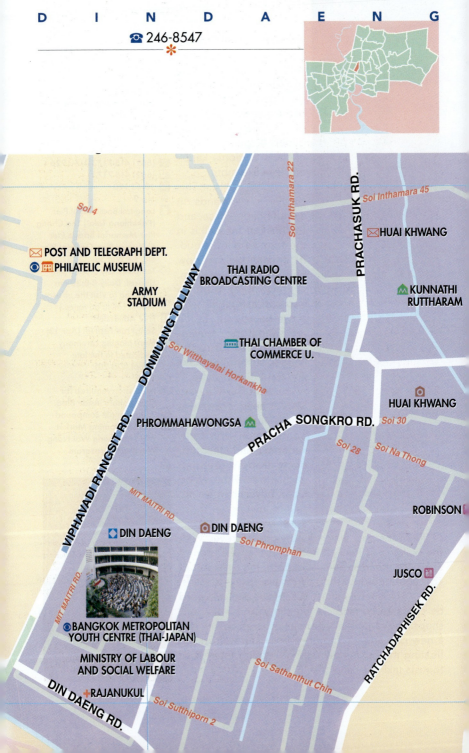

BANGKOK METROPOLITAN YOUTH CENTRE (THAI-JAPAN)

The centre was built with funds from the Bangkok Metropolitan Administration and a gift from the Japanese Government for the Rattanakosin Bicentennial in 1982. Its intention is to give Thai children the opportunity to join in cultural and sports activities as an aid to development, and to strengthen links between Thailand and Japan.

◉ Sports Centre: This provides training in Thai and international sports, martial arts, and aerobic dance, etc.

There are 17 different types of recreational activities such as Thai classical dance, art, music, English and excursions to places of interest.

Community-type activities provide occupational training as well as activities for young and under-privileged members of society.

To participate in the Centre's activities, simply apply for membership or obtain information directly from the Centre.

★ 18
Mitmaitri Road
Dindaeng Sub-District
Dindaeng District
Bangkok 10320
☎ Public Relations:
☎ (662) 245-3360 245-4743
📠 (662) 245-4748
Activity & Sport Centre:
☎ (662) 245-3360: 32 33
📠 (662) 245-4748
Koh2515@hotmail.com
13 24 36 54 61 69 73 92
117 201 204
4 14 15 36 73 Mb 4
🕐 Office: Tues-Sat 10 am-6 pm
Activity & Sport Centre:
Tues-Sat 10 am-9 pm
Sun 1-9 pm
Mon Sun Public Hols.
Free Admission
Acting Exhibition Job Training
Sport Racing Sport Training
Youth Centre:
  8-18 years old 10 Bht/year
  18-24 years old 20 Bht/year
Community Centre:
  Over 18 years old 40 baht/year
In front of the Centre
Ministry of Labour and
Social Welfare
Vibhavadi Rangsit Forest Park

DON MUANG

☎ 929-5463

Map labels

- TECHATUNGKA RD.
- DON MUANG
- SONG PRAPHA RD.
- DON MUANG
- DON MUANG RAILWAY STATION
- DON MUANG
- VIBHAVADI RANGSIT RD.
- DON MUANG
- BANGKOK INTERNATIONAL AIRPORT
- ROYAL THAI AIR FORCE
- ROYAL THAI AIR FORCE ACADEMY
- BHUMIBOL
- PHAHON YOTHIN RD.
- Soi 54
- Soi Talat Phoemsin
- Soi 52
- SAPHAN MAI MARKET
- HANDICRAFT MADE FROM FRAGRANT CLAY
- SUETRONG VILLAGE

BANGKOK INTERNATIONAL AIRPORT

Thailand's first airport was at Sraprathum, but with the rapid growth of air travel, it became necessary to build a new airport. The government purchased land around Don E-yeao for the new Donmuang International Airport, under the supervision of the Airport Authority of Thailand.

◉ **International Airport:** Divided into two buildings, providing service for arrival, departure and transit passengers, as well as for offices and restaurants. In addition, there are airline offices and shops.

Domestic Airport: Divided into two buildings as well. A two-storey building occupied by the offices of Bangkok Airways, and a three-storey building for the offices and service departments of THAI.

★ K2
✉ Vibhavadi Rangsit Road
Sikan Sub-District
Donmuang District
Bangkok 10120
Airport Authority of Thailand
☎ (662) 535-1111
📠 (662) 535-4099
✉ aat bia@ksc15.th.com
www.airportthai.or.th
International Flight:
☎ Arrival: (662) 535-1301
☎ Departure: (662) 535-1123
Domestic Flight:
☎ Arrival: (662) 535-1305
☎ Departure: (662) 535-1277
🚌 29 59 95 356
🚍 4 10 13 13 (Exp.) 29 95
⏰ Daily 24 hrs.
💰 Free Admission
🅿 In the Airport compound
✚ Amari Airport Hotel
Donmuang Railway Station
Mai Market Wat Donmuang

ROYAL THAI AIR FORCE MUSEUM

Established in 1952, with the purpose of conserving various aviation equipment, military aircraft and objects from the beginning of aviation in Thailand up to the present.

◉ **Model I (Corsaire):** This attack aircraft is the only one of its kind left in the world.

Tachikawa Model 6: The one which is on display was Ki-36 type with single wing and only 2 left in the world.

The Bomber Model II (Boripatr) designed by Lieutenant Colonel Luang Vejayantrangsrit was the first aircraft that was designed and built entirely by Thais. King Rama VII gracious named this aircraft the "Boripatr."

★ L2
✉ 171 The Royal Thai Air Force
Phahon Yothin Road
Sikan Sub-District
Donmuang District
Bangkok 10120
☎ (662) 534-1764 534-1853
📠 (662) 534-1936
🚌 2 34 39 114
🚍 3 21 39
⏰ Daily 8:30 am-4:30 pm
Arms Forces Day (Jan 25)
Public Hols.
💰 Free Admission
⚠ Must be in group with written request one week in advance to the Director of Administrative Services
Exhibition
History of Aircraft
⏰ Daily 8:30 am-4:30 pm
🅿 In front of the Museum
✚ RTAF Head Quarters
Royal Thai Air Force Academy

DUSIT

☎ 241-4504

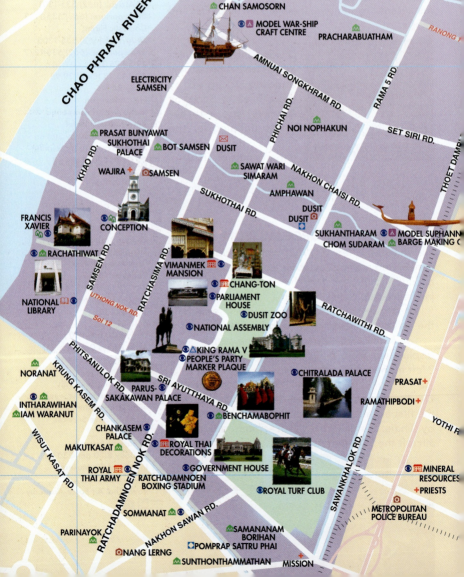

The Must See Sites
In BANGKOK | 153

CHANG-TON MUSEUM
(ROYAL ELEPHANT NATIONAL MUSEUM)

Since the old days "white elephants" have been regarded as the symbol of prestige of the king. When the king received such an elephant, he would command a ceremony to celebrate the registration of the elephant as well as naming it *Phraya Chang-ton*, or *Nang Phraya Chang-ton* if it was a female. The king also had stables for the elephants built in the palace ground.

Formerly an elephant stable, this Thai-style building was built in the reign of King Rama V in Dusit Garden Palace compound. The stable was made into Chang-ton Museum by the Ministry of Education in 1988.

◉ **Building 1:** Artefacts related to elephants such as white elephant figures, tusks, and charms for mahouts are displayed here. There are also pictures and articles about elephants, such as elephant roping in the corral, the birth of an auspicious elephant, and how the elephants are caught.

Building 2: Displayed here is a model of white elephant ceremony. In Thailand, all white elephants belong to the King, and the Royal ceremony is still held when a new one is found.

★ H8
✉ Parliament House compound
Uthong Nai Road
Dusit Sub-District
Dusit District Bangkok 10300
☎ (662) 282-3336
📠 (662) 282-3336
🚌 18 28 70 108
🚍 10 16
🕐 Daily 8:30 am-4:30 pm
💰 5 Bht
• Must be in group
🅿 In front of the Paliament House
• Amphorn Garden
Amphornsathan Palace
Anantasamakom Throne Hall
Chitralada Palace
Dusit Zoo Paliament House
People's Party Marker Plaque
Parus-sakkawan Palace
Royal Thai Army Museum
Royal Thai Decorations Museum
Royal Turf Club
Statue of King Rama V
Wat Benchamabophit
Vimanmek Mansion Museum

CHITRALADARAHOTARN PALACE

★ H8
✉ Rama V Road
Dusit Sub-District
Dusit District
Bangkok 10300
☎ (662) 280-4200
📠 (662) 280-1996
🚌 5 18 28 39 50 72 96 97 108 201
🚐 3 10 16 44 72 Mb 4
Royal Chitralada Projects
☎ (662) 281-1847 282-1850
📠 (662) 280-1996
🕐 Mon-Fri 8:30 am-4:30 pm
Ⓒ Sun Public Hols.
Chitralada
☎ (662) 280-4830-1
📠 (662) 280-3392
🕐 Mon-Fri 8:30 am-5 pm
Ⓒ Sat Sun Public Hols.
SUPPORT Foundation
☎ (662) 281-1111
📠 (662) 281-1202
🕐 Mon-Fri 9 am-4:30 pm
Ⓒ Sun Public Hols.
🅿 In the Palace compound
✠ Anantasamakom Throne Hall
Chang-ton Museum
Paliament House
Royal Turf Club
Statue of King Rama V
Vimanmek Mansion Museum
Wat Benchamabophit
Wat Sommanatwihan

King Rama VI used to write his literary works in this area formerly known as Sompoy Field. He later named the pavilion Chitraladarahotarn Palace, and King Rama VII commanded it to be annexed to Dusit Garden Palace. Today the palace is the residence of *Their Majesties King Bhumibol and Queen Sirikit*

Royal Chitralada Projects: These are the Royal demonstration projects which HM the King has initiated for his subjects. They are non-profit endeavours inside the palace grounds, and include rice growing, rice milling and dairy farming.

Chitralada School: Built in the grounds of the palace, the school was first intended for princes and princesses. Later, however, the school enrolled children of the staff who worked in the palace. Today, the children of people not associated with the palace are admitted, from kindergarten level to the 12th grade.

Dusitalai Pavilian: This all-purpose hall is often used as a venue for HM the King to grant audiences.

SUPPORT Foundation: Many kinds of arts and crafts are taught here, and it is also where local crafts can be preserved and developed. It now houses a collection of handicrafts, from all regions of the country, i.e. gold, silver and lacquerware, Lipao basketry and silk weaving among many others.

BANGKOK METROPOLITAN TOURIST BUREAU

CHURCH OF THE IMMACULATE CONCEPTION

This church was founded by Portuguese residents in 1674 during the reign of *King Narai*. Archbishop Lano named it "Immaculate Conception." The present church was built in 1847, and in its compound there is a smaller, older church known as Wat Noi.

★ H8
167 Soi Mitrakam
Samsen Road
Wachiraphayaban Sub-District
Dusit District Bangkok 10300
☏ (662) 243-2617 243-0064
3 16 19 30 32 33 49 64 65
5 6 16
Chao Phraya Express Boat:
Krung Thon Bridge Pier
Office: Daily 8 am-4 pm
Church: 6-8 pm
Free Admission
Annual Celebration
(Sep 24 Dec 8)
Good Friday (Apr)
Conception
Behind and in front of the Church
Anantasamakom Throne Hall
Dusit Zoo National Library
St. Francis Xavier Church
Vimanmek Mansion Museum
Wat Rachathiwat

DUSIT ZOO

Formerly part of Dusit Royal Garden called *Khaodin-wana*, it was built by command of King Rama V as his private botanical garden. Later, King Rama VIII donated the park to the Bangkok Municipal Administration so that it could be used as a zoo and public park.

Inside is the collection of mammals, birds and reptiles in conditions resembling their natural environments. Several species are rare or close to extinction. As well as its educational value and contribution to breeding and conserving animal species, the zoo has always been a favourite recreational destination for Bangkok people.

★ H8
71 Rama V Road
Dusit Sub-District
Dusit District Bangkok 10300
☏ (662) 281-2000 282-7111-5
FAX (662) 282-6125
5 18 28 70 108
10 16 Mb 4
Daily 9 am-6 pm
Children 5 Bth
Student 1 Bth (In group)
Adult 30 Bth
Motorcycle 10 Bth
Car 30 Bth Bus 40 Bth
In the Zoo compound
Anantasamakom Throne Hall
Chitralada Palace
King Rama VII Museum
Parliament House
Parus-sakkawan Palace
People's Party Marker Plaque
Royal Turf Club
Vimanmek Mansion Museum

GOVERNMENT HOUSE

Originally called Norasingh Residence, King Rama VI commissioned this as a residence for *General Chao Phraya Ram Rakop*. Later, the government bought it and obtained the right of ownership from the general's heir. Since then it has been the Government House and the venue where official guests of the government are entertained.

⊙ **Thaikoofah Mansion:** Formerly named Kraisorn Mansion, this two-storey building combines the Italian Renaissance style with Gothic pointed arches in the exterior walls. There are frescoes on the main ceilings. The building contains an Ivory Room for receiving foreign dignitaries. To its right are the Purple reception room, and the Domed room where official guests may be accommodated.

Nareesmosorn Mansion: formerly called Pra Kan Building, this is the administrative office of the Government House.

Santimaitree Mansion: This is made up of two buildings which surround an open area with a fountain in the centre. The front building was built when *F.M. Plaek Pibulsongkram* was prime minister, the rear building in the time of *F.M. Sarit Thanarat*. Both buildings are used for receptions and seminars.

★ H9
✉ Nakhon Pathom Road
   Dusit Sub-District
   Dusit District
   Bangkok 10300
☎ (662) 281-2240
📠 (662) 282-8147
🚌 10 16 23 99 201
🚤 5 9 16 23 23 (Exp.)
🕐 Mon-Fri 8:30 am-4:30 pm
   Sun Public Holidays
💲 Free Admission
🅿 In front of the Bldg.
   Anantasamakom Throne Hall
   Chang-ton Museum
   Chitralada Palace
   Parliament House
   Parus-sakkawan Palace
   Statue of King Rama V
   Vimanmek Mansion Museum
   Wat Benchamabophit
   Wat Sommanatwihan

MODEL SUPHANNAHONG ROYAL BARGE MAKING CENTRE

Suphannahong Royal barges have been a form of Royal transport since the Sukhothai period. These barges are for the reigning monarch only. They were traditionally used in Royal processions along the waterways during festivals such as Loy krathong, or when the king presented monk robes to monks in temples on the river bank during the Thod Krathin Festival. This was last celebrated on the occasion of HM the King's 6th cycle birthday in 1999.

Mr. Paisal Nettasut has been making models of these Royal barges for more than 20 years. It is delicate work requiring much patience, concentration and and fine craftsmanship. He carves the hull from a solid block of wood which he hollows out. The outside is painted black and decorated with lacquer and gold leaf, while the inside is painted red. The benches for the oarsmen are of bamboo, and the rowers themselves are small, lead figures. Not surprisingly, *Mr. Paisal* can make an average of only five of these model barges in a month.

Models made by *Mr.Paisal* were presented to *Queen Elizabeth II* and *US President Clinton* as souvenirs by the Governor of Bangkok during their respective visits in 1994.

★ H8
✉ 159 Sukhothai Road
Dusit Sub-District
Dusit District Bangkok 10300
☎ (662) 668-8420
🚇 12
🕙 Daily 10 am-9 pm
🅿 In front of the House
✚ Amphorn Garden
Anantasamakom Throne Hall
Chang-ton Museum
Chitralada Palace
Dusit Zoo Government House
Paliament House
Parus-sakkawan Palace
Ratchadamnoen Boxing Stadium
Royal Thai Decorations Museum
Royal Turf Club
Statue of King Rama V
Vimanmek Mansion Museum
Wat Sommanatwihan

MODEL WARSHIP CRAFT CENTRE

Mr. Manoj Musikkabutra, a graduate from Poh Chang Art College, began making model warships after being impressed by some examples in Vienna while on a visit to Austria.

At first, he made only models of foreign vessels, but at the Navy museum in Samut Prakan he was able to sketch a number of Thai warships, and made models based on his sketches. Today, he has more than 20 models in his collection.

The materials used are all local, the hulls made of teak cast-offs obtained from factories. The first step in building a model ship is making the frame, then thin wood planking is pasted onto the frame to make the hull. Some of the models, like the Royal barges, have carving on the hulls which call for very fine craftsmanship; however, the most difficult model to make was "HMS Victory", the British flagship commanded by Lord Nelson at the battle of Trafalgar in 1805.

Mr. Manoj first exhibited his models at the Montien Riverside Hotel in 1996, and he continues to hold annual shows. He also gives training to interested people who pass a selection process. His models are not for sale in shops or exported, because, he says, "the work would then become a business or industry, which is not what I intended."

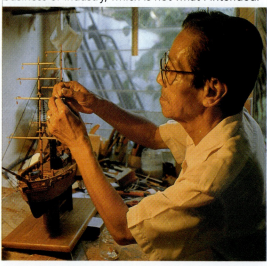

★ H7
✉ 150/4
Phrayaprasit Community
Ongkharak 10 Lane
Samsen 28 Road
Nakhonchaisi Sub-District
Dusit District
Bangkok 10300
☎ (662) 241-3563
🚌 3 16 30 32 49 64 65 66
🚐 3 5 6
⛴ Chao Phraya Express Boat: Kiak Kai Pier
🕒 Mon Wed Fri Sat 6 am-6 pm
  Tue Thu Sun
🎫 Free Admission
📚 Teaching Training
🅿 In front of the House
✚ Boon Rawd Brewery PLC

MUSEUM OF THE ROYAL THAI DECORATIONS, EXHIBITION HALL OF THAI CABINET AND ROYAL GAZETTE

Royal decorations to be worn on court dress or uniform were introduced in the reign of King Rama IV. In 1857, the king ordered medals to be struck to show the status of persons of rank.

The decorations of monarchs were referred to as Royal Decorations of High Rank, while those of the nobility were known as Important Marks of Rank. The term "Royal Decorations" came into use in the reign of King Rama V.

Museum of Royal Thai Decorations: On the ground floor of the museum is a collection of the decorations of various orders arranged in order of rank and displayed on models together with their citations.

Royal Gazette Room: On the northern side of the building, Royal gazettes, seals and documents relating to Thai constitutional law can be seen.

History of Thai Cabinet Room: This is at the southern end of the building and it contains historic articles related to Thai cabinets past and present, showing the origins of the Cabinet and Cabinet orders issued by several governments.

★ H8
Former Chulachomklao Military Academy Bldg.
Government House
Phitsanulok Road
Wat Benchamabophit Sub-District
Dusit District Bangkok 10300
☎ (662) 281-2240 (Public Relations)
280-6262 (Museum)
FAX (662) 282-8147
🚌 10 23 70 201
🚌 3 5 9 23 33 70 201 Mb 8
🕐 Mon-Fri 8:30 am-16:30 pm
Sat Sun Public Hols.
Free Admission, but must be group visits of 10 or more only, with written request one week in advance to the Secretary-General to the Cabinet
Arranged outside the exhibition
Video Presentations
Government House
Government House
P Makkawan-rangsan Bridge
Amphorn Garden
Amphornsathan Palace
Anantasamakom Throne Hall
Chang-ton Museum
Paliament House
Parus-sakkawan Palace
People's Party Marker Plaque
Ratchadamnoen Boxing Stadium
Royal Turf Club
Statue of King Rama V
Vimanmek Mansion Museum
Wat Benchamabophit

★ H8
Uthongnai Road
Dusit Sub-District
Dusit District
Bangkok 10300
☎ (662) 244-1549 244-1557-60
FAX (662) 244-1558
🚌 70 72
3
🕐 Children's Day
(2nd Sat of Jan)
Free Admission
P In front of the Bldg.
Amphorn Garden
Chang-ton Museum
Chitralada Palace
Dusit Zoo Paliament House
People's Party Marker Plaque
Parus-sakkawan Palace
Royal Thai Army Museum
Royal Turf Club
Statue of King Rama V
Wat Benchamabophit
Wat Sommanatwihan
Vimanmek Mansion

NATIONAL ASSEMBLY
(ANANTASAMAKOM THRONE HALL)

This hall was built at the command of King Rama V for visiting foreign dignitaries and for state council meetings. The Italian architecture, *Tamango*, designed it in the Renaissance style.

◉ **Dome Ceiling:** Frescoes depict the monarchs of the Chakri Dynasty and important works of those from King Rama I to King Rama VI are featured on the ceiling of the dome. The rotunda under which the Royal throne is placed has been used for state ceremonies.

The Anantasamakom Throne Hall has played an important role in Thai political history. It reflects the bond between Royal and political institutions since the day when King Rama VII affixed his signature to give the Thai people their first constitution. The first meeting of the Thai parliament was Convened in this hall.

BANGKOK METROPOLITAN TOURIST BUREAU

NATIONAL LIBRARY

Formerly called Wachirayarn Library for the Capital, the National Library was founded in 1905 by the order of King Rama V.

Main Building: Many kinds of reading matter can be found here, from Royal gazettes to novels, newspapers and magazines. The books are classified and arranged according to subject, for example, the Prof. Rapee Sacrik Library provides information on orchids and Luang Vijitvatakarn Library contains rare books.

Wachirayarn Library Hall: Scripture cabinets and religious stone carvings can be seen here.

KING RAMA IX MUSIC LIBRARY HALL

The hall houses a collection of His Majesty's music manuscripts and notebooks, recordings, audio and video tapes and CDs.

Apart from opportunities to study and research His Majesty's literary and musical works, it also enables visitors to listen to His Majesty's music.

CROWN PRINCESS SIRINDHORN MUSIC LIBRARY HALL

The library contains original manuscripts of both classical and contemporary Thai music. It is a centre of information and research for Thai and foreign music, old and new, in a variety of forms and styles.

The Library Hall is divided into a number of rooms such as Luang Vichit-Vadakan Room, HSH Boripatra Music Room, Phra Jane-duriyang Room, Montri Tramote Room and Suntaraporn Room. Each exhibits the works, honours, books and personal effects of the person after whom the room was named.

NATIONAL ARCHIVE HALL

Founded for the purpose of preserving the country's historical documents. The section provides the archive materials for study and research in two categories.

◉ **Official Written Records:** These include Royal decrees, orders, announcements, memos, legislative bills, minutes of meetings, government publications and correspondence.

Audio-Visual Records: These include cassettes, posters, maps, diagrams, slides, photographs, movies and articles related to events of national significance.

NATIONAL FILM HALL

The task of the National Film Hall is to select, review, collect and conserve documents relating to films which are considered to have historical or cultural value. It also offers a comprehensive information service providing documents and references for study and research.

There are approximately 58,000 films including 50,000 items of news footage, 4,000 documentaries and 800 movies. They are now kept at the National Film Hall's facility at Salaya, in Nakhorn Prathom province.

KING VAJIRAVUDH MEMORIAL HALL

This was built at the northern edge of the National Library compound to celebrate the centenary of the birth of King Rama VI in 1891.

◉ **Royal Exhibition of King Vajiravudh:** This contains 12 rooms, divided according to various Royal activities, such as *the Experimenting with Democracy Room*, *the Ascending the Throne Room*, and *the Preserving the Thai Heritate Room*.

Kirtirath Room: Portraits of King Rama V, Queen Saovabha and King Rama VI, as well as commemorative medals and coins from the reign of King Rama VI can be seen here.

Porasurama Room: This room contains two life-size wax models of King Rama VI in full regalia.

★ G8
✉ Samsen Road
Vachiraphayaban Sub-District
Dusit District Bangkok 10300
National Library: Tha Wasukree
☎ (662) 281-5212 281-5313
281-5449
FAX (662) 281-5449
National Archive Hall
☎ (662) 281-1599 282-3829
FAX (662) 281-5341
National Film Hall Salaya
☎ (662) 441-0263-4
FAX (662) 441-0264
🚌 3 9 16 19 30 32 33 64 65 110
🚍 5 6
⚓ Chao Phraya Express Boat:
Thewes Pier
🕐 Daily 9 am-7:30 pm
◐ Public Hols.
🆓 Free Admission
🎫 Student 20 Bht/year
Adult 40 Bht/year
🅿 In the Library compound
✚ Bank of Thailand Museum
Royal Barges Museum
Thewes Market

☎ (662) 282-3264 382-3419
🕐 Mon-Fri 8:30 am-4:30 pm
◐ Sat Sun Public Hols.
📖 Ramachiti Room: King
Rama VI's Literary Works
and Research on His Works
🏛 Huachai Nakrob Room:
Bookshop Specialised in
King Rama VI's and ML Pin
Malakula's Literary Works

★ H8
The Secretariat of the House
of Representatives
2 Uthong Nai Road
Dusit Sub-District
Dusit District Bangkok 10300
☎ (662) 244-1000 244-1500
FAX (662) 244-1019
🚌 12 18 28 70 108
🚐 10 16 Mb 4
⏰ Mon-Fri 8 am-4:30 pm
Sat Sun Public Hols.
Parliament Session: Wed-Fri
Parliament Lib.: Legal Books
  ☎ (662) 244-1287
  FAX (662) 244-1083
King Rama VII Museum
  ☎ (662) 244-1332-3
  FAX (662) 244-1322
  Free Admission, but must
  written request to the
  Secretariat of the House
  of Representative
P Parliament House
Anantasamakom Throne Hall
Chang-ton Museum
Chitralada Palace Dusit Zoo
Parus-sakkawan Palace
People's Party Marker Plaque
Royal Turf Club
Statute of King Rama V
Vimanmek Mansion Museum

PARLIAMENT HOUSE

In the past, parliament meetings were held in the hall on the upper level of Anantasamakom Throne Hall. As the government expanded, permission was requested from the king for a new building, which was erected on the land once belonging to the Tanker Unit of the Police Department.

● **Parliament Building:** Apart from being used for sessions of Parliament, it also houses the office of the house-speaker, government press release room, parliament museum and a library.

Statute of King Rama VII: It is situated at the front of the building. Engraved at the base is the king's signature and a handwritten statement endowing the first permanent constitution of Thailand on December 10, 1932.

King Rama VII Museum: It is located at the Secretariat of the House of Representative office. Displayed in the museum are King Rama VII's personal effects donated by the late *HM Queen Rambhai Barni*, such as collections of lighters, books, clothes and spectacles.

PARUS-SAKKAWAN PALACE

King Rama V ordered the building of the palaces near Dusit Garden Palace. The Chitralada Garden Mansion was intended for *HRH Crown Prince Vajiravudh* and the Parus-sakkawan Garden Mansion, literally "marian plum garden" was intended for *F.M. HRH Prince Chakrabongse.*

When *HRH Crown Prince Vajiravudh* came to the throne as King Rama VI he took up residence at Dusit Garden Palace. He exchanged Chitralada Garden Mansion for a plot of land near Wasukree pier with *F.M. HRH Prince Chakrabongse* and ordered the demolition of the wall separating the two palaces. The king then had a new wall built with the Royal insignia of *F.M. HRH Prince Chakrabongse,* the chakra (or discus) and club, at the gate.

Today, the palace is in the care of the Office of National Police. The Police Museum once located in it has been moved to Police Cadet Academy at Samphran, Nakorn Prathom province.

★ H8
✉ 323 Si Ayutthaya Road
   Dusit District Bangkok 10300
☎ (662) 280-3193
🚌 16 23 70 72 99
🏛 3 5 9
   1989
   1993
🅿 Metropolitan Police Bureau
✚ Amphorn Garden
   Amphornsathan Palace
   Anantasamakom Throne Hall
   Chang-ton Museum
   Chitralada Palace
   Dusit Zoo Parliament House
   People's Party Marker Plaque
   Royal Thai Army Museum
   Royal Thai Decorations Museum
   Royal Turf Club
   Statute of King Rama V
   Vimanmek Mansion Museum
   Wat Benchamabophit

PEOPLE'S PARTY MARKER PLAQUE

"At this point, the People's Party has introduced a constitution for the advancement of the nation on June 24th BE 2475 (1932) at dawn."

This is the historical place where the People's Party read the announcement after it won the revolution that converted the government system from absolute monarchy to democracy with the King as the head of the nation, which signifies the beginning of the democratic system in Thailand.

★ H8
✉ Ground at the side of the
   Statute of King Rama V
   Dusit Sub-District
   Dusit District Bangkok 10300
🚌 70 72
🚇 3
⏰ Daily 24 hrs.
🆓 Free Admission
🅿 In front of Amphorn Garden
✚ Anantasamakom Throne Hall
   Dusit Zoo Parliament House
   Parus-sakkawan Palace
   Royal Thai Army Museum
   Royal Turf Club
   Statute of King Rama V
   Vimanmek Mansion Museum

STATUE OF KING RAMA V
(EQUESTRIAN STATUE)

H8
The plaza in front of Anantasamakom Throne Hall
Dusit District
Bangkok 10300
70 72
3
Free Admission
Daily 24 hrs.
Laying the Wreath: King Chulalongkorn Memorial Day (Oct 23)
In front of Amphorn Garden
Amphorn Garden
Amphornsathan Palace
Anantasamakom Throne Hall
Chang-ton Museum
Chitralada Palace
Dusit Zoo Parliament House
Parus-sakkawan Palace
People's Party Marker Plaque
Ratchadamnoen Boxing Stadium
Royal Thai Army Museum
Royal Thai Decorations Museum
Royal Turf Club
Statute of King Rama V
Vimanmek Mansion Musuem
Wat Benchamabophit

The bronze statue of King Rama V in field marshal's uniform mounted on a horse was cast in Paris by a French sculptor in 1907 when the king visited Europe, and was shipped to Bangkok in 1908.

The statue stands six metres tall from the platform on which the horse stands to the top of the helmet. It is two metres wide and five metres in length. Attached to the front of the marble platform is an engraved bronze plate honouring the King.

King Chulalongkorn is one of the best loved of all Thai kings. On October 23 each year, representatives from government bodies, the military, the police, students and people of all occupations bring garlands, flowers, incense and candles to pay respect to the king and to commemorate the anniversary of his death.

THE ROYAL TURF CLUB

When King Rama V returned from his state visit to Europe in 1897, "The Brine Study Club" which members were civil servants or students who studied in Europe organised a horse racing at the Phramain Ground as an act of allegiance. All the horses used in that race came from the carriage-pulling horses from different stables and this gave rise to the beginning of "the first western-style horse racing in Thailand."

In the reign of King Rama VI, *Phraya Pradipatpubal* and *Phraya Attakarnprasit* asked for the royal permission for the establishment of the horse racing club with the purpose for horse breeding. The king granted the permission and gave the name "Ratchatrinnamai-samakom" and accepted it to be under his patronage.

Today the club manages horse racing, registration of horses as well as owners and associates i.e., stable representatives, trainers, etc. The club is also the centre for horse training and testing. Each year there are approximately 26 races on every other Sunday by alternating with the Royal Bangkok Sports Club. There are 4 cerebrated cups for the club: the Royal *"Darby Cup," Ram Rakop Cup, Phraya Pradipatpubal Cup*, and the *Chairman's Cup*.

★ H8
✉ 183 Phitsanulok Road Suan Chitralada Sub-District Dusit District Bangkok 10300
☎ (662) 628-1810-5: 2129
FAX (662) 280-0415
🚌 10 16 23 99 201
🚇 5 9 Mb 8
🕐 Office: Mon-Fri 8 am-3 pm
   Sat Sun Public Hols.
   Race Course: Daily
   12 noon-6:30 pm
   Golf Course: Daily
   (Except Horse Racing Days)
💵 300 Bht
   Horse Racing
   Life Membership 30,000 Bht
⊘ Under 18 years old Weapons
🅿 In the Club compound

✚ **Anantasamakom Throne Hall**
Chang-ton Museum
Chitralada Palace
Dusit Zoo Parliament House
Parus-sakkawan Palace
People's Party Marker Plaque
Ratchadamnoen Boxing Stadium
Royal Thai Army Museum
Royal Thai Decorations Museum
Statute of King Rama V
Vimanmek Mansion Museum
Wat Benchamabophit

Formerly called Dusit Garden Palace, the palace was built according to the Royal command of King Rama V in 1897, who wished to use it as a summer palace for the Royal family.

The compound contains several small buildings to accommodate the Royal consorts and little princes and princesses. In the time of King Rama V, the compound consisted of:

VIMANMEK MANSION MUSEUM

VIMANMEK MANSION

During the construction of the Dusit Garden Palace, King Rama V commanded *HRH Prince Naris* to dismantle the Mantatrattanarojana Palace from Si Chang Island, and to reassemble and supervise its construction in the Dusit Garden Palace grounds.

Vimanmek Mansion was the residence of King Rama V for some five years. It was built entirely of golden teak in the Western style. The four-storey private section was called Pad-liam, or octagon for its eight-sided shape. Today, 31 rooms are open to the public, and some have been maintained as they were before. These include the Royal bed chamber, the private bathroom and the audience hall.

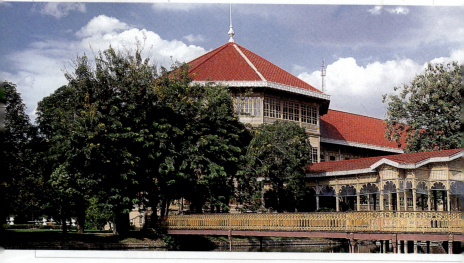

HOR PAVILION

Originally the Hor Mansion was built in Sukhothai Palace. In 1998 *HM King Bhumibol Adulyadej* ordered it to be disassembled and rebuilt in Dusit Garden Palace.

• Inside the pavilion are the personal effects of *HM Queen Rambai Barni*, the consort of King Rama VIII, such as photographs of that King, royal gifts, ceramics such as Sankhaloke ware and artifacts raised from the sea on Thailand's eastern coast, presented by *Mr Anusorn Sapmanu* to HM the King, on the occasion of His Majesty's 72nd birthday.

★ H8
✉ 16 Ratchawithi Road
  Dusit Sub-District
  Dusit District Bangkok 10300
☎ (662) 628-6300-9
FAX (662) 281-6880
🖱 www.palaces.thai.net
🚌 12 18 28 70 108
🚍 10 16 Mb 4
🕘 Daily 9:30 am-4 pm
🎟 Tickets Sold 9:30 am-3:15 pm
  Student Monk Non 20 Bht
  Adult 50 Bht
  Traditional Thai Dancing
  10 am 4 pm
🗣 English
📷 Taking photo inside Bldg.
🅿 Vimanmek Mansion compound
✚ Amphorn Garden
  Amphornsathan Palace
  Anantasamakom Throne Hall
  Chang-ton Museum
  Chitralada Palace
  Dusit Zoo Parliament House
  Parus-sakkawan Mansion
  People's Party Marker Plaque
  Statute of King Rama V
  Royal Turf Club
  Wat Benchamabophit

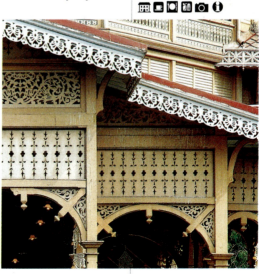

BANGKOK METROPOLITAN
TOURIST BUREAU

Porcelain: During King Rama V's reign, Thailand was significantly influenced by western culture. Porcelain that had been imported from China since the Ayutthaya period was replaced by European-style porcelain. King Rama V, an avid collector of porcelain himself, owned a lot of these items which are on display at Vimanmek Mansion.

Small Artifacts: King Rama V's reign was a prosperous and peaceful period for Thailand. People had time to enjoy art, hobbies and recreation. One of the hobbies which became popular was collecting art and craft items such as picture frames, ivory boxes, porcelain and other rare objects.

Goldware and Silverware: When King Rama V visited Europe to promote international relations, he brought back with him pieces of fine gold-enamel work, especially some pieces from the legendary *Peter Carl Fabergé*, the well-known goldsmith to the Russian court.

Nielloware: Thai nielloware is made by engraving textures on surface of gold or silver and blackening the texture with certain chemical to bring out the beauty. Nielloware has been used to decorate Royal thrones, manuscript covers and wide variety of trays, boxes, bowls, urns, vases and other vessels.

Glassware: This became popular during the reign of King Rama V. In Europe in the late 19th century, the design of glassware developed in the Art Nouveau style, which added colours to the design which had never been seen before. Art Nouveau glass was very popular with Thai aristocrats, who used it for decorating Buddha altars. Imported glass which could be adapted for this use, and for incense burners and flower holders, was much in demand .

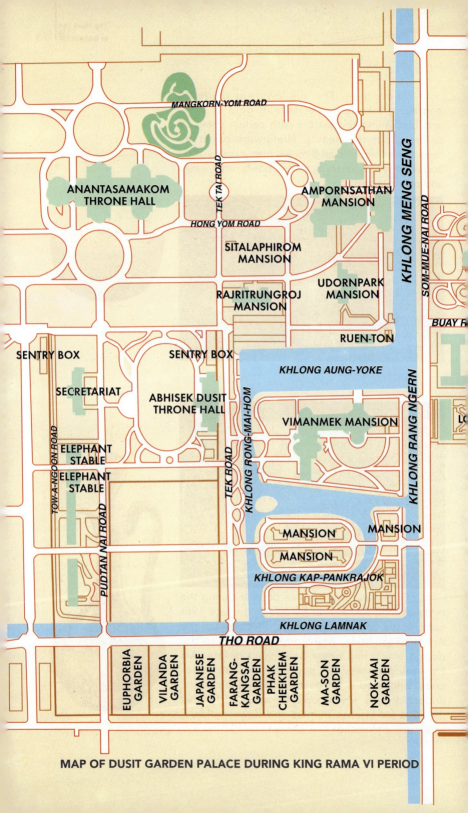

SUAN BUA ROYAL RESIDENTIAL HALL

Originally the residence of *HRH Princess Vimada*, director of the Room for Articles used by the King, it was also a hall of residence for students at Thammasat University.

It was created as a museum to celebrate the 6th Cycle birthday of *HM King Bhumibol* in 1999 displaying works of art presented to His Majesty.

SUAN SI REUDU RESIDENTIAL HALL

In the reign of King Rama VI, the King ordered the moving of Suan Si Reudu Residential Hall formerly the residence of *HM Queen Saovabha* to build in Sukhothai Palace. The palace was subsequently disassembled and rebuilt as Royal Merit for *HM Queen Saovabha* at Wat Rachathiwat.

To celebrate the Golden Jubilee of *HM King Bhumibol*, Suan Si Reudu Residential Hall was rebuilt in its original location. Inside is a display of items presented to HM the King on the occasion of His Majesty's 50th year on the throne.

ABHISEK DUSIT THRONE HALL
SUPPORT MUSEUM

"Abhisek Dusit Throne Hall" was built according to the Royal command of King Rama V in 1903 to serve as a throne hall during his stay in Vimanmek. The throne hall is famous for its Victorian-influenced gingerbread and Moorish porticoes which create a striking and distinctly Thai exterior.

The royal mansion was renovated during the reign of the present king and has been used to display handicrafts made by members of the Promotion of Supplementary Occupations & Related Techniques Foundation (SUPPORT) under the royal patronage of *HM Queen Sirikit*. Among the fine crafts exhibited therein are, silverware, silk, needlework, gold and silver nielloware etc.

SUAN HONG RESIDENCE
ROYAL CEREMONIES' PHOTOGRAPHY MUSEUM

The two-storey green wooden mansion beautifully decorated with ornate fretwork at the eaves and pediment was a former residence of *Queen Srisawarindra*, the royal consort of King Rama V.

It is now used as an exhibition hall where historic photographs documenting the Chakri dynasty are displayed. Among them are pictures of rare court ceremonies such as the one-month-after-birth ceremony and photographs of the king entering the monkhood etc.

HRH PRINCESS BUSSABUN-BUAPHAN'S AND HRH PRINCESS ARUNWADI'S MANSIONS (HIS MAJESTY KING BHUMIBOL'S PHOTOGRAPHIC MUSEUMS I AND II)

Ever since he was young, *HM King Bhumibol* has been interested in taking photographs. His photographic works have both artistic and historical value.

Many of the photos displayed in HRH Princess Bussabun-Buaphan Mansion (Museum I) were taken to use in his development projects. Other pictures displayed in HRH Princess Arunwadi Mansion (Museum II) are photographs of *HM Queen Sirikit*, HRH the Crown Prince and the Princesses, and landscapes.

HRH PRINCESS BUANG SOI-SA-ANG'S MANSION (OLD CLOCK MUSEUM)

King Rama V brought back a number of clocks during his two visits to Europe in the late 19th century. Some of them were for his palaces. Some were specially designed as gifts and souvenirs for members of the Royal family and his staff. Among the clocks displayed are a grandfather clock, 400-day clock (one full winding lasting for 400 days). Apart from clocks, other gifts and souvenirs presented to family, staff and entourage of kings from King Rama V to King Rama VIII are also on display.

HRH PRINCESS ORADAI DEP KANYA'S MANSION (ANCIENT CLOTH MUSEUM)

Most of the textiles displayed in this section are clothes worn by ladies in King Rama V's court. Fabrics displayed are both domestic and imported, for example Tad, gold brocades, silk and Attalad. Those that are domestically woven are in different traditional Thai-styles such as sin, mudmee, Pum Riang, etc. These textiles evolved along with the costume tradition of the ladies in those days. The clothes also signified the status of the wearer.

HRH PRINCESS WORRASETSUDA'S MANSION (ANCIENT ARTIFACT FROM BAN CHIANG MUSEUM)

Ban Chiang is the name of a village in Ban Chiang Sub-District, Nong Wan District of Udorn Thani Province, which has been declared an archaeological site and World Heritage by the UN committee to protect cultural and natural heritage.

Ban Chiang artifacts on display in this pavilion are mostly earthenware vessels. The display area is on two floors. The ground floor displays earthenware utensils, including spoons and ladles. The second floor displays evidence of metallurgical technology such as bronze axes and bangles, chokers and earrings.

SUAN FARANG KANG SAI RESIDENCE (PARAPHERNALIAS OF RANK AND PORTRAITS MUSEUM)

The Mansion was formerly belonged to *HRH Princess Dara Rasmi*. The building was built of brick and plaster with Panya-style roof.

Displayed in this mansion are articles used in royal ceremonies, such as the royal palaquin and the royal sedan chair used in royal barge. Also displayed here are oil paintings ordered from Europe during King Rama V's visit and portraits of senior members of the Royal family.

DUSIT PALACE, ROYAL CARRIAGE MUSEUM

Carriages were introduced into Thailand at the beginning of Rattanakosin period and were popularly used from 1897, after King Rama V's visit to Europe, until they were replaced by automobiles around the period of King Rama VIII. Most of the carriages displayed in the museum are from the periods of King Rama V and VI. Among them are the main royal carriages for the King and minor ones for his entourage, 13 in all.

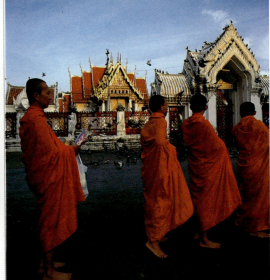

★ H8
✉ 69 Rama V Road Chitralada Sub-District Dusit District Bangkok 10300
☎ (662) 282-7413 281-3277 628-7947 281-4030
🚌 5 16 23 50 70 72 99 201
🚌 3 5 9
🕒 Temple: 8:30 am-5:30 pm
Ubosot: 8 am-5:30 pm
💵 Foreigner 20 Bht
🏛 National Museum Wat Benchamabophit
🕒 Daily 8 am-5 pm
Phra Anusorn
Entering Monkhood Ceremony (Apr)
Hill Tribe Entering Monkhood Ceremony (Jul)
Tan Kuai Salak Festival (Oct)
📖 Thammachinnaratchapan jabophit
🕒 Daily 8 am-6 pm
P. Kittiwan
🏛 1961 1975
⛩ Buddhism: Sun
🕒 1 pm-4:30 pm
Wat Benchamabophit
🚏 In front of the Ubosot
🅿 In front of the Temple
✚ Anantasamakom Throne Hall
Chang-ton Museum
Chitralada Palace
Dusit Zoo Paliament House
Government House
People's Party Marker Plaque
Parus-sakkawan Palace
Royal Turf Club
Statue of King Rama V
Wat Sommanatwihan
Vimanmek Mansion Museum

WAT BENCHAMABOPHIT DUSITWANARAM RATCHAWORAWIHAN

When King Rama V commanded the building of the Dusit Palace, the area belonging to Dusit Temple and another deserted temple were used to construct the hall and for road. The tradition states that a new temple must be built instead; however, the king considered that building several temples would be a big burden for maintenance, but a bigger and more elaborate design would be a better choice. By royal command, HRH Prince Naris Nuvattiwongs designed the temple that was renamed to Wat Benchamabophit, meaning "Wat of King Rama V."

Ubosot: Considered "the perfect architecture of Thai arts", it was built from Italian marble. It is a four-sided structure with a four-tiered roof and a corridor in the back.

A Replica of Pra Buddha Chinnarat: A main Buddha Image, under which placed the ashes of King Rama V.

Wat Benchamabophit National Museum: Local and foreign Buddha images from the period of King Rama V on have been displayed. Among the images, considered two of the most beautiful are the Sukhothai-style in Walking posture, and Subduing Mara (demon) posture.

The Bridges: Between the monk and people area are built in several styles for example cup bridge, tusk bridge and image bridge, etc.

WAT RACHATHIWAT RATCHAWORAWIHAN

The temple was re-established from the former "Wat Samor-rai," by *Somdet Chao Phraya Maha Surasinghanat*. Restoration had been continuously carried on from King Rama I to King Rama III periods. Renovations was made again by King Rama IV who also renamed the temple Wat Rachathiwatwihan, which means "the temple where the king resides."

🔵 Ubosot: The main chapel, was re-designed by *HRH Prince Naris* in Khmer style. The fresco mural was by *Prof. C. Rigoli*, an Italian artist.

Sala Karnparian: The instruction hall, is a large teak Ayutthaya style building also re-designed by *HRH Prince Naris*, who imitated the design of the instruction hall of Wat Suwannaram in Petchburi. The hall is praised "the biggest and most beautiful wooden structure in the Far East."

★ G8
✉ 658 Samsen 9 Lane
   Samsen Road
   Wachira Sub-District
   Dusit District Bangkok 10300
☎ (662) 243-2125
🚌 3 16 19 30 32 33 49 64 65
🚐 5 6
🕐 Temple: Daily 5 am-9 pm
   Ubosot: 8-8:30 am 6-7 pm
   Free Admission
   Buddhist Sermon Day:
   Meditation Class 5:30 pm
🏛 1949
   Second Class
🅿 In the Temple compound
✚ Conception Church
   National Library
   Royal Barge Museum
   St. Francis Xavier Church
   Wat Bot Samsen

HUAI KHWANG

☎ 275-4234

BANGKOK PLAYHOUSE

The private modern-style theatre was opened in July 28, 1993 as a centre for contemporary arts. Among the various arts shown at the centre are: performing arts such as drama, dance, and puppet shows for children, and visual arts such as painting exhibitions by contemporary artists.

The centre also organises lectures, seminars and training courses in order to promote art and culture. Its also cooperates with cultural organisations of various countries in organising shows from abroad.

The centre has been founded on the belief that the development of technology has to go hand in hand with the development of art and culture, which is crucial to the quality of the people in the society.

★ K9
✉ 2884/2 New Petchburi Road
   Bangkapi Sub-District
   Huaikhwang District
   Bangkok 10310
☎ (662) 319-7641-4
FAX (662) 319-7644
🚌 11 23 60 72 93 99 113 506
🚐 12 23 72 206 Mb 3 10
⛴ Passenger Boat:
   Charn Issara Pier
   (SansapCanal)
🕐 Daily 10 am-6 pm.
💳 Admission Change
🏆 Sodsai Award (Dec)
🎬 DASS ENTERTAINMENT
📅 100 Bht/year
ⓘ Theatre: Turn on
   communication equipment
   Taking Food and Drink
🅿 Charn Ilsara II
✚ Pridi Banomyong Institute
   Royal City Avenue Tadu

TADU COMTEMPORARY ART

J9
2nd Fl., Pavilion Y Bldg.
Royal City Avenue
31/4 Soonvijai Lane
Rama IX Road
Bangkok 10310
(662) 203-0926-29: 15-16
(662) 203-0931
taduart@loxinfo.co.th
11 23 60 72 93 99 113 206
12 23 72 206 Mb 3 10
Tue-Sun 10:30 am-7:30 pm
Mon Public Hols.
Free Admission (Except for exhibition event or seminar)
Exhibition Shows Training Group discussion Film shows
In front of the Bldg.
RCA Parking
Bangkok Playhouse
Makkasan Police Station

Art is one of the media that reflects people's culture and style. With awareness of the important role of the arts, Tadu, a private art centre, was established in November 1996 with support from artists, art lovers and collectors to promote Thai contemporary art. Artists and art lovers can meet to discuss, exchange ideas and participate in various exhibitions and activities organised by the centre.

New activities are introduced every month. Activities range from art exhibitions of work of new artists as well as foreign artists, experimental theatre, dance or any kind of integrated performance.

The centre also organises training courses, discussions, public art projects, film shows and critics' events in co-operation with other organisations such as Thai Movie Foundation to promote Thai and Foreign movies.

THAILAND CULTURAL CENTRE

The Thailand Cultural Center organizes both Thai and Foreign cultural performances free to the public with prior reservation. The program and schedule of performances can be checked from the Centre's newsletter.

The Centre contains :

◉ Permanent Exhibition Hall: Open to Thais and foreigners, displays the history, culture and development of Thai people using modern technology such as slide multi-vision etc.

Youth Centre: The purpose of which is to promote the creativity of children. Thai classical dance and Thai music courses are organised for children in the exhibition hall on Saturday, Sunday and during school holidays.

★ J8
✉ Ratchadapisek Road
Huaikwang Sub-District
Huaikwang District
Bangkok 10310
☎ (662) 247-0028
FAX (662) 245-7747
🚌 73 136 137 206
🚌 15 18 136
🕒 Mon-Sat 9:30 am-4:30 pm
🕒 Sun Public Hols.
🎫 Free Admission
(Except Show Seminar
Exhibition Discussion Plays
Training Film Shows)
3rd fl.
☎ (662) 247-0028: 177 183
FAX (662) 247-0061
🏛 Thai Life Permanent
Exhibition Hall
☎ (662) 247-0028: 133 141
FAX (662) 247-0060
Client Services
☎ (662) 247-0028: 102 114
🅿 Cultural Centre compound
✚ Korean Embassy
Robinson Dept. Store
Royal City Avenue
Wat Rama 9 Kanchanapisek

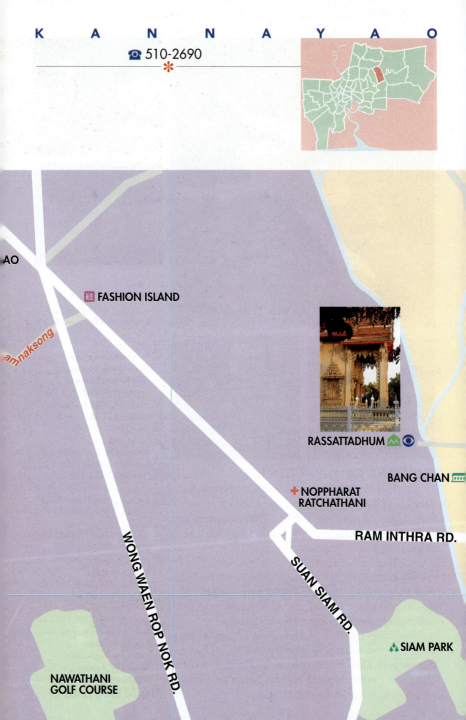

★ P6
✉ 25 Moo 5 Ram Inthra Road
Kannayao Sub-District
Kannayao District
Bangkok 10250
☎ (662) 512-0207 517-5656
📠 (662) 919-0023
🚌 26
🚐 14 26
🕐 Temple: Daily 5 am-8 pm
Ubosot: Weekdays 8-9 am
Buddhist Lent Commencing Day: 4-6 pm
💲 Free Admission
📖 Buddhist Sermon Day: Preaching
Buddhist Lent Commencing Day: Sermon
Songkran Festival (Apr 13)
🅿 In the Temple compound
✚ Nawathani Golf Course
Siam Park

WAT RASSATTADHUM

Formerly known as Wat Bangchan, this civil temple was built in 1882 on land surrounded by rice fields. It is divided into three sections: Phutthawat, where the religious buildings are situated, Sangkhawat, where monks reside, and an area for observing religious practices.

The temple received an award for being an Exemplary Developed Temple in 1973, and in 1993 it was given an Educational Park award by the Department of Religious Affairs for its continuing dedication to the education of the young since the time of its foundation.

Buddhist preaching is held on every Holy Day or *wan phra*, and sermons are given during the Buddhist Lent period. Its peaceful atmosphere, with shade provided by large trees of various kinds make it an ideal place for religious practice.

⊙ Luangpor Suriyothai, standing Buddha image holding an alms bowl, was cast in bronze during the Rattanakosin period. The image was brought to Wat Rassattadhum from the temple of the Golden Buddha, Wat Trimitwitthayaram.

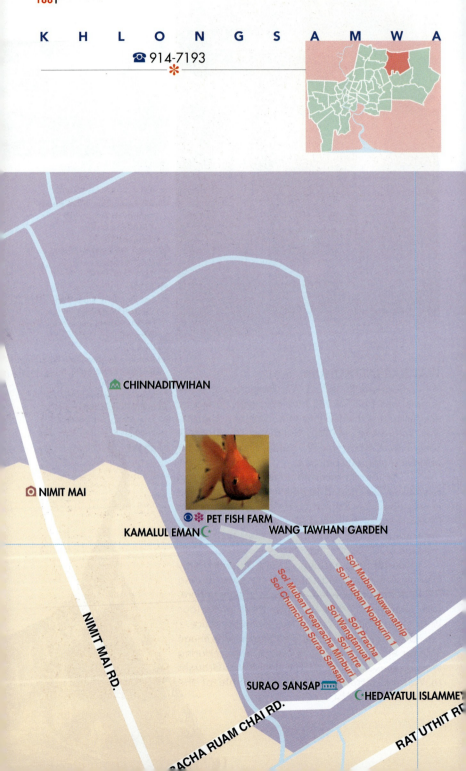

PET FISH FARM

Colourful and exotic fish have become a favourite domestic pet with city-dwellers, and this has introduced a new vocation to some local communities. For some years now, the people of the Bueng Tanode-pattana area have been breeding fish in the traditional way in krachang — large bamboo cages left in the fish's natural habitat, the waterways, which they keep clean for breeding. Today, every family has 30-40 krachang, some even more, with 300-400 fish raised in each. The fish bred in these containers are hardy, easy to care for, and possess all the characteristics of colour, shape and movement which make them a big attraction. There are five kinds of fish bred here, the most popular being the sword-tail or pla sod.

Dealers buy direct from the farm every week, or else fish may be taken to Bangkok's popular Chatuchak market by a local agent or by the farmer himself.

Today, the colourful fish of Thailand are a source of pleasure and relaxation in homes throughout the world, making them a valuable export.

Breeding fish not only provides additional income to the households, but is also a source of enjoyment and relaxation for villagers. They have discovered the value of taking good care of the water resources on which they depend, and this in turn has increased the number of other aquatic animals they can raise.

The Must See Sites
In BANGKOK 189

★ Q5
✉ Moo 5 Tawan Lane
Pracha Ruamchai Road
Saikongdin Sub-District
Khlong Samwa District
Bangkok 10510
☎ (662) 916-9944
🚆 26 27 58 113 131 144
🚌 2 15 Mb 3
🕓 Daily 8 am-6 pm
🆓 Free Admission
🅿 In front of Suraosansap School
✚ Kamalul-e-man Mosque
Safari World
Suraosansap School

KHLONG SAN
☎ 437-5279

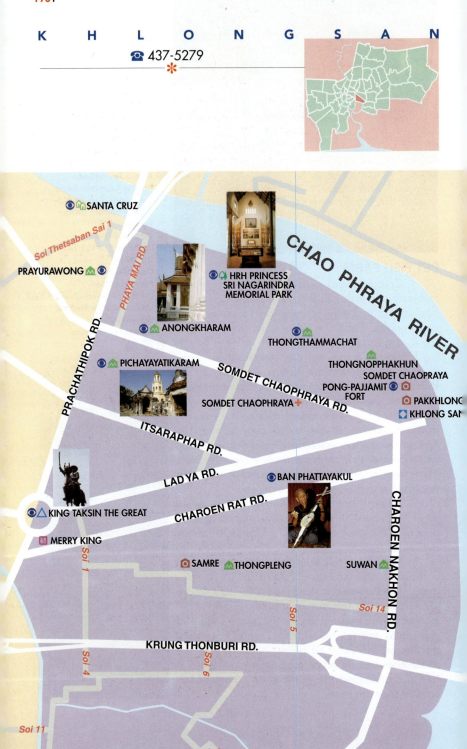

MONUMENT OF KING TAKSIN THE GREAT

King Taksin is the great king who liberated Thailand after Ayutthaya fell to Burma in 1767. In 1937, *Mr. Thongyoo Phuttapat*, the MP of Thonburi Province at that time, proposed the building of King Taksin the Great Monument at Wongwian-yai Circle, Thonburi Province, for *Phraya Phaholpholpha yuhasena*'s government.

The Dept. of Fine Arts, at the government's direction designed seven models and exhibited them to the public at the Constitution Fair of that same year to seek for public opinions and votes. The voting combined with donation was counted by donation cards put for each model without regarding the value of money put in. The winning model, counting 3,932 cards was the form the Monument has taken.

★ G10
✉ Beginning of:
Prajadhipok Road
Intraraphithak Road
Lat Ya Road Somdet
Chaophraya Road
Wongwian-yai Circle
Khlongsan Sub-District
Khlongsan District
Bangkok 10600
🚌 3 4 7 7Kor 9 10 20 21 37 43 84 89 105 120 149
🚐 6 10
🕐 Daily 24 hrs.
💲 Free Admission
🎗 Laying the Wreath: (Dec 28)
🅿 Merry King Dept. Store
✚ HRH Sri Nagarindra Memorial Park
Merry King Dept. Store

PHATTAYAKUL HOUSE

Mr. Tuen Phattayakul, a maestro of Thai Classical music who was appointed National Artist (Performance - Thai Classical Music) in 1991, has opened his house to teach Thai classical music and dance to general public.

Maestro Tuen started playing music when he was 7 years old and has been working in the area for more than 80 years. Apart from being a virtuoso on Thai woodwinds and strings he also composes a great number of Thai classical pieces. He is also skill skillful craftsman who can make every kind of musical instrument and miniature pieces which can produce same quality of sound of normal size pieces.

★ G10
✉ 770 Chareonrath Road
Khlongtonsai Sub-District
Khlongsan District
Bangkok 10600
☎ (662) 437-8575
🚌 6 3 57 84
🚐 3
⚓ Ferry: Khlongsan Pier
🎵 Phattayakul Music and Dance
☎ (662) 281-9857
📠 (662) 281-9857
🚌 3 9 30 32 53
🚐 17 33
🕐 Daily 9 am-4 pm
🅿 In front of the House
✚ Wat Anongkaram

SOMDET PHRA SRI NAGARINDRA THE PRINCESS MOTHER MEMORIAL PARK

Somdet Ya is the title Thai people have given to their late beloved *Somdet Phra Srinagarindra*, HRH the Princess Mother. It literally means "Princess Grandmother" reflecting the closeness of the late Princess Mother to the Thai people.

The HRH Princess Mother Memorial Park was opened by King Bhumibol, Rama IX, *on* January 21, 1997. The park is divided into 2 parts. The shady front part is filled with big old fig tree aged over 100 years, a big fountain bowl and flowers. The inner part is surrounded with pavement which can be used as jogging track. Apart from preserving old trees, an old King Rama V period-style 2-storey building is also maintained and is presently used as the office of the park.

⦿ **Model House:** The Department of Fine Arts made a model of the house in which Somdet Ya used to live during her childhood.

Exhibition Hall 1: Exhibits the pictures of Somdet Ya, places she once lived, a history of Wat Anongkharam Community where she was born and lived, and gifts from people during her funeral. At the middle of the hall, visitors can watch the biographical videos of Somdet Ya and listen to her speech.

Exhibition Hall 2: Exhibits Somdet Ya's personal effects, her dresses, and her handicrafts. The wall at the far end is decorated with paintings.

Sculpture: The bas-relief cut in a huge sand-stone slab features the depiction of numerous activities of HRH the Princess Mother carried out in remote areas, and the scene of Wai Sa Mae Fah Luang procession in celebration for her.

★ G10
✉ Somdet Chao Phraya 3 Lane
  Somdet Chao Phraya Road
  Khlongsan District
  Bangkok 10600
☎ (662) 437-7799 439-0902
  439-0896
📠 (662) 497-1853
🚌 6 42 43
🚐 4 Mb 5 14
🕐 Park: Daily 6 am-6 pm
  Museum: 9 am-4 pm
Ⓒ Museum: Public Hols.
  (Except for special event)
🎫 Free Admission
📅 Anniversary of
  Somdet Ya's Death (Jul 18)
  Mother's Day (Aug 12)
  Somdet Ya's Birthday (Oct 21)
  King's Birthday (Dec 5)
  Monthly productive activities
🅿 50 Bht/year
🅿 In front of the Park
✠ Chao Phor Kuan U Shrine
  Chao Phor Seua Shrine
  Wat Anongkaram
  Wat Pichayayatikaram
  Wat Prayurawongsawat

WAT ANONGKARAM WORAWIHAN

★ G10
✉ 41
Somdet Chao Phraya Road
Somdet Chao Phraya Sub-
District Khlongsan District
Bangkok 10200
☎ (662) 437-3315 437-1033
🚌 6 43 57
⛴ Chao Phraya Express Boat:
Memorial Bridge Pier
🕐 Temple: Daily 5 am-8 pm
Ubosot: Daily 8:30 am-5 pm
💲 Free Admission
📚 Class: Buddhist Thai Culture
  🕐 Sun 8:30-11:30 pm
Thai Dance Thai Culture
  🕐 Sun 1-3 pm
Songkran Festival (Apr 12-15)
📖 Wat Anongkaram Public Lib.
  🕐 Tue-Sat 9 am-5 pm
  🚫 Mon Sun Public Hols.
🏛 1977
🏫 Second Class
🅿 In the Temple compound
✚ HRH Sri Nagarindra
Memorial Park
Wat Pichayayatikaram
Wat Thong Nopphakhun
Wat Thong Pleng
Wat Thong Thammachart

Formerly named Wat Noi Khamtham after its founder, King Rama IV granted it a new name, Wat Anongkaram worawihan.

Ubosot: Built during the Third Reign of brick and mortar in Thai-style. The glazed tile roof is traditionally decorated with chorfa and bairaka. Galleries (made up from outside columns) surround the chapel. Flower patterns decorate the pediments. Doors and windows contain stucco works.

Principal Buddha Image: In Subduing Mara (Demon) posture. The image sits on a throne over a gilded base decorated with glass mosaic.

Wihan: The sermon hall contains outstanding stucco works at the surrounds of doors and windows. The pediments are adorned with flower pattern glass mosaic. The windows depict the Tosachart, literally 10 lives. The stories of the Lord Buddha's reincarnation as the Bodhisatta.

Mondop: The spire roof chapel enshrines the cement replica of the reclining Buddha image of Wat Rachathiwat. The back to the west side contains patterns of metal footprint of the Lord Buddha

Tripitaka Cabinet: The scriptures cabinet is late Ayutthaya period. The beautiful gilded painting on the cabinet depicts royal processions both on land and waterways.

BANGKOK METROPOLITAN
TOURIST BUREAU

WAT PICHAYAYATIKARAM WORAWIHAN

The temple was originally deserted. Later *Somdet Chao Phraya Borommahapichaiyat* renovated the temple and presented it to King Rama III who gave the name Wat Phrayatikaram, and was changed to Wat Pichaiyatikaram by King Rama IV.

Ubosot: The main chapel is in Chinese-style, without the Thai traditional decoration on the roof such as chorfa, garuda head shaped-finial, or bairaka. The Principal Buddha Image enshrined in the ubosot is a Subduing Mara posture image named Somdet Phra Sittharotbuddhachao.

Prang: The main prang enshrining four Buddha Images facing each direction. The other two small minor Prang are in the same size.

Tripitaka: Buddhist scriptures. This is the world's first printed King Rama V's version. The King had granted one copy to the temple.

- G10
- 32 Somdet Chao Phraya Road Somdet Chao Phraya Sub-District Khlongsan District Bangkok 10600
- (662) 861-4489 861-5781
- FAX (662) 861-4530
- 6 9 43 57 82Kor
- Temple: Daily 5 am-8 pm Ubosot: Daily 8 am 6 pm
- Free Admission
- Devo Alming (Dec 31-Jan 1) Songkran Festival: Religious Rite dedicated to the ancestors. (Apr 16)
- 1949
- Second Class
- Sukumalai
- In the Temple compound
- HRH Sri Nagarindra Memorial Park
  Wat Anongkaram
  Wat Thong Nopphakhun
  Wat Thong Pleng
  Wat Thong Thammachart

KHLONG TOEI

☎ 244-2487

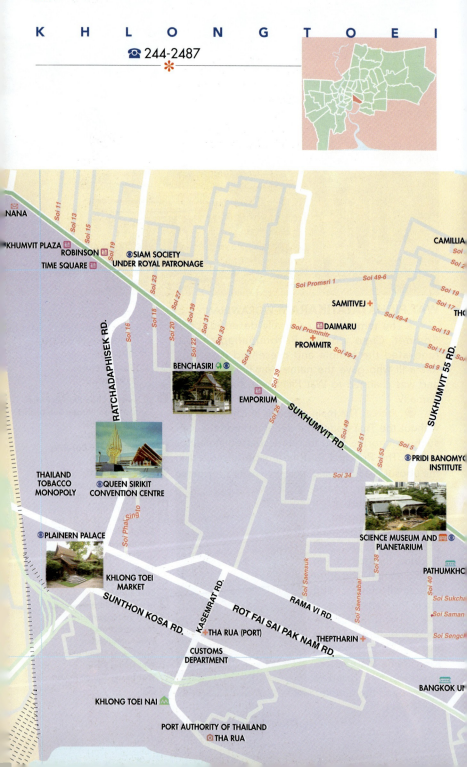

BENJASIRI PARK

Benjasiri Park was built on a 29-rai plot of land donated to the BMA who turned it into a park to commemorate the 60th Birthday of HM Queen Sirikit on August 12, 1992.

◉ Sculptures: There are 12 pieces of contemporary sculptures including children's works in the park.

Chalerm Phrakiet Square: This contains a big coin sculpture depicting a 3 metre-tall standing image of Queen Sirikit in low relief, two Thai-style pavilions displaying pictures of the queen performing her various duties, and jumping fountains.

Inside the park is a forest garden, a big pond, Thai style pavilions, a multi-purpose open space, a health garden, children's playground, a skating rink, basketball and tra-kraw courts, and swimming pools.

★ J10
✉ Between Sukhumvit 22/24 Lanes Sukhumvit Road Khlong Tan Sub-District Khlong Toei Bangkok 10110
☎ (662) 262-0810
📠 (662) 262-1810
🚇 2 25 38 40 48 98
🚌 1 Sai 2 8 11 13 25 38 Mb. 6
🕒 Office: Mon-Fri 7:30 am-3:30 pm
🕒 Sat Sun Public Hols. Park: DAily 5 am-8 pm
💳 Free Admission
🏊 Swimming Pool: Member Only
  ⏱ Daily 5 pm-8 pm
  💵 40 Bht/person/year Swimming 15 Bht/time
🅿 Behind the Park
✚ Emporium Complex Imperial Queen's Park Hotel

★ 110
✉ 1164 Rama 4 Road
Khlong Toei Sub-District
Khlong Toei District
Bangkok 10110
☎ (662) 249-4280
📠 (662) 249-6846
🚌 4 13 22 45 46 47 74 106
109 115 116 149
🚕 7 35 141 (Exp.)
🕐 Apr 28 of every year
9 am-6 pm
💰 Free Admission
📅 Naris Day (Apr 28):
Play from Naris's
Literary works
Thai Music Show
🏛 1982
🎵 Teaching Thai Music
📷 Permission required for
taking photo inside Bldg.
🅿 Outside the Palace compound
➕ Khlong Toei Market
Lumphini Boxing Stadium
Lumphini Park
Old House on Sathon Road
Queen Sirikit Convention
Centre
Thailand Tobacco Monopoly

PLAINERN PALACE

When *HRH Prince Naris* decided to move from Tha Phra Palace to take residence at Khlong Toei permanently, he bought several Thai wooden houses, restored, remodelled and reassembled them in the compound as one house.

When the railway was cut to Rama IV road, the road had been levelled up to the railway and thus, commuters had to push their carriages up the "hilly" land when passing to the area. For people who were not familiar with the palace, the "hill" has been used as a landmark when giving directions to the palace. Therefore, it was named "Plainern" literally, "the end of the hill."

◉ **Tumnak Thoong, literally Hall House:** The east wing was used for receiving guests. On the wall are original paintings of the Lord Buddha, his disciples and celestial beings which the prince used as models for the mural painting in the ubosot of Wat Rachathivas. The west wing, originally used by the prince as a dining area, is now used for exhibiting bussabok or thrones, and lai-rod-nam or gilded lacquerware. The north room is used to store khon masks and wooden sculpture. The prince's study exhibits his paintings and desk.

Tumnak Bunthom, literally, Sleeping House: The west wing room, formerly the prince's bed chamber, contained a bed once belong to *HRH Princess Phannarai*.

HRH Prince Naris was the 62nd son of King Rama IV and *HRH Princess Phannarai*. He was known as "The Great Artist of Siam" for his talent and knowledge in painting, sculpture, architecture, interior decoration, music, archaeology and history. In 1963, he was honoured by UNESCO as "National Artist."

QUEEN SIRIKIT CONVENTION CENTRE

Queen Sirikit Convention Centre is situated in the heart of Bangkok. The beautiful contemporary Thai-style building is enhanced by a large artificial lake providing a scenic view. The interior and exterior of the building are decorated with art works representing Thai styles, cultures and concepts. Among these art works are:

◉ Lokutra: At a small pond in front of the east entrance is "Lokutra," an outdoor sculpture. Its form can be interpreted as a flame or a lotus petal or the Thai gesture of respect, the wai, in which hands are pressed together, which is intended to symbolise prosperity, supreme spiritual perfection or respect according to one's interpretation.

Globe over Elephant Pillar: Another sculpture situated at reception area.

Indrapisek Royal Ceremony: A combination of low and high relief wooden sculpture depicting the Hindu god Indra creating the universe, a Thai interpretation of Hindu belief.

Sala Thai: A 5-room Thai-style pavilion situated in a small garden at the northern side of the building. The sala contains richly decorated pediments and roof.

In addition, there are a post office, banks, restaurants, tourist and hotel information services, a press room, a medical centre, and a transportation service

★ J10
✉ 60 Ratchadaphisek Road
Khlong Toei Sub-District
Khlong Toei District
Bangkok 10110
☎ (662) 229-3000
FAX (662) 229-4253
🖱 http.://www.qsncc.co.th.
🚌 136
🚌 22
⏰ Office: Daily 8:30 Am-5 Pm
Free Admission
Exhibition Meeting Seminar
P In the Covention compound
✚ The Stock Exchange of Thailand
Grand Pacific Hotel
Plainern Palace
Robinson Dept. Store
Siam Society
Sherraton G. Sukhumvit Hotel
Thailand Tobacco Monopoly
Time Square

SCIENCE MUSEUM AND PLANETARIUM

As the Solar System, astronomy, outer space, nature and the environment, and technology are part of reality and human ways of life, the Science Centre was established for the purpose of educating the youth and the general public in these subjects. Here can be found multimedia presentations, exhibits of models and real objects, and educational processes giving experience with various activities at every opportunity.

Bangkok Planetarium: Shows programmes divided into two parts: showing of stars in the sky between twilight and dawn, and multi-vision slide shows for which the programme changes every month.

Science and Technology Building: This has a permanent exhibition on four floors about the bases of human life, where visitors can do experiments and make tests, and otherwise interact with the exhibits. For instance, the first floor displays the world of science, satellite communications, and the miracle of laser light. The second floor opens up the world of energy, the history of timekeeping,

★ K10
928 Sukhumvit Road
Phrakanong Sub-District
Khlong Toei District
Bangkok 10110
☎ (662) 392-1773 392-5951-9: 1034 2008 2009
FAX (662) 391-0522
www.sci-edug.nfe.go
🚌 2 23 25 38 40 48 72 98
🚐 1 Sai 2 8 11 13 23 25 38 Mb 6
🕐 Tue-Sun 8:30 Am-4:30 Pm
Mon Public Hols.
Planetarium: Children 5 Bht
Adult 10 Bht
Exhibition and Planetarium:
Children 15 Bht
Adult 30 Bht
Monk: Free Admission

BANGKOK METROPOLITAN
TOURIST BUREAU

and robot technology.

Nature and Environment Building: This has permanent exhibitions using diverse and modern media. Visitors can learn by participating in activities inside the exhibition on six floors. Floors three to eight start with the prehistoric world and fossils, going on to humans and the environment, and natural disasters, the world of insects, the Discovery Room Cyber Club, and natural heritage.

Underwater World Building: Shows the evolution of aquatic animals and many species of beautiful fish

Exhibition of Sports Science: Displays the importance of our bodies, the history of sports science, knowledge of exercise and tests of the body's capabilities,. Outdoor exercise equipment includes an artificial climbing wall, which tests various parts of the body.

The Centre also has arranged training, demonstration lectures, field trips and sports events as well as regular activities on important days for both students and the general public.

Daily Show
- Tue-Fri 11 Am-2:30 Pm
  Sat-Sun 10 Am 1:30 Pm
  2:30 Pm

Booking special (Student):
- Tue-Fri 10 Am-1 Pm

English :
- Tue 10 Am
- Lectureer 300 Bht
- 7th fl. Bldg. 4
- 1st fl. Bldg. 4
- 1st fl. Planetarium
- In the Centre compound
- Eastern Bus Terminal (Ekkamai)
- Banomyong Institute
- Benchasiri Park
- Unesco Organization

L A K S I

☎ 576-1447

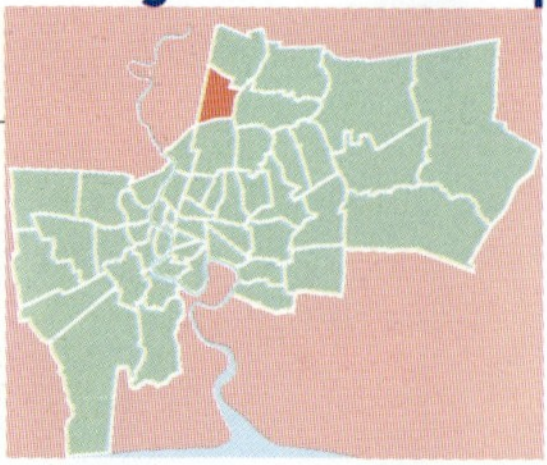

RATCHAPHUEK GOLF COURSE

CHIDCHON RD.

THAI KITE CENTRE

BANG BO

VIBHAVADI RANGSIT RD.

TEWASUNTORN

KHON MASK CENTRE
AT TALAT BANGKHEN

OFFICE OF ATOMIC ENERGY FOR PEACE (OAPE)

KHON MASK CENTRE

Khon mask-making requires both expertise and meticulous care. Because of its ancient tradition and detailed form, it is difficult to find successors to keep up the tradition. Today, there are only a few venues where one can see Khon performances, notably the National Theatre, the Cultural Centre, or at special festivals or occasions.

Mr. Thanom Meethao and his family in the Bangkhen Market community have been making Khon masks and accessories like the Chada headdresses and Sungwan jewelled sashes for more than 20 years. Each piece is made to the customer's requirements. Some like them as a form of interior decoration, and many shops sell them to tourists.

Khon masks come in different sizes and qualities, but those used for a performance demand the most detailed precision in the making.

★ J5
✉ 55/2 Moo 1
Talat Bangkhen Community
Vibhavadi Rangsit Road
Thung Songhong Sub-District
Laksi District Bangkok 10210
☎ (662) 953-0259
🚌 29 52
🚍 10 29
🕘 Daily 9 am-6 pm
🅿 In front of the House
✚ Office of Atomic Energy for Peace
Wat Devasoontorn
Wat Lak Si

THAI KITE CENTRE

During his career in the Civil Service, *Mr. Kul Boonnok*, a native of Nakorn Sawan Province, used to teach handicrafts. With a special fascination for kites, he began making them for sale after his retirement, and invented several new types and designs.

Kite-making begins with a journey to Nakorn Sawan, Lopburi or Ayutthaya to acquire some See-sook bamboo. *Mr. Kul* personally oversees the cutting of the bamboo, selecting trees which are more than three years old. Their skin will be black or dark green. After slicing the bamboo, it is soaked in water for a month to strengthen it and protect it from weevils. It is then dried in the sun and cut to size according to the types of kite to be built. The framework of the kite is bound together with good, strong cord to reinforce it, and the final step is to paste the paper onto the framework.

In addition to kites for general sale, there are several new kinds in the form of owls, butterflies, goldfish and dragons. The most difficult shape to make is the garuda kite, whose intricate frame requires a large amount of bamboo, as well as skill.

Mr. Kul teaches kite-making to small groups within the community. He is also pleased to talk on making kites to all those who are interested, especially to anyone who would like to take up kite-making as a living. In that way, this ancient folk craft will be conserved for future generations.

★ J4
✉ 304/686 Moo 3
 Bangbua National Housing Org.
 Phahonyothin 49/1 Lane
 Phahonyothin Road
 Talat Bangkhen Sub-District
 Laksi District Bangkok 10210
☎ (662) 561-4212
 26 39 59 107 114 126 129
🚌 3 13 21 22 39 Mb 2 16
🕒 Daily 8 am-8 pm
 Free Admission
 Exhibition Trade Fair
🅿 In front of the House
 Bangbua Kindergarten
 Bangbua Sport Complex

LATKRABANG
☎ 326-6288

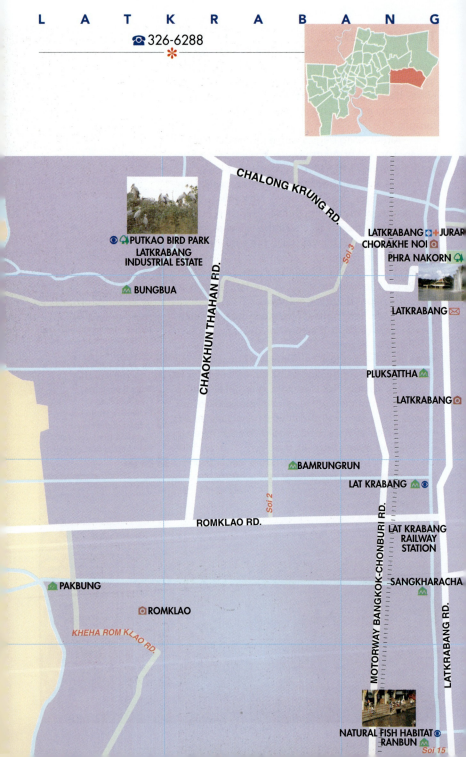

NATURAL FISH HABITAT

Pravet-Burirom Canal, the long waterway which runs through the district, is a natural habitat of fresh water fish such as, serpent-head fish, catfish, carp, *Pangasius larnaudii*, and most of all *Pangasius fowleri*.

Thousand of *Pangasius fowleri* can be found residing in temple compounds since most temples have established sheltered areas where catching fish is prohibited. The fish are well fed each day with rice left from the alms bowls of the monks. Larnboon, Latkrabang, Sankaracha, and Sutthapoth are temples where large numbers of fish can be found.

★ P10
✉ Wat Larnboon1 Moo 7 Km 15
Latkrabang Sub-District
Latkrabang District
Bangkok 10520
☎ (332) 329-0283
🚌 1013 Minibus from mount of Sukhumvit Soi 77
🚌 18 Mb 23
🕐 Temple: 8:30 am-6 pm
💳 Free Admission
🅿 In the Temple compound
✚ Phra Nakhon Park
Wat Latkrabang

★ S10
✉ Moo 1 Onnut Road
Latkrabang Sub-District
Latkra bang District
Bangkok 10520
☎ (662) 326-9994
FAX (662) 326-9994
🚌 143
🚌 18 Mb 23
🕐 Office: Mon-Fri
  8:30 am-4:30 pm
  Sat Sun Public Hols.
  Park: 5 am-8 pm
🎟 Free Admission
  Latkrabang Youth Centre:
  🕐 Mon-Fri 10 am- 6 pm
  Sat Sun Public Hols
  ☎ (662) 326-6828
  FAX (662) 326-6828
  Activities: Arobic Thai Music
  Thai Dance Western Music
  Handicraft
  📖 Latkrabang Youth Centre:
  🕐 Mon-Fri 10 am-6 pm
  💰 Children 8-17 years old
    10 Bht/year
    Adult 40 Bht/year
  🅿 In the Park compound
  ✚ Hau-take Market
    Latkrabang District Office

PHRA NAKHON PARK

This was once a field inundated by flood water every year, until the Public Parks Division decided to develop it in a three-year project from 1985-1987. Now the once-flooded field has been rescued and turned into a beautiful park. Shady trees, flowering shrubs, animal-like trimmed bushes as well as the serenity of a forest park have made Phra Nakorn Park a favourite with families in the evenings.

There is also a multi-purpose field for family activities, a gazebo, fountains, and a youth centre. The nursery provides information for visitors on varieties of plants and how to take care of them.

BANGKOK
BANGKOK METROPOLITAN
TOURIST BUREAU

PUTKAO BIRD PARK

The 35,800 sq. m. plot of land is a natural habitat for birds such as egrets, mynas, night herons, owls and seasonal birds such as open billed storks (*Anustomus oscitans*) and cormorants. Thousands of birds have found this place as their sanctuary.

Open billed storks come in winter, and while most fly back in the rainy season, some stay behind to take care of their nests.

Cormorants come during rainy season and fly back in winter. These birds have been coming here for more than 30 years.

★ S8
✉ Near Latkrabang Industrial Estate Project 3 Lamplathiew Sub-District Latkrabang District Bangkok 10520
☎ (662) 749-5259 (Pol. Lt. Col. Prasit Putkao)
FAX (662) 398-4034
⏱ Daily 6 am-6 pm
🎟 Free Admission
● Disturb Animal
🅿 In the Park compound
✚ Wat Latkrabang

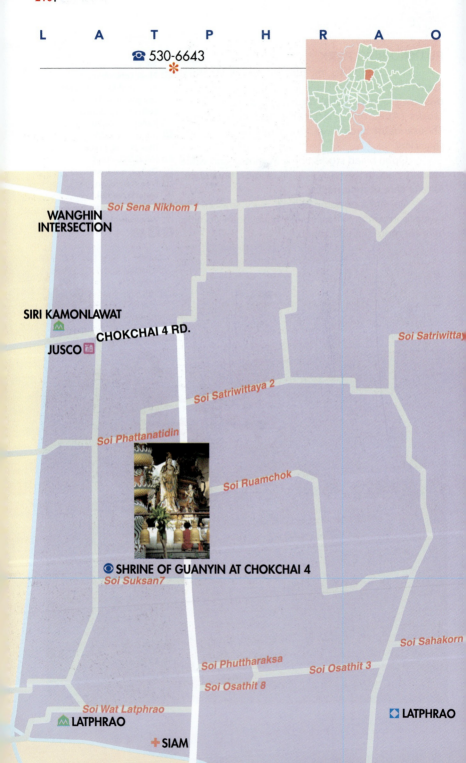

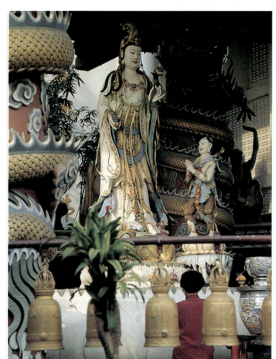

★ K6
✉ 4/37 Suksanti 7 Lane
Latphrao 53 Road (Chokchai 4)
Latphrao District
Bangkok 10230
☎ (662) 539-3951 514-0715
FAX (662) 538-8178
🚌 8 27 44 92 96 122 126 137 145
🚐 2 15 27 92 126 137 145
Mb 15 20
🕐 Daily 7 am-9 pm
🎫 Free Admission
📅 Chinese New Year's Day
(Late Jan-Feb)
Vegetarian Days
Guanyin Procession
(Held on the 9th day after
Chinese New Year's Day)
🅿 In front of the Temple
⊕ Wat Latphrao
🚻 📷

SHRINE OF GUANYIN AT CHOKCHAI 4

Built in 1983 by the *Venerable Kuang Seng*, this is a Mahayana Buddhist shrine. The regimen of devotees to the shrine is very strict: Ordinands must eat vegetarian food and are not allowed to disrobe. They must meditate and abandon worldly life to seek Dhamma, and study and practice meditation.

◉ Architecture: The shrine is in the Chinese style. At the yard in front is the Sukhavati building are shrines to Chinese gods and dragon pillars.

The Main Shrine: This contains an image of the *Bodhisattva Kuan Yin* and the *Bodhisattva Prince Ang Hai Yi*. The interior is decorated with many traditional Chinese deities and Buddha images, such as the 12 Chinese year signs, *Tang Sam Chang Lang*, *Lang Tai Su* and figures of Guanyin in 32 positions. There is also a vegetarian hall and an insight meditation building where ceremonies for those coming to meditate are performed.

MINBURI

☎ 543-7169

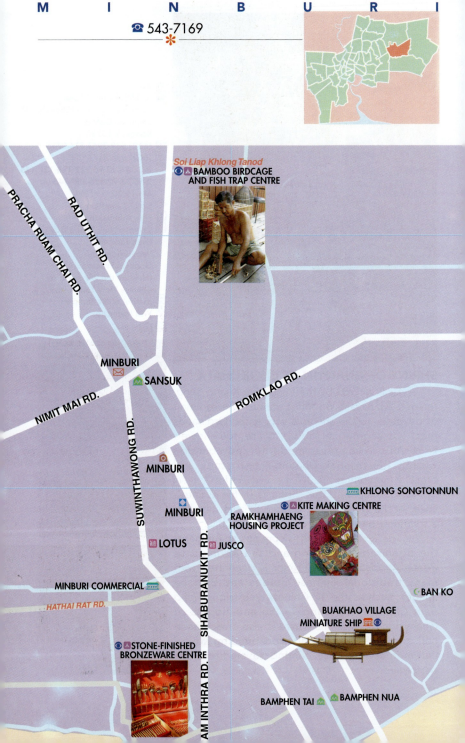

BAMBOO BIRDCAGE
AND FISH TRAP CENTRE

Fish traps are traditional tools associated with Thai agricultural society for centuries. They were made by small household industries using local materials such as bamboo and rattan. The same materials are used to make birdcages, as keeping birds is one of the traditional Thai hobbies. Some are kept for their beauty, others for their singing. Turtle doves in particular are pampered with special care for the annual singing competitions.

In our changing society, fish traps once so important for making a living, are now things of the past. However, they resurrect again as a popular form of decoration which links the new with the old.

The workshop of *Mr. Boonchuay Gasun* makes beautiful birdcages and fish traps using natural materials such as bamboo and rattan. It is a folk craft which still functions, bringing traditional village life into contact with modern society.

★ R6
✉ 42/110 Moo 4
Khlong Tanode Community
Suwinthawong Road
Sansap Sub-District
Minburi District
Bangkok 10510
☎ (662) 914-8763
🚖 131
⏲ Daily 8 am-5 pm
🅿 In front of the House
✚ Hedayatul Islammeyah Mosque

★ P7
✉ 9/9 Moo 7
Samakki Community at
Khlong Songtonnoon
Ramkamhaeng Road
Minburi Sub-District
Minburi District
Bangkok 10510
☎ (662) 916-5409
58 113
🚌 14 15 19 20 Mb 4
🕘 Daily 9 am-8 pm
Teaching Training
🅿 In front of the House
Miniature Ship Museum

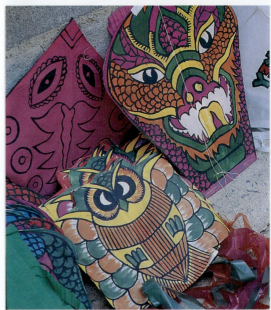

KITE MAKING CENTRE

Kite-flying has been documented since the Sukhothai period, although there is no record when kites made their way into Thailand. Apart from being an enjoyable pastime, kites were used in warfare and in fortune telling. The popularity of kite-flying flourished even among Royalty and the nobility. Today, kite-flying is very much alive as a popular sport, for which the biggest competition is held at Sanam Luang every year.

Since Thai kites developed their own particular characteristics, the art of kite-making here is filtered through tradition and experience as well as skill. No texts or rules for kite-making have been handed down, so kite-maker *Mr. Suay Siankratoke* uses new materials, forms and designs.

For example, he uses vinyl to make glider and stingray kites; and silk screen printing instead of hand-painting in designing. This makes his kites more striking and more accessible to local craftsmen. Most of *Mr. Suay's* kites are on sale at Bo-bae and Mahanark markets. In the community, you can buy his kites every day at the foot of Khlong Song-ton-noon Bridge.

MINIATURE SHIP MUSEUM

In former times, most people were agriculturists who settled along the water ways, some living on rafts. Rivers and canals were avenues for trade and transport, resulting in the emergence of floating markets in many areas. Boats were the most important means of transport in the water-based culture of Siam.

Mr. Kamol Vibulthanakorn has been in the boat-building business for decades. With his enthusiasm and skill, he is commissioned to make small boats for use as flower baskets. This was the origin of the model boats which led to the Model Boat Museum demonstrating exactly how boats are made. The museum also offers courses for those interested in boat-building.

The first step in making a model boat is to dismantle an old boat to use as a prototype. Then, each section must be scaled down in proportion to the real boat. Every detail in boat-building is observed, such as starting with the keel first. The materials used are all locally acquired, notably teak, which comes from unused bits and pieces in furniture factories.

Different kinds of boats modelled include *Kra Sang*, *Sadej Prapas Ton*, *Moo*, *E-Pong* and *Chinese junks*. Some of these ancient boats no longer exist, except in the form of models like these.

★ P7
✉ 2/173-177 Buakao Village
22 Lane Sukhaphiban 3 Road
Minburi Sub-District
Minburi District Bangkok 10150
☎ (662) 517-2080 517-4856
FAX (662) 517-0597
🚌 58 113
🚍 14 15 19 20 Mb 4
🕐 Mon-Fri 8 am-5 pm
☼ Sun Public Hols.
🆓 Free Admission
📚 Teaching Training
🅿 In front of the Museum
✚ Bamboo Birdcage and Fish Trap Centre

NONGCHOK
☎ 543-1099

DARULMUTTAGEEN MOSQUE

The former Darulmuttageen Mosque or Surao Koo used for praying and teaching was built from wood gathered from the area and covered with a thatched roof. Later on, the villagers raised funds from Muslims living in that area and employed Chinese contractors to build a new mosque. The new mosque which appears today was completed in 1893, over 100 years ago. Inside stands Mimbul, or pulpit, which is more than 100 years old.

★ T2
✉ 18 Moo11 Khu-khwa Road Khokfad Sub-District Nongchok District Bangkok 10530
☎ (662) 543-1153 543-2239
🚌 131
🚍 1108
🕐 Daily 9 am-5 pm
🎟 Free Admission
📿 Eidil Fitri: Sermon Pray
Eidil Adha: Sermon Pray
🏫 Muhamadir School: Religious Course
🕐 Daily 3-6 pm
📚 Kuvidhaya Mosque School Wat Sapsamosornnikornkasem
☪ 📷

★ V2
✉ 28 Community Moo 5 Sangkhasantisuk Road Kratumrai Sub-District Nongchok District Bangkok 10530
☎ (662) 988-3530 (Mr. Bang Laaeh Chehmad)
🚌 131
🕘 Daily 8 am-5 pm
🅿 In front of the House
✚ Nong Chok Market

HORN BIRDCAGE MAKING

Raising Java doves is a longstanding tradition, an art of training which the enthusiast must study and carry out corectly. The bird's home is a cage, which is very important, and some bird fanciers are happy to pay high prices for fine cages, as they consider making birdcages to be an art, especially old cages with fine handiwork, such as the specialised "Sa-teng" shape from Yala and "Ko-yi" form Pattani. The older are rarer they are, the more expensive they get.

The area around Community 5 in Nong Jork has many people making beautiful birdcages that are very popular with the dove fanciers, whose tastes determine the shape and size of the cages. For instance, a classic Sa-teng or Ko-yi cage might start at 3,000 Baht and go up to as much as 50,000 Baht.

◉ **Material:** Choice of material is characteristic of this kind of birdcage, such as rattan, ivory and talipot tree stem, and wood from the woody climber Dalbergia for the bars.

Hook: Cast in metal and carved, and it is popular to carve in shapes of auspicious animals such as swans and dragons.

Roof: Made from wood or ivory sawed and turned on a lathe. Sometimes it is carved with intricate patterns, and sometimes ivory is also used to make the patch.

Bars: Made from the horns of an albino buffalo which are translucent, shiny, and extremely rare, or wood is used such as *Plerocapus* or *Dalbergia*.

LIKAE RIAB

Likae riab is a kind of native performance, a tradition belonging to Muslim villagers who lived around Darul-imadas Mosque. They carried the folk theatre with them from Patthani, the southern province of Thailand from where they migrated. Likae riab is performed only during festivals or ceremonies such as Gone Pom Fai, first hair shaving ceremony, house-warming, wedding, and kitun or circumcision ceremony.

Unlike the ordinary likae performance in which performers are dressed in elaborate attire and accompanied by a full band, likae riab, literally "plain likae," has 10-15 performers dressed in traditional costume, each carrying a small drum and only accompanied by another drum called Rammana drum. Performers sit properly in a circle, singing and beating their drums, and there is no dancing. The charm of likae riab is in its lyrics and the style of singing which are In Arabic, telling the life story of Nabi Mohammed, the prophet of Islam.

★ V2
- Kruabungtoei Restaurant 8/6 Moo 3 Prachasamran Road Nongchok Sub-District Nong Chok District Bangkok 10530
- (662) 543-2939 (Mr. Aree Barohemi)
- 131 Disembarking in front of Government Savings Bank Nongchok Branch ◄ ► Mini Bus
- 1180 Disembarking in front of Government Savings Bank Nongchok Branch ◄ ► Mini Bus
- Daily 10 am-7 pm
- Nongchok Market Nong Chok District Office

NATIVE THAI CHICKEN FARM

In the old days, Thai people raised chickens mostly for consumption. However, some good and strong chickens were selected for cock-fighting as well as breeding. Kai chon or fighting cock is one of a native Thai chicken containing special characteristics that other chickens lack. The special features of kai chon are: yield lots of tasty meat, strong, patient, and high tolerance to disease, beautiful, and is a good fighter, part of Thai culture uniquely Thai.

★ U4
- Kamnan Vichien's Fighting Cock Farm 3 Moo 9 Chuam Samphan Road Nongchok Sub-District Nongchok District Bangkok 10530
- (662) 543-1425 989-6432
- (662) 989-6432
- 1108
- Daily 8:30 am-6 pm
- Nongchok Market Nongchok District Office

NONGKHAEM

☎ ๔๒๑-๓๘๔๐

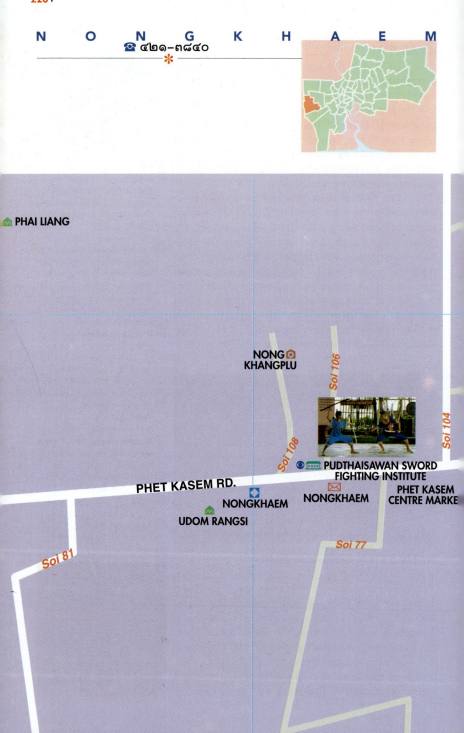

PUDTHAISAWAN SWORD FIGHTING INSTITUTE

The ancient arts of fighting either bare-handed or with weapons are part of Thailand's cultural heritage and have played an important role in Thai history since the Sukhothai period.

With the aim of upholding the tradition of Thai martial arts and improving the standard of performance, *Mr. Samai Mesaman* established the Pudthaisawan Sword Fighting Institute in 1957.

The school is registered with the Ministry of Education, and the subjects taught include Thai boxing, one-handed and two-handed swordsmanship, and the art of using stick, wooden and iron swords, and pike. Both Thais and non-Thais, male and female are invited to join mixed classes in three age groups: 6-9 years old, 10-14 years old and 15 and over.

Apprentices also have opportunities to give demonstrations and performances of martial arts as an outside activity.

★ B12
✉ 5/1 Phet Kasem Road
Nongkangplu Sub-District
Nongkhaem District
Bangkok 10160
☎ (662) 421-1906 808-8461
7 7Kor 80 81 84 91 101 146 147
🚌 7 9 38 84 101 Mb 5 12
🕐 Daily 8 am-6 pm
🆓 Free Admission
Waikhru Ceremony: Paying respect to teachers (May 5)
🅿 In the Institute compound
✚ Wat Nongkhaem
Wat Pa-Thongniam

PATHUMWAN
☎ 214-1330

CHULALONGKORN UNIVERSITY

The history of Chulalongkorn University goes back to 1899 when King Chulalongkorn, King Rama V, ordered the conversion of a long building inside the palace into a civil officer's training school. Later on, with the intention of improving Thailand's standard of education, King Rama VI made the school into Chulalongkorn University.

◉ Faculty of Liberal Arts Bldg.: This building represents the history of the university. The stucco designs on the north and south gables show the Royal insignia of the Chakri Dynasty.

Chakrabongse Bldg.: Located between the Faculty of Engineering and Faculty of Science, this was established by HRH Prince Chulachakrabongse as a memorial to his father. Today, an exhibition of the university's history is on show there.

Sala Phra Kiew: A multi-purpose building using for performances, exhibitions, meetings, lectures, and as a meeting place for faculties and students. The lower level houses offices, the post office and students' associations.

Chulalongkorn University Book Centre: One of Bangkok biggest bookstores, the centre contains a selection of both academic and non-academic books as well as other printed matter. Computer searches can be made here.

Art Centre: Located on seventh floor of the Centre of Academic Resources (Central Library) building, the centre organizes regular exhibitions by both local and foreign artists.

★ H10
✉ Phayathai Road
Pathumwan Sub-District
Pathumwan District
Bangkok 10330
☎ (662) 218-3200
FAX (662) 218-7098
🚌 21 25 29 34 36 40 47 50 93
🚌 1 Sai 25 29 34 36 47 93
🖱 www.car.chula.ac.th
🕐 Mon-Fri 8:30 am-4 Pm
○ Sat Sun Public Hols.
🆓 Free Admission
📋 Exhibition Meeting Seminar
The Art Centre
☎ (662) 218-2964-5
FAX (662) 215-3617
🕐 Class: Mon-Fri
9 am-7 pm
Sat 9 am-4 pm
📖 Centre of Academic Resources (Central Library)
☎ (662) 218-2929
FAX (662) 218-2929
🕐 Mon-Fri 8 am-9 pm
Sat 9 am-4 pm
💰 Non-Member 20 Bht/day
🖼 1987
🅿 In the University compound
✚ Chulalongkorn Hosp.
MBK Centre Snake Farm
Siam Centre Siam Discovery
Siam Square Srapathum Palace
Suphachalasai National Stadium
Wat Pathumwanaram
World Trade Centre

ERAWAN SHRINE

★ 19
494 Ratchawithi Road
Lumphini Sub-District
Pathumwan District
Bangkok 10330
☎ (662) 252-8754
🚌 2 13 14 17 25 48 54 73 74 76 77 204
🚐 5 11 13 15 Mb 20 23
Passenger Boat: Patunam Pier (Sansap Canal)
🕐 Daily 8 am-7 pm
Free Admission
Devasathan Sacrification Ceremony (Nov 9)
Sacrification Dance
P Grand Hyatt Erawan Hotel
Gaysorn Plaza
Grand Hyatt Erawan Hotel
Le Royal Meridian Hotel
Narayana Phand
Peninsula Plaza
World Trade Centre

In 1953 the Thai Hotel and Tourism Co. started the construction of Erawan Hotel. When it was near completion in 1956, the management consulted an astrologer for an auspicious date for its grand opening. As it turned out, the astrologer pointed out that the date when the foundation stone was laid was not suitable, and advised that a Brahman shrine and a guardian spirit shrine should be built to correct the error.

The management brought in the Dept. of Fine Arts to design and build the statue of Brahma according to the traditions of the department. The gilded plaster statue was enshrined at the Erawan Hotel on November 9, 1956.

Both Thais and foreign visitors come to pay their respects at the Shrine, which is widely known as the Erawan shrine. The number of worshippers is increasing every year. They come to pray to Brahma to grant their wishes, or simply to enjoy the exotic sights, sounds and atmosphere.

JIM THOMPSON'S HOUSE

Jim Thompson House is a house belong to the late *James H.W. Thompson* who came to Thailand as an officer in the US forces during World War II. When the war ended, he decided to settle in the Kingdom.

During his stay, *Thompson* became interested in traditional Thai textiles, and being trained as an architect, he used his talent to create new designs and colour schemes for his textiles. The name *Jim Thompson* became synonymous with Thai silk after he introduced the traditional silk to the international market. He had arranged for dismantling of ancient teak houses from various places and reassembled them on the bank of Sansap Canal in Bangkok, today known as Jim Thompson's House. He mysteriously disappeared during a visit to the Cameron Highlands in Malaysia in 1967, leaving behind him this house of historical value as his memorial in Thailand.

◉ **Ban Thai Museum:** Apart from Thompson's splendid art collection and personal belongings exhibited here, the rooms were arranged to reflect the life of Thai people in former times. The garden, featuring various native Thai flowers, is maintained in a natural way and to reflect Thai art and living culture.

★ H9
✉ 6 Kasemsan 2 Lane
Rama 1 Road
Wangmai Sub-District
Pathumwan District
Bangkok 10330
☎ (662) 216-7368
📠 (662) 612-3744
🚌 15 47 48 73 204
🚌 8 (Exp.) Sai 38 Mb 1
⛴ Passenger: Tha Chang Pier (Sansap Canal)
🕐 Daily 9 am-4:30 pm
🎫 Under 25 year old/ 50 Bht
Adult 100 Bht
🗣 English French Japanease
🅿 In the House compound
✞ Ban Krua-nua Community
Chulalongkorn U.
MBK Centre Srapathum Palace
Siam Centre Siam Discovery
Siam Square Wat Boromniwat
Wat Pathumwanaram

BANGKOK RAILWAY STATION
(HUALAMPONG)

    The coming of the Royal railway brought a great change to the Thai way of life at that time. Since then, trains have become an important form of transport and play a great role in trade across the country and beyond.

    Bangkok's Hualampong station was built 14 years after railways were introduced to Thailand. The seven-year construction period started in 1910 and finished in 1916. The station was renovated and modernised in 1998, and this has made made a vast improvement in all its aspects.

The Must See Sites In BANGKOK

★ H10
✉ Rama IV Road
  Rongmuang Sub-District
  Pathumwan District
  Bangkok 10300
☎ (662) 220-4334 (Reservation)
  220-4268 (Public Relations)
  Hot Line: 1690
FAX (662) 222-4211
🖱 www.srt.motc.go.th
🚌 4 7 21 25 29 34 40 53
  73 109 113
🚌 1 4 7 29 73 Mb 5 4
  Passenger Boat:
  Hualampong Pier
  (Phadung Krung
  Kasem Canal)
⏱ Daily 24 hrs.
🅿 At the side of the Station
  About Cafe
  Boe-bae Market
  Mahanak Market
  Wat Kalawar
  Wat Thepsirin
  Wat Trimit Yaowarat

The station provides 24-hour service. There are regular trains, rapid trains, express trains, and the Sprinter or special express train. Trains are divided into 3rd class, 2nd class sleeping car, 2nd class car and 1st class sleeping car with or without air-conditioning. There are 24 ticket windows and a computer system for passengers to buy tickets and making reservations.

The station is complete with a post office, money exchange service, shops, bookstores, restaurants, and food and drink outlets. Services such as luggage deposit and hotel reservation are also available for travellers' convenience.

LUMPHINI PARK

This 360-rai (about 58-hectare) plot of land was formerly known as the Saladaeng field, and was the private property of King Rama VI. In 1925 the King donated the land to the nation to be used as a public park and fair ground. The Siamrath Phiphitthapan Trade Fair held here to promote Thai products among Thais and foreigners was discontinued after the death of the king. The name Lumphini given by the King came from the name of the birthplace of the Lord Buddha.

◉ **Koh Loy or "Floating Island":** King Rama VI arranged for examples of native plants from all regions of the country to be planted here for the

BANGKOK
BANGKOK METROPOLITAN
TOURIST BUREAU

★ 110
✉ Rama IV Road
Wangmai Sub-District
Pathumwan District
Bangkok 10300
☎ (662) 252-7006
📠 (662) 252-7006
🚌 4 13 14 15 17 25 (Samyak)
45 46 47 62 67 74 76 106
109 115 116 149
🚌 4 5 15 62 67 76 Mb 14 17
🕐 Office: Mon-Fri 8 am-4 pm
   Sat Sun Public Hols.
   Park: Daily 4:30 am-8 pm
💲 Park: Free Admission
   Boat Pedal Boat: 40 Baht/hrs.
   Aerobic Dance: Daily 6-7 am
   Music in the Park: Sat Sun
📖 Lumphini Park Public Lib.
  ☎ (662) 252-8030
  📠 (662) 252-8030
  🕐 Tue-Sun 8:30 am-8 pm
     Mon Public Hols.
🚇 Suan Lumphini
🅿 Inside and In front of the Park
✚ Central Dept. Store
   Chula.Hosp. Dusit Thani Hotel
   Lumphini Boxing Stadium
   Pan Pacific Hotel
   Robinson Dept. Store
   Royal Bangkok Sports Club
   Silom Road

education of the people.

Royal Monument of King Rama VI: Located at the park's main entrance. Alumni of Vajiravudh College built the memorial with additional funding from the government of *F.M. Plaek Pibulsongkram* and public donations.

Clock Tower: This Chinese style stucture was built in 1925 as preparations for the Siamrath Phiphitthapan Trade Fair.

Lumphini Park Public Library: This is the first public library in Thailand. It has 30,000 books and has opened audio and visual educational services, promotions to encourage reading, and book exhibitions etc.

★ 19
✉ Faculty of Science
  Chulalongkorn U.
  Phayathai Road
  Pathumwan Sub-District
  Pathumwan District
  Bangkok 10330
☎ (662) 218-5581-3
FAX (662) 255-3021
🚌 21 25 29 34 36 40 47 50 93
🚌 1 25 29
🕘 Mon-Fri 9 am-3 pm
🚫 Sat Sun Public Hols.
💲 Student 10 Baht
  Thai Visitor: 20 Baht
  Foreigner Visitor: 100 Baht
  Photograph Exhibition
🏛 Faculty of Science
  ☎ (662) 218-5045-7
  FAX (662) 218-5045
  🕘 Mon-Fri 8 am-7:30 pm
    Sat 8 am-4 pm
    School Hols.
  Mon-Fri 8 am-4 pm
🅿 In the University compound
✚ MBK Centre Siam Centre
  Siam Square
  Wat Pathumwanaram

MUSEUM OF IMAGING TECHNOLOGY

Evidence at the Missionary Centre in Paris reveals that Bishop Pallegoix ordered a Daguerreotype camera from Paris in the reign of King Rama IV. The first to bring this camera to Bangkok was the priest Lanaudi, who also became a teacher of photography.

As photography has become increasingly important, and photographs have become a part of everyday life around the world, whether as historical record or just as a hobby, the Photography Museum collects, exhibits, maintains, studies and gives knowledge about the evolution of cameras. equipment and techniques of developing and printing photographs for the education of interested members of the public. This is so they can develop techniques of taking photographs and using other imaging technology for themselves.

The exhibition area is divided into 10 rooms, such as the Printing Technology Gallery, a Camera Gallery, a Portrait and Advertising Studios, a Kodak Multi-Image and Cine Theater, a Gallery Photography, an Agfa Gallery and Ilford Holographic and Cibachrome Gallery etc.

BANGKOK
BANGKOK METROPOLITAN
TOURIST BUREAU

NARAYANA PHAND

Narayana Phand is Thailand's biggest handicraft store. Quality Thai handicrafts such as Thai dolls, puppets, khon masks, silk, silverware, bencharong-ware, pearl-inlay ware, lacquerware and wooden sculpture suitable for souvenirs and gifts can be obtained at a reasonable price here.

★ I9
127 Naraya Phand Bldg.
Ratchadamri Road
Lumphini Sub-District
Pathumwan District
Bangkok 10330
☎ (662) 252-4670-9
FAX (662) 255-7247
narayana@box1.a-net.net.th
www.narayana-phand.co.th
2 14 17 23 54 77 79 204
5 11 13 15 Mb 20 23
Passenger Boat: Pratunam Pier (Sansap Canal)
Daily 10 am-9 pm
P Grand Hyatt Erawan Hotel
Gaysorn Plaza Erawan Shrine
Wat Pathumwanaram
World Trade Centre

NATIONAL STADIUM

The national stadium was given the name Subhachalasai Stadium to honour Commander Luang Subhachalasai (Bung Subhachalasai) who dedicated himself to the advance of physical education in Thailand.

He introduced sports, public health, Scouts and Young Red Cross Volunteer programmes which are basic features of Thai education today.

The stadium consists of a number of smaller stadia and sports fields, such as the Nimitbutr multi-purpose gym, Thephas-din practice stadium, the Chindarak ground for football matches and for the Thai national football team to hold practice sessions.

★ H9
154 Department of Physical Education Rama 4 Road
Pathumwan Sub-District
Pathumwan District
Bangkok 10330:
☎ (662) 214-0129:
1508 (Dept. of Physical Education & Sports Division)
1512 (Training & Excercise)
FAX (662) 215-5942
15 47 48 73 204
8 (Exp.) Sai 38 Mb 1
Mon-Fri 8:30 am-4:30 pm
Sat Sun Public Hols.
Free Admission
(Except during sport events)
P In the Stadium Compound
Chulalongkorn U.
Jim Thompson's House
MBK Centre Siam Centre
Siam Discovery Siam Square
Wat Boromniwart
Wat Pathumwanaram

QUEEN SAOVABHA MEMORIAL INSTITUTE

In 1912, *HRH Prince Dumrong* proposed the establishment of an institute for the prevention of rabies in Thailand.

King Rama VI granted permission and gave a building on Bamrung Muang road to be used for the purpose of producing and testing rabies vaccines. Later, the King ordered the smallpox vaccine lab to be moved from Nakorn Pathom province to the building and named the institute Pasteura Sabha or Pasteur Institute in honour of Louis Pasteur, the inventor of rabies vaccine. The King later changed its name to Queen Saovabha Memorial Institute or Sathan Saovabha.

Snake Farm: Slide presentations, snake catching, milking and feeding can be seen here, with information on snakes for the general public.

In 1923 *Dr. Leopold Robert*, the first director of Queen Saovabha Memorial Institute, raised funds from foreign residents in Thailand for the building of this snake farm in order to use the venom milked from snakes for the production of anti-snake bite serum, because imported serum imported was not suitable for bites of Thai snakes. The farm is open to the public everyday.

★ 110
✉ 1871 Rama IV Road
  Lumphini Sub-District
  Pathumwan District
  Bangkok 10330
☎ (662) 252-0161-4 252-016: 7
📠 (662) 254-0212
🚌 4 16 21 45 46 47 50 67 109
🚐 2 4 7 7 (Exp.) 26 Mb 1
🕐 Office: Mon-Fri
  8:30 am-4:30 pm
  Sat Sun Public Hols.
  8:30 am-12:00 noon
  Snake Farm:
  Mon-Fri 8:30 am-4 pm
  Sat Sun Public Hols
  8:30 am-12:00 noon
💵 Thai 20 Bht Foreigner 70 Bht
  Free admission for children
  under 10 years old
📖 Bldg. 2nd fl.: Books of Snake
  Children's Day Public Hols.
  Estabblish Day (Dec 7)
🏥 1. Checking and treating
  patients, dressing wounds
  and vaccination.
  2. Immunisation against
  rabies for animals.
  3. Autopsies for tracing
  rabies.
  4. Pet quarantine for
  tracing rabies.
  5. Vaccination for protection
  from Cholera and Typhoid
  for the general public.
📷 1987
🗣 English Thai
⊘ Disturb Animal
🅿 In the Institute compound
✚ Chulalongkorn U.
  Lumphini Park Silom Road

WAT BOROMNIWART RATCHAWORAWIHAN

The temple has been known as Wat Nok, literally the "outside temple", because of its location outside the city wall. It was founded by the order of King Rama IV in 1834 when he was in the monkhood. It was to serve as a Aranyavasi, literally a "forest" temple for meditation, while Wat Bowon niwet was to serve as Kamvasi, literally a "city" temple for scripture study.

⊙ Kuti: The 14 monks' residences are examples of the Rama IV and V period style, of which there are very few left nowadays.

Murals: These are by the famous Rama IV period artist, Khrua In Khong. He abandoned "the traditional story-telling style in favour of a newer conceptual style." The pictures depict Buddhist symbolism rather then the life of the Lord Buddha.

Ubosot: Built in front of the Chedi in the Ayutthaya style. The tiled roof is decorated with chorfa, bairaka and hanghong, and the gables are decorated with stucco. The principal Subduing Mara Buddha image named Phra Thospolyarn is in the Sukhothai style. The mural, which is divided into two parts, is by Khrua In Khong.

Chedi: Situated on a square base, the chedi is decorated with gilded tiles. The door to the room inside the chedi is inlaid with mother-of-pearl depictions of Royal regalia.

Sala Karnparian: The instruction hall is a Thai-style raised wooden building. The gilded stone Phra Pichitmaramatthayomphuttakorn Buddha image is enshrined here.

★ H9
✉ 2 Rama I Road
Rongmuang Sub-District
Pathumwan District
Bangkok 10300
☎ (662) 214-0708
🚋 47 67 204
🚌 Sai 38 67 204
👤 Passenger Boat: Wat Phraya yang Pier ◄ ► walk across Yotsay bridge
⏱ Temple: Daily 8 am-8 pm (Wishing to visit the ubosot should call in advance.)
💲 Free Admission
 Religious rite dedicated to the late Abbot (Oct)
Meditation Training:
⏱ Every Other Sunday 2 pm
📖 Sirichantho: Religious Books
⏱ Daily 8 am-4 pm
🏛 1949
🏠 Second Class
🚋 Wat Boromniwat
🅿 In the Temple compound
📷 Permission required for taking photo inside Bldg.
✚ Boe-bae Market
Wat Phraya-yang
⛩

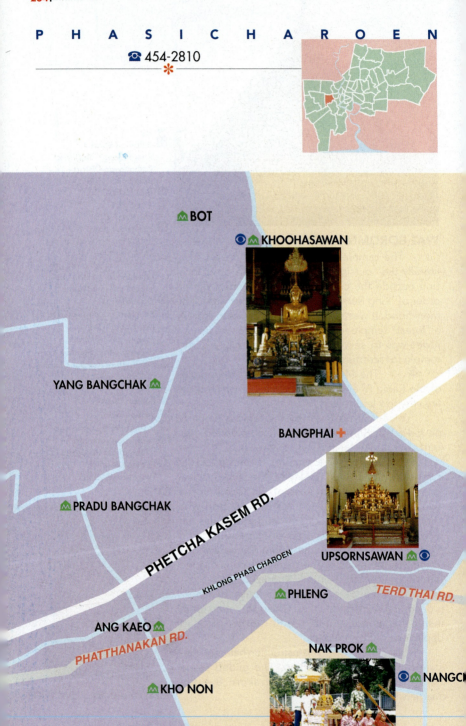

★ F10
✉ 541 Kuhasawan Sub-District
Phasicharoen District
Bangkok 10160
☎ (662) 467-2000 467-4585
80 81 84 91
🚌 9
⛴ 1. Chao Phraya Express Boat
(Yellow and Green Flags):
Memorial Bridge Pier ◄ ►
Wat Sala Seena Pier
2. Chao Phraya Express Boat
(Green Flag): Rajini Pier ◄ ►
(Pakklong Talat)
Wat Sala Sina Pier
🕐 Temple: Daily 8 am-6 pm
Ubosot: Daily 8 am-6 pm
💳 Free Admission
Maha Chart Sermon (Sep)
🏛 1977
Third Class
Dhamma School
🅿 Inside the Temple compound
✚ Wat Bot Wat Kampaeng
Wat Thong Salangarm
Wat Yang

WAT KHOOHASAWAN WORAWIHAN

The temple was formerly called Wat Sala Seena. The twin sandstone sema and wooden sculptures on the front and rear gables of the main chapel suggest that it was built in the Ayutthaya period. King Rama I ordered the temple to be renovated and renamed it Wat Koohasawan.

Ubosot: A brick and stucco Thai-style building of the Ayutthaya period, with three doors at the front. The doors and windows are decorated with gilded paintings of Chinese-style trees on a black background. The principle Buddha image in the Meditation posture is called Phra Phutthadheva.

Sema: The boundary stones are sandstone and placed in small alcoves around the chapel. Twin semas are usually found only in Royal temples.

Prayer Hall: A wooden, Thai-style building with traditional roof decorations and wooden pillars decorated with gilded paintings of the life of the Lord Buddha.

Kuti: The monks's residences with ancient wooden walls are at the side and rear of the main chapel outside the temple area.

WAT NANGCHEE SHOTIKARAM

★ F10
✉ 312 Thoet Thai Road
Pakkhlong Sub-District
Phasichareon District
☎ (662) 467-4540 467-4093
🚌 4 9 10 103
🚕 4
⛴ 1. Passenger Boat:
Wat Paknam Pier
2. Taxi Boat:
Wat Nangchee Pier
🕐 Temple: Daily 5 am-10 pm
Ubosot: Daily 5-6 am 5-7 pm
🆓 Free Admission
🎉 Chakphra Festival
(Late Nov-Dec)
Thod Krathin Festival (Nov)
Procession of Flower
Decorated Boats
🚌 Third Class Ordinary
🅿 In the Temple compound
✚ Wat Paknamphasichareon
Wat Rajkruh
Wat Upsornsawan

There is no record of the founding of this temple, but *Phraya Rajanuchit (Jong)* re-established it in the style popular in the reign of King Rama III. The king named the temple Wat Nangchee Shotikaram.

Ubosot: The statue of a deity stands on a lion at the door of the main chapel, in the Chinese style prevalent during the Third Reign. The building has a two-tiered roof, and the main Buddha image is made of plaster in the Meditation posture.

Wihan: The prayer hall stands on the right of the ubosot. Its door and window arches are decorated with glazed tiles. The main Buddha image is in the Laylia posture.

Chakphra Festival: Since the early Rattanakosin period, relics of the Buddha and his disciples are carried in procession by boat from Wat Nangchee to Wat Kaitere in Talingchan on the second day of the waning moon in the 12th lunar month.

The procession begins at Wat Nangchee on the Daan Canal and continues along the Bangwag, Chakpra and Mon Canals. The return route to is by Bangkoknoi Canal to the Chao Phraya River, then along the Bangluang Canal.

The festival also features boat racing, flower parades on boats, and pleng rue, traditional singers leading the boat containing the Buddha's relics.

WAT UPSORNSAWAN WORAWIHAN

The ancient temple was formerly called Wat Moo, moo meaning pig, as it was built on land used for a pig farm and pigs were allowed to remain in the area. It was restored by King Rama III from his private funds and renamed Wat Upsornsawan in honour of the celebrated actress, Jaojomnoi. Her portrayal of Suranakong in "Eanao", the royal play from Indonesia, was so impressive that she became known as *"Chaochom Noi Suranakong."*

Ubosot: Built in the Chinese style with a single-tier roof and pediments decorated with Chinese patterns. Enshrined within it are 28 Buddha images in the Subduing Mara posture created by order of King Rama III.

Wihan: The prayer hall is in the same style as the ubosot, and houses two Buddha images also in the Subduing Mara posture.

Phra Mondop: The alcove contains a Buddha image in the Chansamore posture holding an Indian olive.

Hor Trai: This ancient Ayutthaya-style hall is registered as a preserved building by the Fine Arts Department. It is "the original" of the Hor Khien, which can be seen at Suan Pakkad Palace.

- H10
- 174 Thoet Thai Road Pakkhlong Sub-District Phasichareon District Bangkok 10160
- (662) 467-5392 458-0917
- 4 9 10 103
- 4
- Passenger Boat: Rajini (Pakkhlong Talat) Pier ◄►
  Wat Paknam Pier
- Temple: Daily 5 am-10 pm
  Ubosot: Daily 8-9 am 4–5 pm
- Free Admission
- Songkran Festival (Apr13)
- 1977
- Third Class
- Satri Upsornsawan Supapromsuksa
- In the Temple compound
- Wat Khunjan
  Wat Koohasawan
  Wat Nakprok
  Wat Nangchee Shotikaram
  Wat Paknamphasichareon
  Wat Thongsalangam

PHAYATHAI
☎ 270-1395

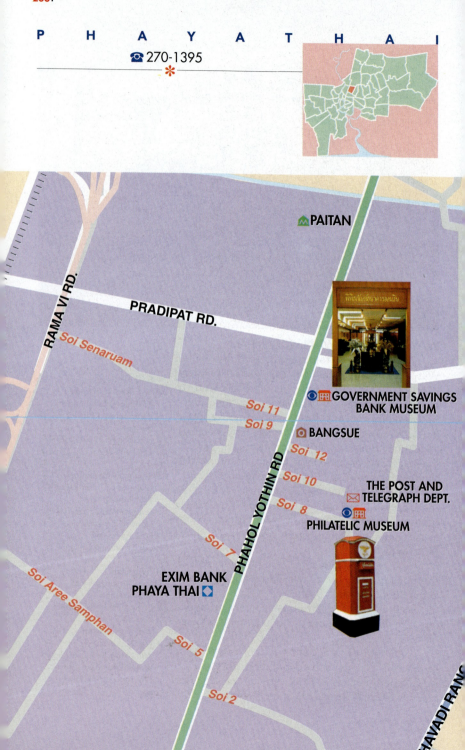

PHILATELIC MUSEUM

Collecting stamps is one of the all-time favourite hobbies worldwide. It has continuously evolved since the early days of the postal system, and the number and variety of stamps has multiplied over the years.

The postal service in Bangkok was established in 1881, and the first Thai postage stamps were made in London using woodblock prints.

The museum shows how the postal service developed in Thailand. It displays postage stamps from the first examples to those of the present day, as well as the advances which have been made in printing.

Here, history is depicted on small pieces of paper which become more and more valuable as time goes by.

★ 18
✉ The Communications Authority of Thailand Northern Metropolitan District Building Phaholyothin Road Samsen Sub-District Phayathai District Bangkok 10400 (Behind Samsen Nai Telegraph)
☎ (662) 506-3344
FAX (662) 573-4494
🚌 3 8 26 27 28 29 34 38 39 52 59 63 77 90 97 108 204
🚐 2 3 9 10 13 19 29 44 Mb 1 Kor 2 Kor 2 8
🕐 Tue-Sat 8:30 am-4:30 pm
   Mon Sun Public Hols.
   Free Admission
   Outside Exhibition
   Postage Stamps Collection of Thai and Foreign Books related to postage stamps
P In the Bldg. compound
✚ Chatuchak Park Government Saving Bank Museum Paolo Hosp. Wat Phaiton

240

★ 17
✉ The Government Saving
   Bank Head Office
   72 Year Bldg. (Bldg. 4) 7th fl.
   470 Phaholyothin Road
   Samsen Nai Sub-District
   Phayathai District
   Bangkok 10400
☎ (662) 299-8000: 9108 9243
FAX (662) 270-1441
🚌 8 26 27 28 29 34 38 39 54
   59 63 74 77 97 108
🚐 2 3 9 10 13 Mb 2 8
🕐 Mon-Fri 8:30 am-4:30 pm
   Sat-Sun Public Hols.
   Bank Mid-year Hol. (Jul 1)
🆓 Free Admission
📅 Exhibition Children's Day
📖 3rd fl.
   Government Saving Bank
🅿 In the Bank compound
✚ Chatuchak Park EXIM Bank
   Philatalia Museum
   Queen Sirikit Park

THE GOVERNMENT SAVINGS BANK MUSEUM

While studying in England, King Rama VI took the opportunity to see how English savings banks accumulated money for the government's use. On his accession to the throne, the king expressed his intention of establishing a savings bank in Thailand.

The bank was founded in 1913 with the name Klang Omsin. Initially under the Finance Ministry, it has undergone many changes during the course of Thai history, and finally became the Government Savings Bank, or Thanakhan Omsin, in 1991.

In the same year, after 78 years of operation, the management decided that the bank should have its own museum. Among the items from the past to the present which can be seen, there are deposit books, Savings Bank Lottery tickets, calendars, souvenirs of special occasions, ancient money, printed matter of all kinds, and even piggy banks.

BANGKOK
BANGKOK METROPOLITAN
TOURIST BUREAU

PHRAKANONG

☎ 332-9458

- Soi Onnut 44
- PROJECT TO PRESERVE THAI SWEETMEATS
- RASSATTADHUM
- Soi 30
- Soi Tabkaeo
- Soi 12
- Soi Chula 3
- Soi Wachira 16
- Soi 10
- Soi Chula 2
- Soi 101/1
- Soi Mahasin
- Soi Wachira 6
- CHEDIPHRATHAT
- THAMMONGKHON THAOBUNNONTHAWIHAN
- Soi 101
- Soi 101/2
- UDOMSUK
- Soi 66/1
- Soi 97/1
- Soi 64
- SUKHUMVIT RD.
- Soi 93
- Soi 62/1
- Soi 89
- Soi 62
- Soi 85
- Soi 60/2
- Soi 81
- PHRAKANONG
- PHRAKANONG
- Soi 50
- Soi 54
- Soi 56
- BANGCHAK BIRDWATCHING CLUB
- BANGCHAK OIL REFINERY

BANGCHAK BIRDWATCHING CLUB

Lectures are given by specialists from the Birdwatching Club of Thailand, and birdwatching trips are frequently organised.

Bangchak Birdwatching Club is one of the activities of Bangchak Oil Plc's One Family Project, whose aim is to promote family togetherness and nature appreciation.

The club's activities take place in natural surroundings near the factory area which is the habitat of thousands of birds. It provides general information on nature and specific information on birds and birdwatching. It conducts bird watching tours within the area, and keeps records of the birds observed and identified there.

★ K12
✉ Bangchak Oil Refinery Sukhumvit 64 Lane Bangchak Sub-District Phrakanong District Bankok 10250
☎ (662) 301-2750
FAX (662) 301-2750
🚌 2 23 25 38 46 48 116 132
🚐 2 7 8 11 13
🕘 Mon-Fri 8:30 am-4:30 pm
⊘ Sat Sun Public Hols.
 Basic Birdwatching Course Member: Children 120 Bht Adult 200 Bht
 Expert on Birdwatching from the Association of the Preservation of Birds and Nature of Thailand
🅿 In the Bangchak Oil Refinery
✠ Wat Wachirathamsathit

WAT THAMMONGKON THAOBUNNONTHAWIHAN

Within the temple area is Nakorn Tham, literally "the Land of Dhamma", founded in 1962 by *Phra Rajthamjetiyacharn*. It can be described as a centre of technology in the service of Buddhist studies, and it contains films detailing the history of Buddhism, Internet facilities, a high-tech library, a meeting room and a canteen.

Meditation Cave: This is man-made, modelled after the natural caves found in Thailand's forests and mountains. This forms an appropriate setting for the teaching of meditation.

Chedi: Phra Viriyamongkonmahachedi, is the tallest stupa in Thailand, 14 storeys high, and relics of the Lord Buddha brought from Bangladesh are kept there. It is a replica of Bodhgaya in India, and ornamented with diamonds. The nine-tier golden parasol at the top of the stupa is decorated with Thai motifs and 1,063 diamonds. The top of the parasol is made from 17 kg. of gold. In the chedi are museums, libraries, and meditation rooms.

Buddhamongkolthamsrithai Pavilion: A three-storey glass structure whose third floor houses Phra Buddhamongkolthamsrithai and statue of the goddess Guanyin pictured above. The figure was sculpted by *Paolo Viaggii* from a massive jade boulder found in Canada.

★ L12
✉ 132 Punna 6 Lane
Sukhumvit 101 Road
Bangchak Sub-District
Phrakanong District
Bangkok 10260
☎ (662) 332-8226 741-3552
FAX (662) 311-3994
🖱 www.thai@vision.com
🚌 2 23 25 38 46 48 116 132
🚐 2 7 8 11 13 23 Mb 6
🕐 Temple: Daily 8 am-6 pm
Ubosot: Buddhist Sermon Day 12 am-3 pm
Wihan: Daily 8 am-6 pm
Free Admission
10,000-Nun Initiation Ceremony (Jan 7-10)
Wat Thammongkon's Job Training Centre
Will Power Institute
Will Power Meditation Course:
🕐 Mon-Fri 6 am-8:30 pPm
Course in Community Development:
🕐 Sat Sun 9 am-5 pm
Buddhist Sermon Day: Sermon 3rd fl. Phra Viriyamongkon mahachedi
Wax: 1st fl. Phra Viriyamongkonmahachedi
Buddha Image Antique: 10th-12th fl. Nakorn Tham Wat Thammongkol
Thamsala Kindergaten Child Development Centre
💰 500 Bht/person
1st fl. Phra Viriyamongkon mahachedi
1st fl. Phra Viriyamongkon mahachedi
P In the Temple compound
Bangchak Birdwatching Club Phrakanong Canal
Wat Wachirathamsathit

GEMOPOLIS

    Gems and jewellery are among Thailand's most important export products. The Gemopolis Industrial Estate and Free Trade Zone was established with the support of the Thai government to promote the local and international trade in gems, jewellery and accessories.

    Within the industrial estate are factories and workshops of different sizes, diamond production and trading facilities, exhibition halls, wholesale and retail outlets, customs offices, a safety vault with deposit services and a museum.

    Investors in the poject are entitled to privileges such as tax breaks and exemption from customs duty on importing machinery and raw materials.

    In its first phase, 20 companies opened in Gemopolis with 2,500 workers employed in gem-cutting, the making of accessories, and in the gold purification works.

★ P10
- IGS Place 47/31 Moo 4 Sukhaphiban 2 Road Dokmai Sub-District Pravet District Bangkok 10260
- ☎ (662) 727-0022
- FAX (662) 727-0500
- igs-gemo@samart.co
- 11 1013 (Minibus)
- 11 18 Mb 23
- Mon-Fri 8:30 am-5 pm
- Sat Sun Public Hols.
- Free Admission
- In the Estate compound
- Pravet District Office Phra Nakorn Park Wat Lanboon

★ N12
✉ Sukhumvit 103 Road
  Nongbon Sub-District
  Pravet District
  Bangkok 10250
☎ (662) 328-1972 328-1395
📠 (662) 328-1395
🚌 40 133 145 206 207
🚐 145 206 Mb 15
🕐 Daily 6 am-6 pm
💲 10 Bht (9 am-5 pm)
  Motorcycle 5 Bht
  Sightseeing Bus 10 bht
  Van 20 Bht
  Bus 30 Bht
🎪 Flower Festival (Dec 1-10)
  Caladium Contest
  (2nd Sun of the month)
📖 Hor Prucksasart: Herbarium
  🕐 Mon-Sat 8:30 am-4:30 pm
🏛 Herbarium: Dried Plant & Fruit
  🕐 Daily 8:30 am-4:30 pm
🚣 Boat Paddle Boat
🆓 Free Admission: Group of
  students in uniform, with
  written request in advance.
🅿 In the Park compound
👁 Birdwatching site at
  Nongbon Pond
  Phra Nakorn Park
  Seacon Square Seri Center

SUAN LUANG RAMA IX PARK

Rama IX Royal Park was built by the Bangkok Metropolitan Administration, the Rama IX Park Foundation and the people of Thailand to honour HM the King on the occasion of his 60th Birthday on December 5, 1987. The 500-rai (81-hectare) park is divided into six areas:

◉ **Chalerm Prakiat Area:** Consisting of Hor Ratchamongkol, a nonagonal plan tower (as HM the King is Rama IX) and Uttayarn Maharaj (Park of the Great King);

Botanical Garden: Located at the northern side. The plants in this area are classified according to their ecological regions, which is the main feature of a metropolitan park.

Traphang Kaeo Kep Num (Water Resevoir): The pond is being used to retain water to alleviate the flooding which affects the area during the rainy season. At the same time it can be used for water sports, recreations and preservation of aquatic animals;

Rommanee Park: With its waterfalls, streams and flowers arranged to imitate the natural atmosphere of the countryside.

The Must See Sites In BANGKOK

Water Garden: A water park which was added recently. The area looks out to a stream with plants growing on both sides. This is where water plants are collected and preserved.

Sanam Rat Field: Consists of a large public space and an open stage. This area is used for cultural performances and agricultural fairs where competitions for various kinds of farm produce are held.

POMPRAPSATTRUPHAI

☎ 282-5826

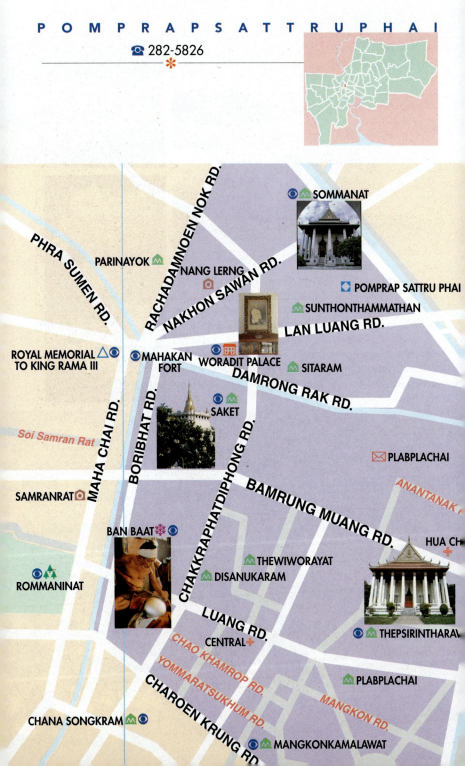

BAN BAAT COMMUNITY

Ban Baat is a community well-known for making baat, the alms bowl used by monks to receive donations of food in the morning.

The community is believed to have started as a settlement of refugees fleeing from the war in Ayutthaya. The refugees were taught to make baat by a Khmer master whom they called *Por-kru*, literally "father-teacher." Por-kru has always been revered by people in the community, and his shrine was to be seen in front of every household that contains the special piped stove which is traditionally used for baat making.

Sadly, the craft is in danger of dying out, as there are now only three households still making baat in the traditional way.

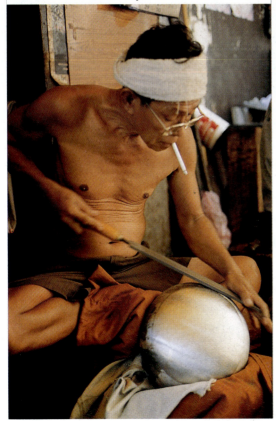

★ H9
✉ 71 Ban Baat Lane
   Poriphat Road
   Ban Baat Sub-District
   Pomprap Sattruphai District
   Bangkok 10100
☎ (662) 223-7970 621-1317
🚌 5 8 21 37 47 48 49 56
🚐 8
🕐 Daily 10 am-8 pm
🆓 Free Admission
🎎 Waikhru Ceremony: Paying respect to teachers (Apr)
🅿 Poriphat Road compound
✚ BMA Bldg. Devasathan
   Democracy Monument
   Giant Swing Mahakan Fort
   Rommaninat Park
   Wat Mahannaparam
   Wat Ratchanatdaram
   Wat Suthat

★ H9
344
Chakkraphatdiphong Road
Ban Baat Sub-District
Pomprap Sattruphai District
Bangkok 10100
☎ (662) 233-4561 (Office)
621-0576 (Golden Mount)
🚌 8 15 37 47 49
🚐 Sai 38 49
⛴ Passenger Boat: Phanfalilat Pier (Sansap Canal)
Phukhawthong Pier (Phadung Krung Kasem Canal)
🕒 Temple: Daily 4 am-9 pm
Golden Mount:
7:30 am-5:30 pm
🎫 Golden Mount:
Foreigner 10 Bht
🎉 Loykrathong Festival
🏛 1949
🏯 Second Class
🅿 In the Temple compound
✚ Ban Baat Mahakan Fort
Memorial of King III
Phanfalilat Bridge
Wat Ratchanaddaram
Ⓜ 🚻 📷

WAT SAKET RATCHAWORAMAHAWIHAN

This Ayutthaya-period temple was formerly known as Wat Sakae. It was restored during the reign of King Rama I who renamed it Wat Saket.

◉ **Chedi Pookhaothong:** The chedi, whose name means "golden mountain" is a replica of Chedi Pookkhaothong in Ayutthaya, and was added in the reign of King Rama III. The chedi was completed in the reign of King Rama V and was named Suwannabanphot, which has the same meaning, golden mountain.

Lanka-style Chedis: Several small stupas in Sri Lanka style were added to the top of the Golden Mountain during King Rama IV's reign.

Ubosot: The main chapel contains murals by artists in King Rama III's period.

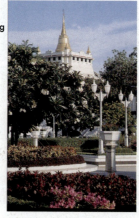

BANGKOK METROPOLITAN TOURIST BUREAU

★ H9
✉ 646 Krungkasem Road
Wat Sommanat Sub-District
Pomprap Sattruphai District
Bangkok 10200
☎ (662) 282-7944 282-9137
📠 (662) 282-0462
🚌 5 10 15 47 48 53 70 201
🚐 3 5 9
⛴ Passenger Boat: Wat Sommanat Pier (Phadung Krung Kasem Canal)
🕐 Temple: Daily 5 am-8 pm
Ubosot: Daily 8:30-9 am 6-7 pm
🆓 Free Admission
📅 Meditation Seminar: 7-Day (Apr Jul Oct)
📖 Wat Sommanat
🏛 Second Class
🅿 In the Temple compound
➕ Amphorn Garden
Amphornsathan Palace
Chankasem Palace
Government House
Parus-sakkawan Palace
Ratchadamnoen Boxing Stadium
Wat Benchamabophit

SOMMANATWIHAN RATCHAWORAWIHAN

This Dhammayut sect Royal temple was built in 1853 by command of King Rama IV as a memorial to *Queen Sommanat Vadhanawadi*.

◉ **Bell and Drum Tower:** This is a round tower with a Chinese-style roof.

Wihan, Wihankot and Chedi: The prayer hall, cloisters and stupas were built together as a group.

Ubosot: The main chapel is surrounded by a traditional boundary wall. Placed on the wall facing in eight directions are semas, ogival stones used to indicate the boundary of the ubosot.

Stone Statues: Chinese stone figures decorate the monks' residential area.

Kuti-senasana: The residences of the monks is built of brick and mortar and has a wooden roof, in accordance with the traditional Thai style.

WAT THEPSIRINTHARAWAT
RATCHAWORAWIHAN

The temple was built by command of King Rama V. The king dedicated it to his mother, the late *Queen Thepsirindhra*, and named it in her memory.

◉ Ubosot: This chapel is one of the most outstanding architectural treasures of the Rama V period. The doors and windows are decorated with gilded lacquer, the ceiling is decorated with carvings depicting Royal decorations, and many famous Buddha images are enshrined in it.

Royal Cemetery: King Rama V ordered this to be built as a crematorium for those members of the Royal family who had no special crematory pavilion in Sanam Luang in front of the Grand Palace.

Memorial Shrines: Two shrines were built to house clothed Buddha images and the ashes of *HRH Prince Chakrabhadibhong* and *HRH Prince Bhanubhandu-wongworadej*. The shrines are called Chaturana-Annussaree and Bhanurangsi-Annusorn.

There are other interesting buildings and objects in the temple and residential areas. They include monks' residences built in European style, bronze Buddha Image in the Subduing Mara posture, and an image wearing the attire of the late *Queen Thepsirindhra*.

★ H9
✉ 423 Luang Road
   Yotse Sub-District
   Pomprap Sattruphai District
   Bangkok 10100
☎ (662) 221-8877 222-0700
FAX (662) 223-3992
🚌 7 15 47 48 53 204
🚌 8 15 Sai 38 47
🕐 Temple: Daily 6 am-6 pm
   Ubosot: Daily 7 am-9 pm
Ⓟ Free Admission
   Chinese New Year
   (Late Jan-Feb)
   Mid-Autumn Festival:
   Coin Casting Ceremony
   Vegetarian Festival (Oct)
🚆 Wat Thepsirin
Ⓟ Inside the Temple compound
✚ Bangkok Railway Station
   BMA General Hosp.
   Boe-bae Market
   Mahanak Market
   Wat Phraya-yang

★ H9
✉ 182 Lan Luang Road
Khlong Mahanak Sub-District
Pomprap Sattruphai District
Bangkok 10100
☎ (662) 282-9110
📠 (662) 282-9110
2 8 39 44 59 60 79
Sai 2 11 39 44 60 Mb 1
🕓 Mon-Fri 8:30 am-4:30 pm
🚫 Sat Sun Public Hols.
🎟 Free Admission, but must be in group, with written request to the Chairman of Woradit Palace Foundation
🎉 Anniversary of Somdet Krom Phraya Dumrong-rajanuphab (Dec 1)
📖 Dumrong-rajanuphab: His literary works Manuscripts Books
🏛 1984
📷 1984
📸 Permission required for taking photo inside Bldg.
🅿 In the Museum compound
🍴 Sapan Khao Market
Mahanak Market

WORADIT PALACE AND DUMRONG-RAJANUPHAB LIBRARY

The palace was the residence of *HRH Prince Dumrong-rajanuphab* until the 1932 Revolution in which the coup changed the form of government of Thailand from an absolute to a constitutional monarchy.

At that time, Prince Dumrong went into exile in Penang. In 1942, he returned to Woradit Palace and lived there until his death over a year later. The architectural style of the palace is that of King Rama VI's period, in which Western influences were prevalent.

Today, the residential apartments of Prince Dumrong have been made into a museum, of which the Dumrong-rajanuphab Library is a part.

◉ **Dumrong-rajanuphab Library:** After World War II, Prince Dumrong's daughter, *HSH Princess Poonpisamai Diskul*, donated the Prince's valuable collection of books on archeology, history, art and culture to the government. Later, government funds were made available for the establishing of the library.

Dumrong-rajanuphab Library was part of the National Library until it was moved to Woradit Palace compound in 1989. The library contains 7,000 volumes, 3,871 in Thai and 3,061 in other languages. There are also 156 books of pictures and two cabinets containing manuscripts. It is an invaluable repository of information on the life and culture of Thailand, and an important resource for scholars.

RATBURANA
☎ 427-7878

WAT JANG-RON

Wat Jang-ron is a civil temple built beside the Chao Phraya River in the U-Thong or Lopburi period and originally called Wat Hong-ron.

◉ Luangphor Hin Dang's Wihan: This is the shrine of Luangphor Hin Dang. The Buddha image in the Meditation posture is made from laterite. The gable's frame has no decoration, but there are beautiful stucco reliefs on the pediments and door frames in the style of the Third Reign.

Ubosot: The door and window arches of the main chapel date from 1926, early in the reign of King Rama VII. Their stucco decorations are in the shape of fruit such as pomegranates, sugar apples, mangos and pineapples; animals such as bats, rabbits, elephants and goats; and aquatic creatures like goldfish, squid, crabs and frogs.

Hor Trai: The two scripture cabinets were built in the First Reign.

Sala Karnparian: This was built in 1927. The stucco decoration of the gable depicts a wild boar emerging from a cave in a forest of coloured glass.

★ H12
✉ 2 Ratburana Road
   Ratburana Sub-District
   Ratburana District
   Bangkok 10140
☎ (662) 463-6581 463-1172
   6 17 37 85
🚌 37
🕐 Temple: Daily 5 am-8 pm
   Ubosot: Daily 8-9 am 5-6 pm
   (Wishing to see the ubosot should call in advance.)
   Free Admission
   Songkran Festival (Apr 13)
   Jang-ron Wittaya
   Wat Jang-ron
Ⓟ In the Temple compound
✚ Thai Farmers Bank Head Office
   Wat Ratburana Wat Ruag
   Wat Ruangpueng Wat Soan

★ G12
✉ 10 Moo 4 Suksawat 27
Bangpakok Sub-Disctrict
Ratburana District
Bangkok 10140
☎ (662) 427-4591
🚌 37 88
🚍 37
⛴ Chao Phraya Express Boat:
Ratburana (Big C) Pier
🕐 Temple: Daily 5 am-8 pm
Ubosot: Daily 8:30 am-6 pm
(Wishing to visit the ubosot
should call in advance.)
💰 Free Admission
📅 Songkran Festival (Apr 13-15)
Buddhist Lent Commencing
Day: Dharma study for 3
months (Late Jul) 1-4 pm
🏛 1995
🚏 Wat Prasertsutthawat
🅿 In the Temple compound
➕ Big C Dept. Store
Ratburana Hosp.
Wat Bangpakok
Wat Ratburana
🚇 📷

WAT PRASERTSUTTHAWAT

Wat Prasertsutthawat is an Ayutthaya-period temple built in the Chinese style and restored once during the reign of King Rama III. According to the story, a Chinese pig farmer found three large jars full of coins while he was foraging for food for his pigs. He used the money to found the temple and dedicated it to the king. Temple records of 1838 indicate that the Chinese farmer might be *Phra Prasertwanit*, who was rewarded with a post after the temple was completed.

🔵 **Sema:** The ogival stones placed around the ubosot to mark its boundary are of red sandstone. The single-style sema dates before the Ayutthaya period.

The Principal Buddha Image: The name of the image is Pra Soisuwannarat, and it is in the Medita-

tion posture. It is made of red sandstone decorated with gold in the U-Thong style, as can be seen by its angular face, layered chin and tightly-curled hair. The rasmi, or flame finial on top of the head is in Sukhothai style.

Wihan: The prayer hall retains its original structure but has been restored. The stucco relief on its pediments and the ceramic and other decorations on the roof are pure Chinese in style.

Ubosot: In the main chapel are murals in early Rattanakosin style with Chinese influences. They depict stories from the Romance of the Three Kingdoms, a classic work of Chinese literature translated into Thai during the First Reign. The gable and roof are decorated with stucco tiles in the Chinese style.

RATCHATEWI

☎ 246-8982

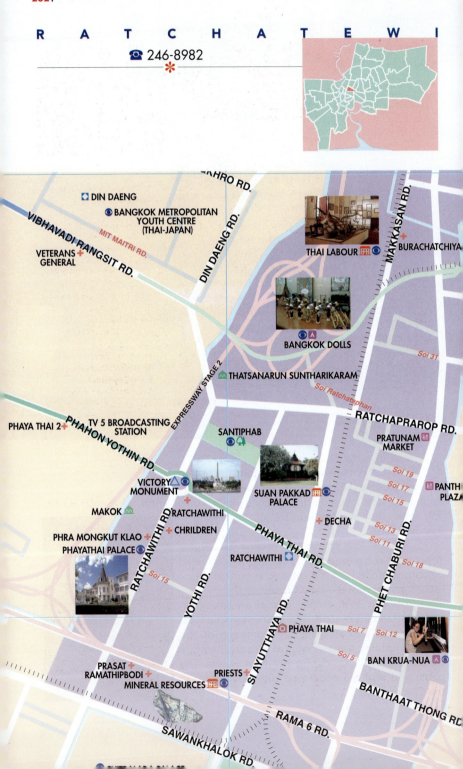

BANGKOK DOLLS

The museum was founded in 1956 by *Khunying Thongkorn Chanthavimon*. Having been trained at the Osawa Dool School in Tokyo, Khunying Thongkorn began making dolls herself. At first, they resembled Japanese dolls, but the Khunying tried to adapt a Thai style with the assistance of well-known artists such as *Prof. Silpa Bhirasri*, the founder of Silpakorn University, *Luang Wisarnsilapagum*, *Mr. Chit Rianpreecha* and *Mr. Prachum Mana*. Finally, she succeeded in making the beautiful Thai-style dolls which won her an award in the 3rd International Traditional Dolls Competition held in Poland in 1978.

Today, the products of the factory are in eight categories: Khons and Khon masks, village life, hill tribe people, dolls for children, puppets, dolls in the style of neighbouring countries, and dolls made to order.

Part of the factory compound has been made into a museum where dolls from Thailand and other countries are exhibited.

★ I9
✉ 85 Ratchataphan Lane
Ratchaprarop Road
Makkasan Sub-District
Ratchatewi District
Bangkok 10400
☎ (662) 235-3008
FAX (662) 235-3008
🚌 13 14 54 62 63 72 73 74
🚐 13 15 62 72 73 Mb 20
🕐 Mon-Sat 8:30 am-5 pm
    Sun Public Hols.
💲 Free Admission
🅿 In front of the Factory
✚ Baiyoke Tower
    Pratunam Market
    Santiphab Park
    Siam City Hotel
    Suan Pakkad Palace
    Thai Labour Museum
    Victory Monument

BAN KRUA-NUA COMMUNITY: CENTRE OF SILK WEAVING

The community has been well-known for its skill for more than 50 years. In the old days every household in the community woved silk as a means of living. *Jim Thompson* used to order large quantities of the silk made in this area. His mysterious disappearance in 1967 caused the community's income to plunge. Today, only a handful of households still carry on the unique silk weaving tradition of the community.

★ H9
✉ Ban Krua-nua Community
Sansap Canal-Bank
Kasemsant 3 Lane
Ratchatewi Sub-District
Ratchatewi District
Bangkok 10400
☎ (662) 216-6517
🚌 16 29 34 36 50 54 79 93 113
🚐 2 29 36
⛴ Passenger Boat: Saphan
    Huachang Pier (Sansap Canal)
🕐 Daily 9 am-11 pm
💲 Free Admission
✚ Jim Thompson's House
    MBK Centre Siam Discovery
    Siam Square

MUSEUM OF MINERAL RESOURCES

In the past, mining was mostly carried out by foreign companies as Thais had little knowledge or experience of the industry. The museum was built to give Thai people an opportunity to study minerals in order to be able to make use of them. Apart from the study of and geology, it is also a museum of Thai natural history.

The museum was started in 1924-1925 but the systematic collection was not begun until 1933 by the Geology Section, Mining Industry Division, Department of Land and Mining Industry. The permanent establishment of the museum came afterwards. Today, it is in the care of the Geology Museum Section of the Department of Mineral Resources.

Geology: This section shows the evolution of the earth, fossils, rocks and minerals, earthquakes, and underground water.

Mineral Resources: This section exhibits gemstones, and the various commercial and domestic uses of minerals, such as for fuel.

Exhibition: These change every three to six months. The theme of each exhibition is related to a topic of current interest.

★ H8
✉ 75/10 Department of Mineral Resources Rama VI Road Ratchatewi District Bangkok 10300
☎ (662) 202-3670 202-3669
FAX (662) 202-3754
🚌 8 44 67 72 92 96 97
🚐 9 44 67 92
🕐 Mon-Fri 8:30 am-4:30 pm
🚫 Sat Sun Public Hols.
💰 Free Admission
🎬 Lecture Film Shows Mineral Stone Rented for Exhibition Science Day (Aug 18)
📖 Dept. of Mineral Resources
  🕐 Mon-Fri 8:30 am-4:30 pm
👥 Must be in group, with written request one week in advance to the Director-General of the Department of Mineral Resources
🅿 In front of the Museum Priests Hosp.
✚ Foreign Ministry Ramathibodi Hosp. Suan Pakkad Palace

PHAYATHAI PALACE

Formerly the area was gardens and fields called Phayathai Field. King Rama V ordered a new residence to be built there for relaxation, and also for conducting agricultural experiments. The Royal Ploughing Ceremony was held at this palace several times.

After King Rama V passed away, *Queen Saovabha* moved to take up residence here. King Rama VI later ordered the building of five Western-style throne halls.

On their completion, King Rama VI named the palace Phayathai Royal Palace and moved Dusit Thani, a demonstration city established by the King to introduce the Thai people to the democratic system, into the palace compound.

During the reign of King Rama VII, the State Railways of Thailand asked Royal permission to turn the palace into the Phayathai Hotel. When radio broadcasting was introduced, it became the Bangkok Radio Broadcasting Station.

The palace was later presented to the Royal Thai Army to be used as a hospital. Today, it is part of King Mongkut Hospital.

Some of the old buildings now are being maintained by the Department of Fine Arts, but the demonstration city of Dusit Thani no longer remains.

★ 18
✉ 315 Ratchathewi Road
Phayathai Sub-District
Ratchatewi District
Bangkok 10400
☎ (662) 246-1400-17: 93694
(Palace Lover Club)
245-9770 (Direct Line)
FAX (662) 246-7876
🚌 8 12 14 18 28 92 97 108
🚐 9 10 16 92 Mb 4 8
🕒 Mon-Fri 8:30 am-4:30 pm
Sat Sun Public Hols.
Arms Forces Day (Jan 25)
🚪 Free Admission, but must be in group with written request one week in advance to the Director of the Medical Centre. King Mongkut Hosp.
📷 Permission required for taking photo inside Bldg.
🅿 King Mongkut Hosp.
✚ Rajvithi Hosp.
Santiphab Park
Suan Pakkad Palace
Victory Monument

★ 19
✉ 352-354 Si Ayutthaya Road
Phayathai Sub-District
Ratchatewi District
Bangkok 10400
☎ (662) 245-0568 245-6368
246-1775-6
FAX (662) 247-2079
14 17 63 72 74 77 204
13 72 Mb. 2
⏰ Daily 9 am-4 pm
💰 Student 20 Bht Thai 50 Bht
Foreigner 80 Bht
Free Admission: Student
group in uniform with
written request in advance.
Anniversary of HRH Prince
Chumbhot's Birthday (Dec 5)
1994
Marasi Gallery 2nd fl.
Chumbhot-Pantip Centre of Arts
☎ (662) 245-6368: 138 139
FAX (662) 245-6369
<cpflib1@ksc.th.com>
⏰ Daily 10 am-6 pm
Free Admission
Khon Ban Chiang
Taking photo inside Bldg.
In the Museum compound
Bangkok Dolls
Mineral Resources Museum
Pratunam Market
Siam City Hotel
Santiphab Park
Thai Labour Museum
Victory Monument

SUAN PAKKAD PALACE

On the site of what was once a cabbage field (suan pakkad), *Maj. Gen. HRH Prince Chumbhotpong Paripatra of Nagor Svarga* and his consort, *MR Pantip*, built the palace as a weekend resort, and after World War II was over, they moved in permanently.

The museum started as an exhibition of their superb collection of antiques for friends and acquaintances in the Thai-style houses. Artifacts on display date from prehistoric times to the Ratanakosin period, and include objects from other Asian nations.

⦿ House 1: This building contains images of the Thai Royal Family, model boats and six drums. Upstairs are artifacts such as an image of the goddess Uma, Buddha images from the U-Thong period of Thailand, India and Myanmar.

House 2: This was was originally a reception area, and displays personal effects, such as ivory boxes and bowls inlaid mother-of-pearl.

House 3: Thai musical instruments, nielloware, Bencharong ceramics and a palanquin are displayed here.

House 4: Originally a dining room in the in

Japanese style, this house has a mother-of-pearl inlaid door frame dating from the 17th century. On the lower floor is "The Cave of Ali Baba," showing the Princess' extensive mineral collection.

House 5: The upper room displays ancient Ban Chiang pottrty, while downstairs there are sea shells, rocks and fossils.

House 6: Sawankhalok ceramics, ancient stone axes, earthenware utensils and figurines from the Sukhothai period can be seen here.

House 7: This is a Khon Museum with masks, costumes and accessories, and a model of a Ramayana troupe playing a scene from the battle of Kumphakan, as well as video presentations.

Lacquer Pavilion: This is the perhaps the most exquisite building in Suan Pakkad Palace. Outside are carvings, lacquer patterns. Inside are pictures in lacquer.

Marasi Gallery: On the first floor of the Chumbhot-Pantip Art Gallery, exhibitions are held here regularly to promote contemporary art, photography, ceramics, mixed media, installation and performance. The Ban Chiang Museum on the second floor displays ancient artifacts and has an information system which explains Ban Chiang art and culture.

THAI LABOUR MUSEUM

★ 19
✉ Makkasan Road
Makasan Sub-District
Ratchatewi District
Bangkok 10400
☎ (662) 251-3173
🚌 11
🕐 Wed-Sun 10 am-5 pm
⏰ Mon Tue Public Hols.
🎫 Free Admission
📋 Exhibition Meeting Seminar
📖 Labour Prof. Nikom Chandravithun: A collection of documents books and research concerning Thai labour.
🅿 Beside the Museum
✚ Amari Watergate Hotel
Bangkok Dolls
Empress Hotel Bangkok
Indra Hotel
Makkasan Railway Station
Murcure Hotel
Pratunam Market
Suan Pakkad Palace
Santiphab Park

This is the first museum in Thailand where story of working-class people is represented. The museum was officially opened on October 17, 1993 under the name of Anusawaree Saksi Raeng-ngarn, "Monument to the Dignity of Labour," the name reflecting the glory of the Thai labour.

The exhibit is divided into 6 rooms demonstrating the development of Thai labour from the serf-slave period up to the present time.

Inside the building is the all-purpose hall used for meeting, seminar, exhibition as well as a souvenir shop. On the wall displays the mural depicting the history of the evolution of Thai Labour. There is a traditional rickshaw once drawn by a Chinese labourer, the symbol of the Thai society and its working class. Former cells inside the building have been adapted as a library in honour of *Prof. Nikom Chandravithun*, the foremost expert on Thai Labour.

VICTORY MONUMENT

The Victory Monument was built in the reign of the present King, *HM King Bhumibol Adulyadej* to commemorate soldiers, policemen and civilians who gave their lives in the service of the country. The monument is built of reinforced concrete and marble in the shape of five bayonets 50 metres high. Around the base of the bayonets are statues representing the army, navy, air-force, police and civilian services. Under the statues are bronze plates engraved with the names of people who died during the Franco-Thai dispute in 1943.

When a foreign dignitary pays a state visit to Thailand, laying a wreath at the monument is one of the ceremonies included in his schedule.

The monument area is also a major centre for buses going to all parts of Bangkok.

★ 18
✉ Between Dindaeng Road
Phahonyothin Road
Ratchawithi Road
Phayathai Road
Thung Phayathai Sub-District
Ratchatewi District
Bangkok 10400
🚌 12 14 17 18 24 26 27 28 29 34 36 38 61 62 63 92 97 104 108
🚐 2 3 9 10 13 14 16 19 24 29 30 32 33 36 38 62 92 104 112 140 Mb 2 4 12
🕐 Daily 24 hrs.
🅿 Around Victory Monument
✚ King Mongkut Hosp.
Phayathai Palace Rajvithi Hosp.
Robinson Dept. Store
Santiphab Park

S A I M A I

☎ 991-4926-7

- FISH HABITAT AT HOK-WA CANAL
- SAIMAI
- YUDIBAMRUNGTHAM
- KUKOT
- HAROENTAMMARAM
- SAIMAI
- SAIMAI
- KOSUWANNARAM
- ROYAL THAI AIR FORCE ACADEMY
- ROYAL THAI AIR FORCE
- BHUMIBOL
- HANDICRAFT MADE FROM FRAGRANT CLAY
- AMARAWARARAM
- SUETRONG VILLAGE

LAMLUKKA RD.
SAIMAI RD.
Soi Kilometer 25
SUKHAPHIBAN 5 RD.
SUKHAPHIBAN 3 RD.
RATTANA KOSINSOMPHOT RD.
TALAT PHOEM SUK RD.
PHAHON YOTHIN RD.

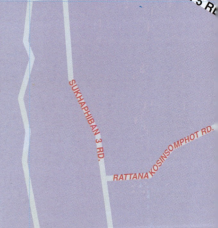

HANDICRAFTS MADE FROM FRAGRANT CLAY

Using flowers to make garlands, sweets and objects for religious ceremonies has been a part of Thai life since the golden era of Sukhothai.

The art has undergone change and development since then. Items made from jasmine-perfumed clay are one of the more recent developments. Nowadays, craftsmen can make fragrant clay garlands and other knickknacks as beautiful as those made of flowers and natural materials.

The process starts by preparing the clay, kneading it, dividing into smaller cakes according to design, and mixing it with oil, chalk or acrylic paint. The clay is then shaped into garlands and flower moulds. These products can be found in Sampeng market, in the shops selling religious products, and at some department stores.

★ L3
✉ Saimai Garland Centre
64 Lane 4 Suetrong Village
Phahonyothin 52 Lane
Phaholyothin Road
Khlong Thanon Sub-District
Saimai District Bangkok 10210
☎ (662) 972-1065
(Ms. Sasithorn Kanjanathat)
FAX (662) 972-1065
🚌 34 39 114
🚐 3 21 22 24 25 39 Mb16
🕘 Mon-Sat 9 am-5 pm
Sun Public Hols.
Teaching Training
P In front of the House
✚ Royal Thai Air Force
Royal Thai Air Force Museum
Saphan-Mai Market
Wat Amrawararam

N2
✉ Saimai School
  Khlong Thanon Sub-District
  Saimai District
  Bangkok 10210
  Saimai District Office
☎ (662) 991-4923-7: 204 205
📠 (662) 991-4923-7: 208
🚌 1. Minibus: Yingchareon
     Market Bangkhen District
     ◁▷ Wat Saimai
   2. Bus: Lamlookka Road
     Thupathemee Stadium
     ◁▷ Wat Saimai
🕐 Daily 6 am-5 pm
💲 Free Admission
🅿 In Saimai School compound
✚ Saimai District Office
  Wat Saimai

SAWAI FISH HABITAT AT HOK-WA CANAL

Hok-wa is an ancient man-made canal joining Song Canal and Phraya Suren Canal with a length of 3.4 km. King Rama V ordered its construction to disperse flood waters in Bangkok.

In the past the canal had a width of "hok wa" or six wa (approximately 12 metres), but currents have expanded this to 14-20 wa, or 30-40 metres.

In the serene countryside around the canal the people still farm rice and catch fish, raise chickens and carry on such cottage industries as making sweets, with traders coming to their doors.

With water transport playing an everdecreasing role, the water in the canal is quite clean. In fact, Klong Hok-wa is now the habitat of many fish, especially at the Pla Sawai Sanctuary in front of Wat Saimai School. There are thousands of Sawai fish (*Pangasius fowleri*) here, and people come to feed them regularly.

BANGKOK METROPOLITAN TOURIST BUREAU

WAT AMARAWARARAM

The temple was built in 1987 on land belonging to *Dr. Amara Chandrapanon* which he donated for the Amarawanaram meditation centre. The temple was built at a later date and named Wat Amara-wararam after the donor.

🔵 **Sala Chedi-Ubosot:** This is a multi-purpose pavilion built in imitation of Bodhkaya in India, and is used for various religious ceremonies and meditation. Inside is a copy of the famous Phra Putta Sihing image, images for the days of the week, and other Buddha images.

★ L3
✉ 1/13 Moo 5 Tahanakard Lane Khlongthanon Sub-District Saimai District Bangkok Bangkok 10210
☎ (662) 552-5020 972-7735
🚌 34 39 114
🚐 3 21 22 24 25 39 Mb 16
🚢 Passenger Boat: Saphanmai Pier
🕐 Temple: Daily 5 am-8 pm
Ubosot: Daily 5 am-8 pm
💳 Free Admission
📅 Buddhist Lent Final Day: Devo Alming
Meditation Training:
🕐 Daily 2 pm-4 pm
🅿 In the Temple compound
✠ Royal Thai Air Force Museum Saphanmai Market Saimai Garland Centre
Ⓜ 📷

SAMPHANTHAWONG

☎ 235-9127

- CENTRAL
- THEPSIRIN
- LUANG RD.
- PHLAPPHLA CHAI
- PHLAPPHLA CHAI
- WORACHAK RD.
- CHAROEN KRUNG RD.
- MAITRI CHIT RD.
- MANGKON RD.
- KRUNG KASAE RD.
- CHAICHANA SONGKHRAM
- CHAKKRAWAT RD.
- CHAKKRAWAT RACHAWAT
- KANMATUYARAM
- MANGKON KAMALAWAT
- MONGKHON SAMAKHOM
- MITTRAPHAN RD.
- CHAKKRAWAT
- RATCHAWONG RD.
- MANGKON RD.
- YAOWARAT RD.
- YAOWARAT (CHINA TOWN)
- TRIMIT
- SAMPHANTHAWONG
- SONGWAT RD.
- TRIMIT RD.
- CHAO PHRAYA RIVER
- PATHUMKHONGKHA
- UPHAIRATCHA BAMRUNG
- THONGTHAMMACHAT
- THONGNOPPHAKHUN
- THAILAND'S COMMERCIA
- SOMDET CHAO PHRAYA
- SOMDET CHAO PHRAYA
- PONG-PAJJAMIT FORT
- TAKSIN
- PAKKHLONG SAN
- SAMP THAWO
- KALAWAR
- KHLONG SAN

THAILAND'S FIRST COMMERCIAL BANK

After Siam made trade treaties with foreign powers in the reign of King Rama IV, trade and the economy changed greatly, as well as the internal monetary system. New financial institutions were needed, and foreign banks began to play a role in the city in 1898.

For Siam's financial independence, *Prince Mahissara Ratchaharuthai*, "the Father of Thai Banking," experimented with a small bank in 1904 called the Book Club in Bang Mor district. This was incorporated as the Siam Commercial Bank, which is today known to Thais as Thai Panich, although the English name is still official.

When World War II reached Thailand in 1941, Thailand was obliged to cooperate with the Imperial Japanese Army. The bank's American executives were replaced by Thais, while the branch offices of banks from Allied countries had to close. Many Thai-owned banks were founded at this point.

★ H10
✉ Siam Commercial Bank
Talat Noi Branch
Talat Noi Sub-District
Samphanthawong District
Bangkok 10100
☎ (662) 237-5000
FAX (662) 235-7020
🚌 1 73 75
⛴ Chao Phraya Express Boat:
Hapour Dept. Pier
Si Phraya Pier.
🕘 Mon-Fri 9 am-3:30 pm
Sat Sun Public Hols.
Bank Mid-year Hol. (Jul 1)
💰 Free Admission
🖼 1982
🏧 All services are available
📷 Permission required for taking photo inside Bldg.
🅿 In front of the Bank
✚ Khlong Tom Old Market
Nakhonkasem Market
Phahurat Market
Saphanhan Market
Saphanlek Market
Sampeng Market
Wangburapa
Wat Chaichanasongkhram
Wat Kalawar Wat Mongkorn
Wat Ratchaburana
Wat Samphantowong
Wat Trimit Yaowarat

★ G9
✉ 225 Chakkrawat Road
Chakkrawat Sub-District
Samphanthawong District
Bangkok 10100
☎ (662) 221-8906 225-3564
🚌 4 5 7 8 21 37 40 56 73 82
🚌 4 Sai 7 73 82
⛴ 1. Chao Phraya Express
   Boat: Rachavongse Pier
   2. Ferry: Din Deang Pier
🕐 Temple: Daily 6 am-6 pm
   Ubosot: Daily 8 am-6 pm
🆓 Free Admission
🛕 Buddha's Footprint Festival
   (Mar)
🏛 1990
🔰 Second Class
🔰 Bali Class
   Buddisht Sunday School
🕐 8:30 am-3 pm
📷 Permission required for
   taking photo inside Bldg.
🅿 In the Temple compound
➕ Nakhonkasem Market
   Thai Commercial Bank
   (Talat Noi Branch)
   Wat Kalawar]
   Wat Ratchburana
   Wangburapa
   Wat Phatumkongka
   Yaowarat (Chinatown)

WAT CHAKKRAWATRACHAWAT
WORAMAHAWIHAN

Formerly called Wat Nang Pluem or Sam Pluem, the temple has existed since the Ayutthaya period. After *Chao Phraya Bodindecha* mobilised his troops to suppress the coup d'etat in Vientiane, Laos, he brought back with the news of his victory the Buddha image called "Phra Bang", which he presented to King Rama III.

Ubosot: The main chapel has a Chinese-style roof with two superimposed surrounded balconies. The interior is decorated with murals.

Prang: The stupa is decorated with coloured ceramic in the Chinese style. The prang stands on a Tarn Singha, or lion-style base.

Wihan Phra Nark: The sermon hall was formerly where the Buddha image Phra Bang was enshrined. King Rama IV ordered the return of Phra Nark to take the place of Phra Bang in the Grand Palace.

Mondop of the Buddha's Footprint: This chapel situated on a man-made hill houses the Footprint of the Lord Buddha and a gilded Buddha image in Pa Laylai posture.

WAT KALAWAR (THE HOLY ROSARY CHURCH)

This church was built in 1787 on the bank of Chao Phraya River on a plot of land given by King Rama I to the Portuguese in recognition of their assistance in the defence of Ayutthaya against the Burmese.

Since then the church has been centre of worship for Catholics in Bangkok. The present neo-Gothic brick and stucco building was built in 1890 to replace the original wooden church which was burned down earlier. One of the oldest and most beautiful Roman Catholic churches in Thailand, it is is being registered as an historical site by the Department of Fine Arts.

★ H10
✉ 1318 Wanit 2 Yotha Road
Talat Noi Sub-District
Samphanthawong District
Bangkok 10100
☎ (662) 266-4849 236-2727
FAX (662) 236-2727
🚌 1 35 36 75 93
🚌 36 Mb 3 6
⚓ 1 Chao Phraya Express Boat:
Si Phraya Pier
2. Ferry: Khlong San Pier
◄► Si Phraya Pier
🕐 Office: Mon-Fri
8:30 am-5:30 pm
🚫 Sat Sun Public Hols.
Church: 6 am-9 pm
🎟 Free Admission
⛪ Mass: Mon-Sat 6 am 7:30 pm
Sun 6:15 am 8 am 10 am
(Chinese) 7:30 pm
Parish Feast (First week of Oct)
Holy Week (Late Mar-Apr)
Good Friday:
Corpus Christi Procession
Christmas (Dec 24)
🖼 1987
📷 Permission required for
taking photo inside Bldg.
🅿 In front of the Church
Habour Dept.
✠ About Cafe Central Post Office
River City
Royal Orchid Sheraton Hotel
Samphanthawong District Office
Thai Commercial Bank
(Talat Noi Branch)
Wat Mahaphruettharam

★ H9
✉ 661 Charoenkrung Road
Talat Noi Sub-District
Samphanthawong District
Bangkok 10110
☎ (662) 225-9775 623-1279
📠 (662) 623-1279
🚇 1 4 25 35 40 49 53 73 75
🚌 4 Mb 5 14
Passenger Boat:
Hualampong Pier (Phadung
Krung Kasem Canal)
🕐 Temple: Daily 5 am-8 pm
Ubosot: Daily 8 am-5 pm
💰 Golden Buddha:
Foreigner 20 Bht
Chinese Opera Festival
(Late Jan)
Mother's Day (Aug 12)
King's Birthday (Dec 5)
Amazing Chinatown
(Chinese New Year)
📖 Worakun: 6-8 pm
Woratham: 11 am-8 pm
🏛 1956
Second Class
Maha Veranuwat
Trimit Wittayalai
🅿 In the Temple compound
About Cafe
Bangkok Railway Station
Thai Commercial Bank
(Talat Noi Branch)
Wat Kalawar
Wat Phatumkongka
Yaowarat (Chinatown)
Ⓜ 📷

WAT TRIMITWITTHAYARAM WORAWIHAN

Formerly called "Wat Samjeentai, this temple was built by three Chinese comrades around 150 years ago. It was restored in 1937 and granted the new name of Wat Trimitwitthayaram.

◉ **Phra Sukhothaitrimit:** The main attraction of the temple is the five-ton, three-metre tall Sukhothai-style Buddha image in the Subduing Mara position made of solid gold known as the Golden Buddha. The image was once believed to be of ordinary stucco until it fell from a crane while being moved to a new building and the gold inside was revealed. The theory is that the covering was a means of protecting it from the Burmese while the capital of Ayutthaya was under siege.

BANGKOK METROPOLITAN
TOURIST BUREAU

YAOWARAT (CHINATOWN)

The 1.43-km. street of Yaowarat where the Chinese community is located was built in the reign of King Rama V and has since been the centre of both local and international business.

Known as the Chinatown of Thailand, Yaowarat Road consists of a crowded array of gold, hardware, food and fabric shops as well as dozens of other small businesses. Today, it is also Thailand's best known and biggest gold trading centre with 132 gold shops scattered along it. The standard of gold and its daily retail price are set by the Gold Traders Association, an organisation formed by gold traders, most of them in the Chinatown area . Gold and jewellery from Yaowarat are well-known both locally and aboard for their fine craftsmanship and good quality, in which a certain percentage of gold is guaranteed.

"During the night time, this busy thoroughfare turns into one of the city's longest food streets, with shops and food stalls selling various kinds of food, especially Chinese delicacies such as shark's fin soup, bird's nest soup and roast chestnuts."

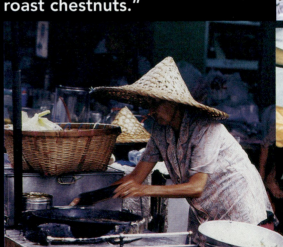

★ H9
Yaowarat Road
Yaowarat Sub-District
Samphanthawong District
Bangkok 10110
1 4 7 25 35 40 73
1 4 7 25
Chao Phraya Express Boat:
Rachavongse Pier
Amazing Chinatown
Chinese New year
(Late Jan-Feb)
Lunar New year's Day (Sep)
Vegetarian Festival (Oct)
Khlong Tom Old Market
Nakhonkasem Market
Phahurat Market
Saphanhan Market
Sampeng Market Wangburapa
Wat Chaichanasongkhram
Wat Chakkrawat Wat Kalawar
Wat Mongkorn Wat Trimit

SAPHANSOONG
☎ 373-0213

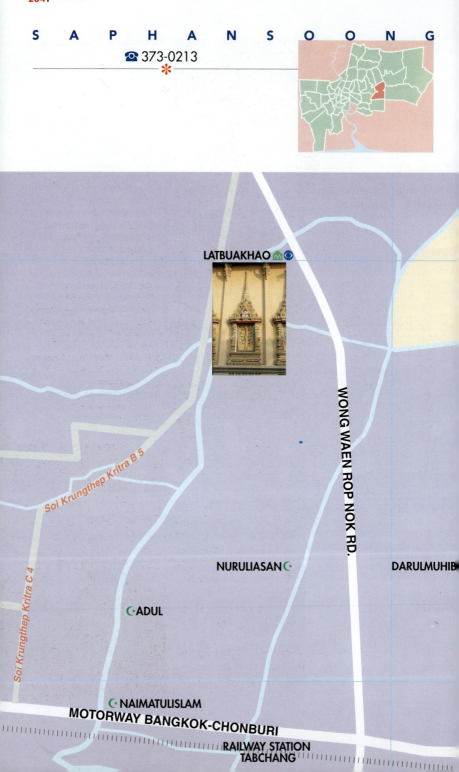

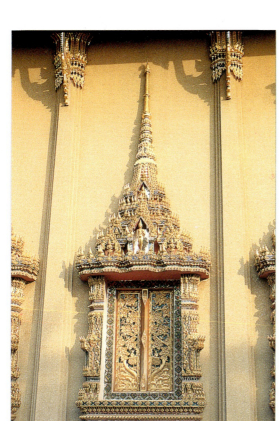

- P8
- 33 Moo 9
  Saphansoong Sub-District
  Saphansoong District
  Bangkok 10250
- (662) 373-8899
- Passenger Boat:
- Wat Latbuakhao Pier
  Temple: Daily 5 am-8 pm
  Ubosot: Daily 8 am-4:30 pm
  (Wishing to visit the ubosot
  should call in advance.)
- Free Admission
- Buddhist Holy Days: Sermon
- Meditation Training:
- Wat Latbuakhao
- In the Temple compound
  Birdwatching site at
  Mae-chan Canal

WAT LATBUAKHAO

This temple was built by *Phraya Rachayotha (Niam Singhaseni)* in 1882 at the suggestion of *Chao Phraya Bodindecha (Sing)* who once rested his army in the area. First, the monks' residences were built, then later the temple was granted the name of Wat Latbuakhao by the king, buakhao meaning white lotus. There is a profusion of these flowers in the area, but even today, local people still call the temple Wat Rachayotha or Wat Phraya Rachayotha.

Luangphor Thong, invited by *Phraya Rachayotha* to take up residence at the temple, was the first abbot revered by villagers and the people living around the area.

SATHON

☎ 211-8714

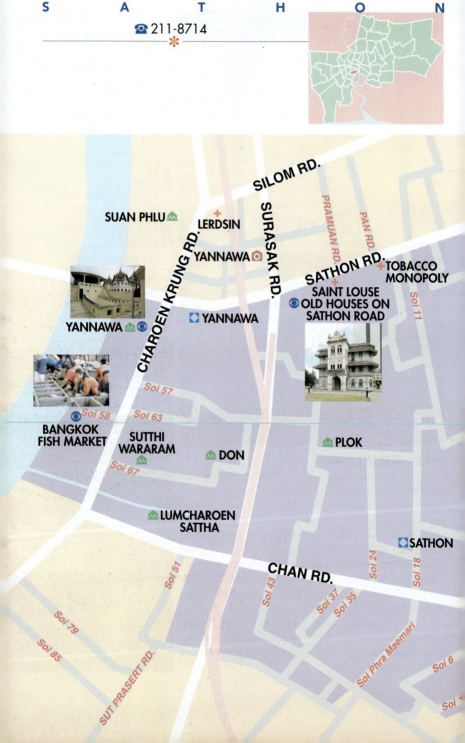

BANGKOK FISH MARKET

In the past, Bangkok's wholesale seafood market was at Songwat Road in Sampanthawong, while the wholesale freshwater fish market was at Hualampong, along Phadung Krung Kasem Canal. For convenience and efficiency, the present fish market was built in Yannawa District to combine the two.

Apart from this one, there are two more fish markets serving Bangkok, one in Samutprakarn and the other in Samutsongkram province. All fish markets are under the Fish Marketing Organisation, a state enterprise belonging to Ministry of Agriculture and Agricultural Cooperatives.

Most of the sea fish come from the south and east of Thailand, and the coastal areas near Bangkok. These days, most of the freshwater fish are likely to come from fish farms.

Trading is done through brokers who act as middlemen between the fishermen, the retailers and the processing companies. Large-scale buying is done by auction, but for smaller lots, buyers choose the fish they want and bring them to the manager for appraisal. Price levels are not fixed, but changed daily in accordance with the state of the market.

- H10
- 211 Chareonkrung Road Yannawa Sub-District Sathon District Bangkok 10120
- (662) 211-0300 (Information) 211-4394 (Brokers)
- (662) 212-5899
- 1 15 17 35 75
- 4 Sai 38 75 Mb 9 20
- Fish Marketing Organisation: 8:30-4:30 pm
  Bangkok Fish Market:
  Freshwater Fish; 11 am
  Sea Fish; 2 am
- Fish Marketing Organisation: Sat Sun Public Hols.
- Free Admission
- In the Market compound
- Bangrak Market
  Shangri-La Hotel
  Wat Yannawa

★ H10
✉ Sathon Nua Road
   Sathon Tai Road
   Yannawa Sub-District
   Sathon District
   Bangkok 10120
☎ 17 22 62 67 76 77 106 116 149
🚌 22 35 62 67 Mb 12
🅿 Office Bldg. on Sathon Nua and Sathon Tai Road
✚ Alliance Francaise Bangkok
   Apostolic Nunclature Vatican
   Australia Embassy
   Austria Embassy
   Embassy of the Republic of Singapore
   Evergreen Hotel Bangkok
   Germany Embassy
   Goethe Institute
   Royal Dennish Embassy
   Slovak Republic Embassy
   Sukhothai Hotel
   The Embassy of Brazil
   Westin Banyan Tree Hotel
   Y.W.C.A
📷

OLD HOUSES ON SATHON ROAD

Sathon Road was built in 1888 during the reign of King Rama V by *Jao Sua Yom*, a Chinese land developer who hired Chinese labourers to dig a canal to link the Chao Phraya River with Hualampong Canal. They then built the road on either side of the canal.

At first, the canal was known as Jao Sua Canal and the road, Phor Yom Road. When both were complete, *Jao Sua Yom* sold the land to wealthy Chinese and Europeans. *Jao Sua Yom* was later elevated to the nobility, and was given the title *"Khaluang Sathon Ratchayuk."* The road then became known as Sathon Road.

The road building policies of Kings Rama IV and V were the starting point of changes in Bangkok's transport system. As water travel gave way to road transport, people preferred to build houses by the roads rather than the waterways.

European Colonial styles influenced the architecture of these stately houses along Sathon Road, although a mixture of styles is evident. Mostly of two storeys, they have tiled hip roofs and porches decorated with glass. The stucco-ornamented gables and balconies had slatted windows or louvred shutters for ventilation, and the awnings, eaves and pillars were decorated with fretwork designs. Most of these residences are now embassies, associations or compamies such as the Thai CC Building and Thai-Chinese Chamber of Commerce. The Russian Embassy is often quoted as a notable example of the style.

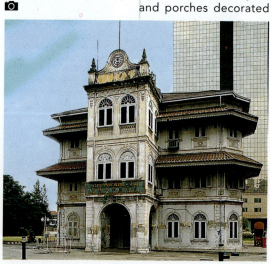

BANGKOK
BANGKOK METROPOLITAN TOURIST BUREAU

WAT YANNAWA

Formerly called Wat Kok-kwai, this temple was built in the Ayutthaya period and was restored and a Greek cruciform ubosot added during the reign of King Rama I. When the ubosot was restored again in the reign of King Rama III, the king supervised the building of a full-size junk to form the base. The king then renamed the temple Wat Yannawa — literally "the boat temple."

Ubosot: The pediments of the main chapel are decorated with animal designs in the style characteristic of the First Reign.

Door Panels: On the panels of the ubosot's door is a painting of a a large krathong made from banana leaf containing flowers, incense and candles. The style of the krathong is the same as those used in the Loykrathong festivals during the reign of King Rama III.

Window Panels: At the back of the ubosot's window panels is the painting of a rice container of the type used in the Sart merit-making ceremonies during the reign of King Rama III.

Model Junk: This boat replica was the first monument built to commemorate Thailand's sea trade.

Maha Jessdabodin Pavilion: This Greek-style cruciform pavilion was built during the reign of King Rama I. It was used by King Rama III when he came to the temple to supervise the building of the junk boat chedi.

★ H10
✉ 1648 Charoen Krung Road Yannawa Sub-District Sathon District Bangkok 10120
☎ (662) 211-9317 675-7895
FAX (662) 675-5473
🚌 1 15 17 35 75
🚐 4 Sai 38 75 Mb 9 20
⛴ Chao Phraya Express Boat: Sathon Pier
🕐 Temple: Daily 5 am-11 pm
Ubosot: Daily 8-9 am 5-6 pm
(Wishing to visit the ubosot should call in advance.)
💲 Free Admission
🎊 Chinese New Year Festival: The junk boat is opened to the public to worship the replica of Buddha's footprint. (Feb) Giving alms to the 108 monks. (Feb)
🏛 1983
🏯 Third Class
🏫 Buddhist School on Sunday
☎ 212-2122
Thetsaban Wat Yannawa
🅿 In the Temple compound
✚ Bangkok Fish Market
Bangrak Market
Shangri-la Hotel
Wat Yannawa

SUANLUANG
☎ 322-4667

WAT MAHA BUT

This temple was built in Phrakhanong in the mid-Ayutthaya period and named for a revered monk, *Phra Mahabut*. However, most people call it Wat Mae Nak Phrakhanong, after the famous Phrakhanong ghost.

The legend of *Mae Nak of Phrakhanong* has been told for many years, and is as influential today as it ever was. Inside the Wat, besides the building of *Mae Nak*, there are statues and a shrine to which many people come to pay respect and ask for help.

Mae Nak was the young wife of a conscript. While she was pregnant with their first child, he was called to the wars. While he was away, the mother and her unborn child died. On his return, however, he found them waiting for him. Little did he realise that both were ghosts!

A film of the story made in 1999 was one of Thailand's most successful movies. And one of the biggest group of *Mae Nak*'s devotees today are the young conscripts who come to ask her to intercede for them.

- ★ L10
- ✉ 749 Moo 11 Onnut 7 Lane Sukhumvit 77 Road Suan Luang Sub-District Suan Luang District Bangkok 10250
- ☎ (662) 311-2183 311-0543
- 🚌 1013 Minibus from mount of Sukhumvit Soi 77
- 🚐 20
- ⛴ Passenger Boat: Wat Maha But Pier (Pravet Burirom-Phrakhanong Canal) Temple: Daily 5:30 am-10 pm
- 🕐 Ubosot: Weekdays 6:30 am-6 pm Buddhist Sermon Day: 4 am-5 pm
- 🆓 Free Admission
- Annual Fair
- 🅿 In the Temple compound
- Bangna Police Station Phrakhanong District Office Wat Tai Wat Thongnai Wat Yang

TALINGCHAN

☎ 434-3148

- TALINGCHAN
- TALINGCHAN
- SIRINDHORN RD.
- CHAK PHRA RD.
- TALINGCHAN
- PRINCESS MAHA CHAKRI SIRINDHORN ANTHROPOLOGY CENTER
- TALINGCHAN FLOATING MARKET
- KHLONG BAN SAI
- CHAN
- MONTHOP
- CHANGREK
- CHIMPHLI-RATCHADATHITHAN RD.
- RERAI
- CHAIYATHIT
- MARI
- INTHARAWAT
- KHLONG BANGBRAHM
- KANCHANASINGHAT
- RATCHADATHITHAN
- Soi 35
- KAEO
- MAI THEPPHON
- PHLENG
- SAPHAN
- KHLONG BANGNOI
- PAKNAM FANG NUA
- PAKNAM FANG TAI
- KO
- BANG SAOTHONG

PRINCESS MAHA CHAKRI SIRINDHORN ANTHROPOLOGY CENTER

The Centre was established in 1991 to commemorate Her Royal Highness Princess Maha Chakri Sirindhorn's 36th birthday, and in response to her wish that Thailand should have centre for collecting information and other material relating to anthropology. It is also an information centre for anthropology students and researchers, as well as the general public both local and overseas, through its computer system.

⦿ HRH Princess Maha Chakri Sirindhorn Hall: (2nd fl.) Contains photographs and portraits telling the life story of the Crown Princess, as well as books, ceramics and paintings by the Princess.

Social and Cultural Development of Thailand Exhibition: (5th fl.) Depicts the social and cultural relations between Thailand and countries of the Southeast Asia Region.

Ethnology and Archeology Exhibition: (5th fl.) Depicts life-styles, society and customs of ancient Thai communities

★ E8
✉ 20 Borommaratchachonnani Road
   Khlong Chakphra Sub-District
   Talingchan District
   Bangkok 10170
☎ (662) 880-9429
📠 (662) 880-9332
🖱 http://www.sac.or.th
🚌 19 40 57 123 124 125 127
🚌 16 17 33
🕐 Office: Mon-Fri 8 am-5 pm
   Exhibition Hall: Tue-Sat
   9 am-4 pm
   Sun Mon Public Hols.
   10 Bht
   Free Admission: Students with
   ID Card Monks
   Must be in group of 10 or more,
   with written request one week
   in advance to the Director of
   the Centre
   Permanent Exhibitions Seminar
   Temporary Exhibitions
   6th-7th fl. Collections of books,
   journals and documents
   related to anthropology
   Membership 300 Bht/year
   Daily service 30 Baht/day
   Telnet:llb.sac.or.th
   www:http://lib.sac.or.th
   Audio-video facilities
   Large meeting room seating 400
   Meeting room seating 30-50
   Lecture Hall seating 72
   Computer Room
   Works of HRH Princess Maha
   Chakri Sirindhorn
🅿 Anthropology Centre compound
   (Visitors coming from Phra
   Nakhon side are advised not
   to take the raised expressway
   after crossing Phra Pinklao
   bridge. Instead, cross
   Bangkoknoi Canal, take the left
   lane and use the parallel road)
   Bicycle House
   New Southern Bus Terminal
   Talingchan Floating Market
   Siamease Cats Farm

from the study of traditional artifacts and utensils.

Anthropological Photographs by Thai Scholars Exhibition: (5th fl.) Subjects include slum dwellers, Likae theatre of Korat province, the world of village drama, and rice cultivation in agricultural communities.

Thai Earthenware Museum: (2nd fl.) Contains both prehistoric and historic earthenware found in the four regions of Thailand, besides tools and other artifacts.

Anthropology Centre Library: (6th & 7th fl.) Contains books, research works, journals, aerial photographs of ancient communities, CD-ROM and Internet.

Computer Room: Provides computer and internet access to information. Meetings, seminars, and lectures by Thai and visiting scholars are arranged at intervals.

TALINGCHAN FLOATING MARKET

On the bank of Bangkhunsri Canal, also known as Chakphra Canal, life still retains the atmosphere and lifestyle of a traditional Thai waterside community: Temples, houses, shops and boats with people selling all manner of goods just as in old Bangkok. There are farms, vegetable gardens and orchards where local fruit such as mangos, jackfruit, plums and kathon are grown.

⊙ Talingchan Floating Market: A semi-rural market in natural surroundings, open on Saturdays and Sundays, from 7 o'clock in the morning. Local farmers bring fresh vegetable, fruit, fish and aquatic animals to sell, each in its season.

There are also floating food shops on rafts selling Thai food, sweets and handicraft from rural craftsmen. Canal boat trips to experience the waterside lifestyle and listen to the old time music are arranged at various times during the day.

★ F8
✉ Pier in front of
   Talingchan District Office
   Khlong Chakphra Sub-District
   Talingchan District
   Bangkok 10170
✉ Talingchan District Office
☎ (662) 424-1712 424-5448
FAX (662) 424-5448
🚌 79 83
🚌 79
🕘 Mon-Sat 9 am-4 pm
   Sun Public Hols.
   Canal Tours: Sat Sun
   🕘 10 am 11 am 1 pm 2 pm
   (2 hrs./Trip)
   Children: 40 Bht
   Adult: 70 Bht
🅿 Talingchan District Office
✚ Princess Maha Chakri Sirindhorn
   Anthropology Center
   Wat Kanjanasingha Wat Laylai
   Wat Ratchadathithan

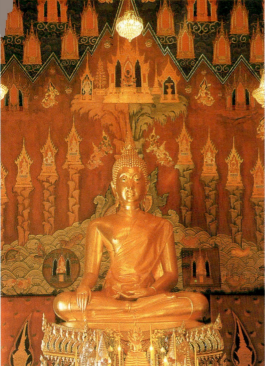

WAT RATCHADATHITHAN
RATCHAWORAWIHAN

★ E9
✉ 692 Charansanitwong 35 Lane Charansanitwong Road Khlong Chakphra Sub-District Talingchan District Bangkok 10170
☎ (662) 418-3445
🚌 28 42 80 81 91 108 146
🚐 9 10 68 Mb 10
🕘 Temple: Daily 9 am-6 pm
Ubosot: Daily 8-9 am 5-6 pm
📖 Wat Ratchadathithan Public Lib.
☎ (662) 412-0702
🕘 Tue-Sat 9 am-5 pm
🚫 Sun Mon Public Hols.
🏛 1952
🛕 Third Class
🍽 Buddhist Lent Final Day: Alms offering (End of Buddhist Lent) Merit Making Day (Oct)
📷 Taking photo inside Bldg.
🅿 In the Temple compound
⛴ Tulingchan Floating Market
Wat Kanchanasinghat

Two brothers, *Ngern* (Silver) and *Thong* (Gold) started the building of Wat Ngern and Wat Thong on the banks of Bangprom Canal, but both died before the temples were completed. In the reign of King Rama I, *Queen Amarindhramart* re-established the temples and the King renamed Wat Ngern as Ratchadathithan and Wat Thong as Kanchanasinghat, in accordance with the old meanings of the names.

◉ Ubosot: Built in the style of the Third Reign it has a two-tiered roof. The gables are decorated in flower designs of yellow-painted stucco. The door and window panels are decorated with gilded lacquer. The principal Buddha image is in Subduing Mara posture.

Wihan: Located at the rear of the ubosot. The hall features beautiful door and window decorations and the Buddha image is in the Meditation position. The mural paintings depict the 10 incarnations of the Lord Buddha.

Stone Throne: This was used by King Rama IV on his visits to the temple to make merit.

THAWI-WATTHANA
☎ 551-1004

SIAMESE CAT FARM
THAMSARA
PHUTTHA MONTHON SAI 2 RD.
BANGKOK NOI-NAKHON CHAISI RD.
LORD BUDDHA IMAGES
WISITBUNYAWAT
THAWI-WATTHANA RD.
RAJDAMNERN COMMERCIAL
KOMUT PUTTARANGSI
PHUTTHA MONTHON SAI 2 RD.
UTTHAYAN AVENUE

LORD BUDDHA IMAGES MUSEUM

The Lord Buddha Image is the symbol of the Buddha, the prophet of Buddhism, before which Buddhists pay homage.

This museum contains 200 large images of the Lord Buddha from the Indian Kupta period to the Rattanakosin period, and 3,000 smaller images. Some are especially highly regarded, such as *Somdet Wat Rakang PimYai A*, *Somdet Bangkhunprom Wat Kejchaiyo*, and the rare *Pra Kring Suriyaworamun*.

The museum is open to everyone who is interested in seeing, discussing and seeking to know more about the images of the Lord Buddha, both large and small.

The process of making Buddha images has evolved over the centuries, in terms of materials, style and imagery. The images are not only beautiful as sculptures, but are also important expressions of the civilisation and cultural life of the nation.

★ C9
✉ 5/9 Phuttha Monthon Sai 2 Road
   Thawi-watthana Sub-District
   Thawi-watthana District
   Bangkok 10170
☎ (662) 448-1795
FAX (662) 448-1795
🚇 123
🚌 33 79
🕐 Daily 10 am-5 pm
   Children Free Admission
   Student 50 Bht
   Adult 100 Bht
   Taking photo inside Bldg.
P In front of the Museum
✣ Bicycle House
   Siamese Cat Farm
   Utthayan Avenue

SIAMESE CAT FARM

★ C8
✉ 103 Moo 10
Pinklao-Nakornchaisri Road
Salatummasop Sub-District
Thawi-watthana District
Bangkok 10170
☎ (662) 889-2030
124 125
16
🕙 Daily 10 am-4 pm
Children & Student 20 Bht
Adult 50 Bht
🅿 In front of the Farm
Bicycle House
Princess Maha Chakri
Sirindhorn Anthropology
Center Utthayan Avenue

The characteristics of the khao-manee breed of Siamese cat are its beautiful form, elegant grace and pure white coat, khao meaning white. Of most importance, however, are its eyes, which must be of different colours. A khao-manee cat may, for example, have one green and one yellow eye, or one blue and one grey. Because of this distinctive colouring they are often called "the cats with diamond eyes."

Every khao-manee cat in this farm is descended from the cats which King Rama V loved to breed in the Royal palace in the care of *HRH Prince Chumphonkhet Udomsak*. The Prince later gave his daughter, *Princess Ruengjitjarang Arpakorn* the responsibility of continuing to breed these prestigious cats. The Princess passed on the duty to *Mr. Namdee Witta* in 1958, when there were 18 of them.

UTTHAYAN AVENUE

Utthayan Avenue is one of the landscaped infrastructure developments along the periphery of Phuttha Monthon. The avenue connects Phuttha Monthon Sai 3 and Sai 4 and runs parallel to Borommaratchachonnani and Phet Kasem Highway. It was opened to the public in 1999.

The avenue has fountains on its bridges and a waterfall with several cascades, as well as flower beds and shady trees. Marking each intersection are tall posts each with a different design. Beside of the road are 979 lamp posts decorated with the Thai phoenix .

The water supply and electricity power lines run underground on both sides of the avenue, which is 90 m. wide and extends for 3.861 km. There are three main traffic lanes on either side and two roads running parallel on each side. The avenue also has a 5.5-metre wide pedestrian walkway and a 2-metre wide bicycle lane on both sides. Along the centre of the avenue is a lotus pond.

★ A8
✉ Utthayan Avenue
Thawi-watthana Sub-District
Thawi-watthana District
Bangkok 10170
🚌 84Kor 91Kor
🕐 Daily 24 hrs.
🅿 Utthayan Avenue
✚ Lord Buddha Images Museum
Phuttha Monthon
Siamese Cat Farm
📷

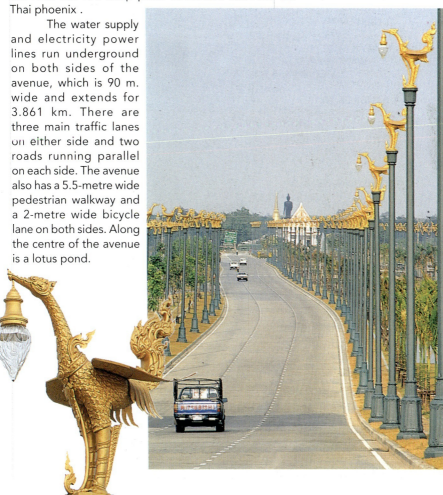

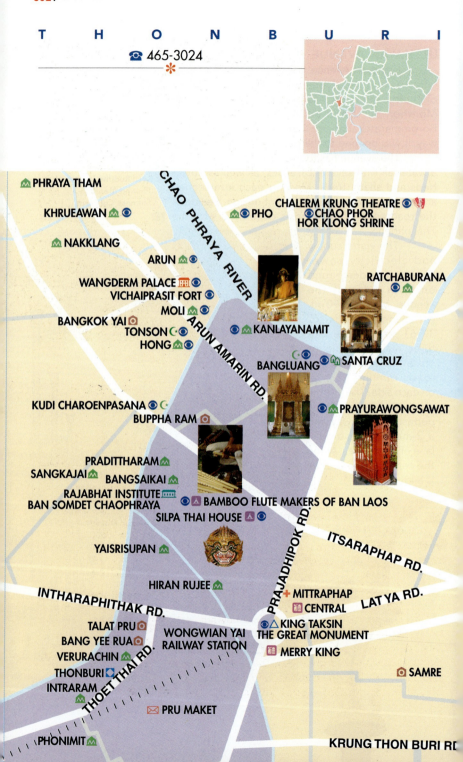

BAMBOO FLUTE MAKERS OF BAN LAOS

The ancestors of the Bangsaikai Laos Community were prisoners of war from Vientiane. They brought with them their knowledge of making traditional woodwind instruments, the khlùi flute and the khaen. Since the Laos made their home there it became known as Muban Laos, or Laos village.

Mr. Jarin Glinbuppha, head of Ban Laos, was taught how to make khlùi by his grandfather. The bamboo comes from Taipikul Puttabaht Village in Saraburi, he said. "First we cut it to length then dry it in the sun. It takes 15 to 20 days for it to dry completely. After that we sort the lengths into the sizes we need, then pierce the bamboo to give us the khaen sound."

We make the patterns on the khlùi by pouring hot lead onto the bamboo with different motifs, like pikul trees (*Bullet wood*) or flowers.

At present there are still 20 or so families still making khlùi. Because of their quality and the good reputation of khlùi Ban Laos, customers come here to buy them direct, and they are also sold at well-known Thai musical instrument shops.

★ G10
343 Behind Rajabhat Institute
Bansomdej Chao Phraya
Itsaraphap 15 Lane
Itsaraphap Road
Hirunrujee Sub-District
Thonburi District
Bangkok 10600
☎ (662) 465-2880
19 40 56 57 149
Mon-Fri 8-11am
Sun
P Behind Rajabhat Institute
Bansomdej Chao Phraya
Silpa Thai House
Wat Bangsaikai
Wat Kanlayanamit
Wat Pradittaram Community
(Mon Community)
Wat Bangsaikai

BANGLUANG MOSQUE

During *King Taksin*'s fight to liberate Thailand from the Burmese in 1767, some Thai Muslims were evacuated by raft down the Chao Phraya River to Thonburi. Some of them chose to live in Bangkok-yai, others in Bangkoknoi. Those living along the Bangluang Canal near Wat Werurashin are known today as the Kudi Khao Community.

🔵 Mosque: Their brick and stucco Thai-style mosque and the monks' residences (kuti) were painted white (khao), which is why the area was called Kudi Khao. It was in fact a new mosque, built to replace the old one which had been painted red (daeng) and was known as Kudi Daeng.

Mimbal: Made at the same time as the summon stand of Wat Prayurawongsawat. Its arch is decorated with stucco in the kanok flame design. It is surmounted by a three-pointed crown. The stucco decoration is in the form of a climbing plant influenced by Thai, Malaysian and Indonesian styles and encrusted with red, blue and white glass.

★ G10
✉ Thetsaban Sai 3 Road
   Wat Kanlaya Sub-District
   Thonburi District
   Bangkok 10600
☎ (662) 466-6159
   19 40 56 57
🕐 Daily 5-5:30 am
   12 noon-12:30 pm
   3-3:30 pm 6-6:30 pm
   8-8:30 pm
   Fri 12 noon-00:30 pm
   Free Admission
   Eidil Fitri: Sermon Pray
   Eidil Adha: Sermon Pray
🅿 Buppharam Police Station
   Bangluang Kudi Kao
   Community
   Bupparam Police Station
   Charoenpaas Bridge
   Wat Bupparam
   Wat Kanlayanamit

BANGKOK METROPOLITAN TOURIST BUREAU

SANTA CRUZ CHURCH

When Ayutthaya fell to Burmese in 1767, most Europeans returned to their own countries. Some of the Portugueses residents, however, remained in Thailand. When *King Taksin* offered them land to found a temple, *Brother Core* chose land in Portuguese Community in the Kuti Jeen area.

In the reign of King Rama III, the temple fell into disrepair. *Cardinal Pallegoix* re-established it and renamed it Santa Cruz Church, or the Church of the Holy Cross. However, it is popularly known as Wat Kudi Jeen.

◉ Church: It is a single-storey building in the Italian style. The rectangular belfry above the dome is decorated with stucco. Inside the church are 14 sculptures depicting scenes from the life of Jesus.

Priest's House: The two-storey, Western-style Priest's House was built in the reign of King Rama VI. Its pediment bears the emblem of the church in stucco.

Waterside Pavilion: The wooden pavilion on the water front is decorated in the "gingerbread" style.

★ G10
✉ 112 Tesaban Sai 1 Road
Wat Kanlaya Sub-District
Thonburi District
Bangkok 10600
☎ (662) 466-0347 472-0153-4
FAX (662) 465-0930
19 40 56 57 149
Ferry: Rajini (Pakkhlong Talat) Pier ↔ Santa Cruz Church Pier
⌚ Daily 5:30-8:30 am 6-8 pm
Free Admission
Mass 6 am 7 pm
Easter Day
Christmas (Dec 24)
P In front of the Church
✠ Bangluang Mosque
Wat Buppharam
Wat Prayurawongsawat

SILPA THAI HOUSE

Suk Phephai and *Chareon Kitrat* have been making khon masks for more than 20 years. Their products sell at Narayana Phand, Suksaphan and shop in Chatuchak market project 24 lane 2.

The making of a Silpa Thai House khon mask begins with modelling the basic mask in clay. This clay original forms the mould on which the mask will be shaped. The base will be made up of strong saa paper or cement-bag paper and rice glue, and when it is finished it will be left to dry in the sun for one or two days. After that, it is removed from the clay mould, trimmed and given its basic coat of colour. Then it is given another day drying in the sun before being painted, gilded and decorated.

Mrs. Suk and Mr. Charoen have received several awards for their outstanding contribution to the preservation of Thai central region culture, and certificates for their contribution to the preservation of Thai art. The most prestigious award they were presented is from the National Culture Commission in the category of the Culture in the Central Region.

★ G10
✉ 539/1 Behind Rajabhat Institue
Bansomdej Chao Phraya
Itsaraphap 15 Lane
Itsaraphap Road
Hirunrujee Sub-District
Thonburi District
Bangkok 10600
☎ (662) 465-0420
📠 19 40 56 57 149
🕐 Daily 8 am-8 pm
🅿 Behind Rajabhat Institue
Bansomdej Chao Phraya
✚ Bangsaikai Community
(Laos Village)
Wat Bangsaikai
Wat Kanlayanamit
Wat Pradittaram Community
(Mon Community)

★ G10
✉ 371
Wat Kanlaya Sub-District
Thonburi District
Bangkok 10600
☎ (662) 466-5018
🚌 3 4 7 7Kor 9 21 37 56 82
🚌 Sai 4 7 21 37 82
⛴ Chao Phraya Express Boat:
Rajini (Pakkhlong Talat) Pier
⇔ Wat Kanlaya Pier
🕐 Temple: 6 am-6 pm
Ubosot: 8:30-9 am 5-6 pm
Wihan: 6 am-6 pm
🎫 Free Admission
🎉 Chinese New-year Festival
(Late Jan-Feb)
Mahachat Celebration
(Before Buddhist Lent Final Day)
Chinese Half-year Festival
(Aug)
Coin Casting Ceremony
(After Chinese Mid-Autumn Festival)
🏛 1949
🛕 Second Class Special
🚌 Wat Kanlaya
🅿 In the Temple compound
➕ Bangluang Mosque
Bupparam Police Station
Kudi Jeen Community
Santa Cruz Church
Wat Bupparam
Wat Prayurawong
Ⓜ 📷

WAT KANLAYANAMIT WORAMAHAWIHAN

Chao Phraya Nikornbordin (Toe Kanlayanamit) dedicated his house and bought land in Kudi Jeen area to found the temple in 1825. King Rama III built Pra Wihan Luang where the principal Buddha image is enshrined. Later, King Rama IV renamed the image Praputthatrirattananayok.

👁 **Pra Wihan Luang:** Built in Thai style, with flower motifs encrusted with coloured glass decorating the pediments.

Pra Wihan Noi: This is on the north of Pra Wihan Luang. Insides there are several Buddha images in different postures.

Ubosot: The brick and stucco ubosot is in the Chinese style, the pediment decorated with stucco work in flower motifs and Chinese glazed tiles. The mural paintings depicting the Buddha's life story have almost completely faded.

Hor Pratammontien-taleungprakiert: King Rama IV ordered this hall to be built in 1865 for the purpose of keeping the Pra tripikata and Buddhist scriptures. The two-storey building has chorfar, bairaka and hanghong decorations. The pediments are carved, gilded and encrusted with coloured glass, with the Royal regalia at the centre. The door and window arches have moulded flower designs with a crown as the central motif.

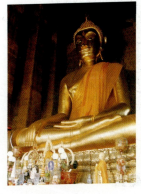

WAT PRAYURAWONGSAWAT WORAWIHAN

Somdet Chao Phraya Maha Prayurawong donated the site of a coffee plantation for the building of this temple in 1828 and presented it to King Rama III, who named it Wat Prayurawongsawat. It is known locally as Wat Rualek, or Iron Fence Temple.

Khao Mor: The miniature mountain, was built in the middle of a turtle pond. A small ubosot and wihan were built on the top of the mountain and a reclining Buddha image placed in the cave at its foot.

Chedi: The large, bell-shaped chedi has 55 compartments surrounding its base, each containing a Buddha image. The upper part contains another small chedi where 18 relics of the Buddha are kept.

Ubosot: This was built in the Thai tradition and the gable is decorated with an Indian rose motif. The murals depict the life story of the Lord Buddha.

Wihan: The pediments are decorated with flower designs. The Buddha image in the Subduing Mara posture enshrined in the hall is Luangpor Nark, believed to be one of a pair with Phra Sri Sakkayamuni, the principal image of Wat Suthat-Thepwararam.

- ★ G10
- ✉ 24 Prajadhipok Road
  Wat Kanlaya Sub-District
  Thonburi District
  Bangkok 10600
- ☎ (662) 465-0439
- FAX (662) 466-1738
- 🚌 3 4 7 9 10 21 37 42 85
- 🚐 6 Sai 3 Sai 4 Sai 7 Sai 21 Sai 37
- ⏰ Temple: 6 am-6 pm
  Ubosot: 8:30-9 am 4-5 pm
- Free Admission
- Songkran Festival (Apr 13)
- 1949
- Second Class
- P In the Temple compound
- ✚ Bangluang Mosque
  Bupparam Police Station
  Kudi Jeen Community
  Santa Cruz Church
  Wat Bupparam
  Wat Kanlayanamit

THUNG KRU

☎ 426-0761

THONBURIROM

KING MONGKUT'S INSTITUTE OF TECHNOLOGY THONBURI

PRACHA UTHIT RD.

Soi 33

BMA VOCATIONAL TRAINING

YOUTH CENTRE RATBURANA

PHUTTHA BUCHA RD.

ATTAKWA

Soi 69

ALISTIKHOMAH

JUSCO

ISLAMIC COLLAGE OF THAILAND

PRACHA UTHIT RD.

Soi 74

Soi 76

BANGMOD TANGERINES

THUNG KRUE

BANGMOD TANGERINES

In 1937 and 1938, experiments were carried out in the cultivation of tangerines in the area of Bangmod, Jomthong, and Bangkhuntien. When the trials proved to be a success, and good quality tangerines were grown, the cultivation of the fruit was extended to Thungkru and Takham.

The tangerine plants came from gardens in Bangkunnon, Talingchan, and Bangkoknoi. In the past, growers used to travel along Khlong Daan to Khlong Chakphra bringing their tangerine plants to the market at Wat Kaitere pier.

Because of the quality of the soil in which they are grown, the tangerines are of high quality: Tasty and juicy, with a thin skin, soft pulp and an attractive appearance. They quickly became a favourite with consumers so that today, Bangmod tangerines are a well-known product of this area.

★ H15
- Development & Social Welfare Dept. Thungkru District 122/673-682 Moo 2 Pracha Uthit Lane 91/2 Thungkru Sub-District Thungkru District Bangkok 10140
- ☎ (662) 426-0761
- FAX (662) 426-0760
- 21 75 88
- 4 Mb 20
- Mr. Surasak Kwanbua 51 Moo 3 Bangmod Sub-District Thungkru District Bangkok 10140
- ☎ (662) 870-5037
- 75
- Mrs. Sarapee Gimoum 207 Moo 4 Thungkru Sub-District Thungkru District Bangkok 10140
- ☎ (662) 873-8727
- 75
- Wul Ophasee Wat Putthabucha Wat Thungkru

THONBURIROM PARK

This land, formerly cultivated as fields and orchards, was developed to become Bangmod Nursery, where trees and shrubs were grown to sell commercially and to plant beside of the road.

In 1968, *Phraya Mahaisawan*, the mayor of the city of Thonburi Municipality made the area into a people's park, with many varieties of plants and flowers, waterfalls, fountains, pavilions, and a recreation area.

★ G14
- Pracha Uthit Road Bangmod Sub-District Thungkru District Bangkok 10140
- ☎ (662) 426-3210
- FAX (662) 426-3210
- 21 75 88
- 4
- Office: Mon-Fri 7:30 am-3:30 pm Park: Daily 5 am-8 pm
- Free Admission
- In the Park compound
- Celebration of the King Youth Centre

VADHANA
☎ 391-0211

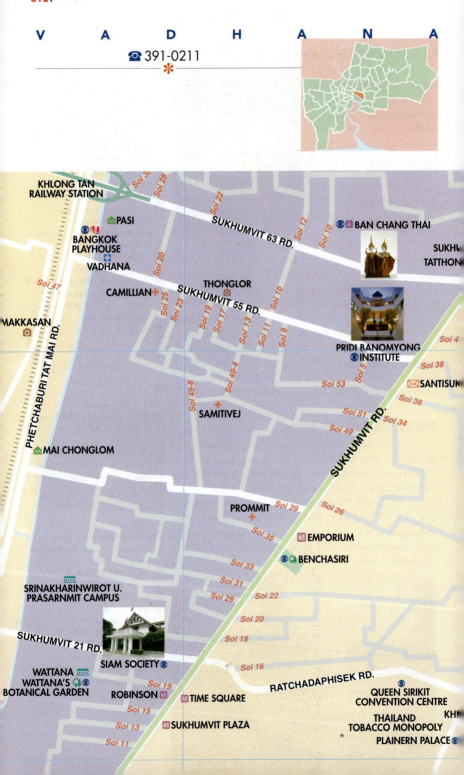

BAN CHANG THAI

From the love and passion of Thai classical puppets, *Mr. Krisda Sodprasert*, a well-known artist, established Ban Chang Thai (House of Thai Artisans) in order to conserve and promote Thai arts and handicrafts. The house provides courses such as puppet making, gilded painting, Thai motif design, Thai style painting, water colours, oils, and chalk drawings for the public.

Ancient Thai martial arts, the Thai boxing Chaiya style of *Master Ketr Sriyabhai*, is also taught on Sunday.

★ K10
✉ 38 Sukhumvit 63 Lane
  Sukhumvit Road
  Khlong Toei Nua Sub-District
  Vadhana District
  Bangkok 10110
☎ (662) 391-3807
📠 (662) 391-3807
🚌 23 72
🚐 126
🕐 Tue-Sun 8 am-5 pm
   Mon Public Hols.
 Free Admission
 Exhibition
🅿 In front of the House
➕ Eastern Bus Station (Ekkamai)
  Pridi Banomyong Institute
  Science Museum and
  Planetarium

PRIDI BANOMYONG INSTITUTE

The Institute was established to commemorate *Dr.Pridi Banomyong*, stateman.

The philosophy of the institute is to promote his idea stating that in a society, morality leads politics. It is a non-government organization dedicated to the research in social studies, such as economics, politics and history. The institute also gives advice and provides legal services to public, and organises activities such as exhibitions and lectures, and performances of music, art and culture.

★ K10
✉ 65/1 Sukhumvit 55 Road
  Khlongtoei Nua Sub-District
  Vadhana District
  Bangkok 10110
☎ (662) 381-3860-1
📠 (662) 381-3859
🖱 pri_institute@hotmail.com
🚌 2 25 38 40 48 71 ‹ › Mini Bus
🚐 2 8 11 13 ‹ › Mini Bus
🕐 Mon-Fri 8:30 am-4:30 pm
   Sat Sun Public Hols.
 Free Admission
 Exhibition Art Exhibition
📖 Sawai Sutthiphitak 2nd fl.
   🕐 Mon-Fri 10 am-4:30 pm
      Sat Sun 9:30 am-12 Noon
   💰 200 Bht/year
   🎫 Student 150 Bht/year
      Adult 300 Bht/year
      Organisation 2,000 Bht/year
🅿 In the Bldg.
➕ Ban Chang Thai
  Eastern Bus Station (Ekkamai)
  Science Museum and Planetarium

★ J9
✉ 131 Sukhumvit 22 Road
Khlong Toei Nua
Vadhana Bangkok 10110
☎ (662) 661-6470-77
FAX (662) 258-3491
🚌 38 98 136
🚌 22 38
🕘 Tue-Sat 9 am-5 pm
🚫 Mon Sat Public Hols.
🎫 Free Admission
📋 Exhibition Lecture Seminar
Study trip Training
📘 Membership Only
🏛 Museum of Ethnology
Kumthiang House
🕘 Mon-Sat 9 am-5 pm
🚫 Sun Public Hols.
🎫 Student 50 Bht
Non-member 100 Bht
💳 Student 500 Bht/year
Adult 2,000 Bht/year
Life Member 40,000 Bht
🅿 In Siam Society compound
➕ Grand Pacific Hotel
Queen Sirikit Convention
Centre
Robinson Dept. Store
Sheraton G. Sukhumvit Hotel
Time Square
Wattana's Botanical Garden

SIAM SOCIETY
UNDER ROYAL PATRONAGE

The society was founded in 1904 during the reign of King Rama V, with the aim of promoting the study of Thailand and her neighbouring countries in their artistic and scientific aspects.

The society has its own library and museum, and publishes journals and academic books. It arranges lectures, seminars, field trips, meetings and exhibitions as well as art, culture and environmental events. It is a centre for study, research and dissemination of information in numerous fields.

Library: This is a treasure trove of original archive material on the anthropology, archeology, sociology, history and natural environment of Thailand and its neighbours.

Museum of Ethnology, Kumthiang House: A northern Lanna style wooden house called Ruen Galae. It demonstrates the culture, community

and life style of the Lanna people. The house shows how space was utilised and the purposes for which it was used, as well as the way utensils were kept according to their use. The museum also has exhibitions on hill tribes, and the wood carvings, musical instruments and utensils of the northern people.

WANGTHONGLANG
☎ 211-8714

- WANGTHONGLANG
- CHAO PHRAYA BODINDECHA (SING SINGHASENI)
- BODINDECHA
- INTHRACHAI
- THAILAND MANGEMENT ASSOCIATION
- THEPLILA
- RAMKHAMHAENG U.
- HUAMARK SPORTS COMPLEX

CHAO PHRAYA BODINDECHA (SING SINGHASENI) MUSEUM

Chao Phraya Bodindecha was born in the Thonburi period and served in the Royal army during the reigns of King Rama I, Rama II and Rama III. He was one of the most influential figures of the early Rattanakosin period, playing an important role in the military, international relations, politics and economics.

A group of golden teak houses where the museum now stands was built in the Ayutthaya period and were dismantled then reassembled on the present site by Ayutthaya artisans. The museum consists of three wooden houses:

- ★ L8
- Bodindecha (Sing Singhaseni) School Latphrao Lane 112 Road Wangthonglang Sub-District Wangthonglang District Bangkok 10310
- ☎ (662) 538-3964
- FAX (662) 538-3964
- 🚌 8 22 27 44 92 96 126 137 145
- 🚐 2 15 92 126
- ⏰ Mon-Fri 9:30 am-3:30 pm
- ⊘ Sat Sun Public Hols.
- 💰 Children 10 Bht Adult 20 Bht Foreigner 100 Bht
- 🅿 In the Museum compound
- ✚ Huamark Sports Complex Ramkhamhaeng U. Shrine of Guanyin at Chokchai 4 Siberian Duck Pond

⊙ **Chao Phraya Bodindecha House:** The central one of the three, housing an exhibition of ancient weapons, bronze casts, personal effects and paintings of the Chao Phraya.

Ratchadabodin House: To the right of the Chao Phraya House, this building displays the history of Bodindecha School, including awards and the stories of people associated with the school since it was founded, as well as the history of its branches.

Silpanithat House: This shows the culture and lifestyle of people in Siam during the reign of King Rama III. Downstairs is a meeting room, the curator's office, library, souvenir shops and information centre.

YANNAWA

☎ 284-2244

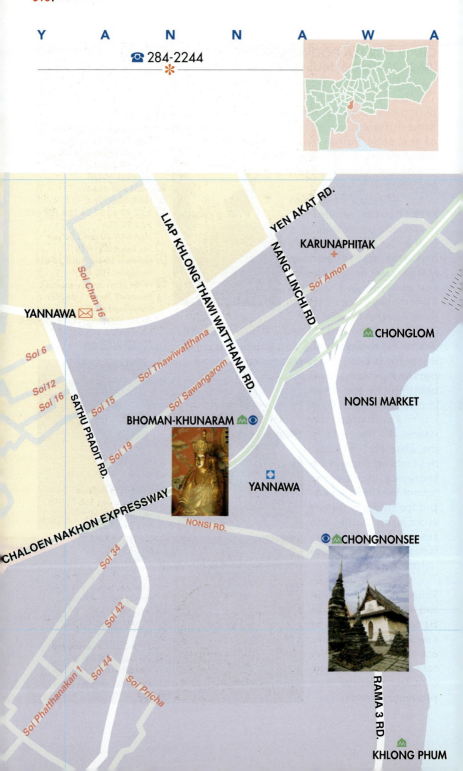

WAT CHONGNONSEE

Wat Chongnonsee is a civil temple. From the style, it is thought to have been built in the mid to late Ayutthaya period.

◉ Chedi: Lining the boundary wall is a group of chedi or stupa, eight angular chedis and six round chedis. Another six angular chedis can be found outside the boundary wall.

Ubosot: Surrounded by boundary wall, it faces eastward according to ancient tradition. The pointed arch windows and the architectural style resembles that of the period of King Narai of Ayutthaya.

Mural paintings: These are in five sections. Examples of erotic art can be seen in some of the murals, and the overall style is surrealistic. Only four or five colours were used, with red as the predominant colour.

★ 111
✉ 463 Rama III Road
   Chongnonsee Sub-District
   Yannawa District
   Bangkok 12120
☎ (662) 284-1667
🚇 67 89 205
🚌 67 205
🕐 Temple: Daily 6 am-6 pm
   (Wishing to visit the ubosot
   should call in advance.)
💲 Free Admission
🎎 Songkran Festival (Apr 13)
🏛 1977
🅿 In the Temple compound
✚ Central Dept. Store
   Wat Bhoman-Khunaram
   Yannawa Distict office

WAT BHOMAN-KHUNARAM

Thammasamathiwat or *Phochang*, a Chinese spiritual master who was also the first abbot of the temple, built this Chinese-Tibetan style temple in 1959.

Ubosot: The architectural style of the main chapel is a mixture of Chinese and Thai styles. Door and window panels are decorated with fine painting and sculpture.

Principal Buddha Image: Named by King Rama IX Phra Phutthawatcharaphothikhun, it is enshrined in the chapel which contains 500 other Buddha images.

Sala Thammanusorn: The pavilion houses 7,240 texts of the Mahayanist version of the Tripitaka, the Chinese Republic version.

Wihan of the Guardian Angels: Contains gilded stucco statues of four Chinese angels and the Maitriya, the next incarnation of the Lord Buddha. The Wihan of the Great Teachers houses the image of the first abbot.

- 111
- 323 Sathupradit 19 Lane Sathupradit Road Chongnonsee Sub-District Yannawa District Bangkok 10120
- (662) 211-7885 211-2363
- FAX (662) 212-7777
- 35 62 77
- 62
- Temple: Daily 7 am-6 pm Ubosot: Daily 8 am-5 pm
- Free Admission
- Chinese New Year Festival: Dhamma Practice
  Annual Dhamma Practice Ceremony (Jul)
  Mid-Autumn Festival: Coin Casting Ceremony
  Vegetarian Festival (Oct)
- In the Temple compound
- Central Dept. Store Wat Chongnonsee